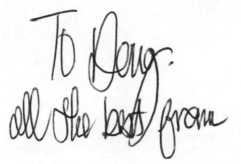

To Doug:
all the best from

A FART IN A COLANDER

A FART IN A COLANDER
THE AUTOBIOGRAPHY

ROY HUDD

Michael O'Mara Books

First published in Great Britain in 2010 by
Michael O'Mara Books Limited
9 Lion Yard
Tremadoc Road
London SW4 7NQ

A CIP catalogue record for this book is available from the British Library.

Papers used by Michael O'Mara Books Limited are natural, recyclable products made from wood grown in sustainable forests. The manufacturing processes conform to the environmental regulations of the country of origin.

ISBN: 978-1-84317-494-3

1 2 3 4 5 6 7 8 9 10

www.mombooks.com

Every effort has been made to trace the copyright holders of the images in this book. Any errors or omissions that may have occurred are inadvertent, and anyone with any copyright queries is invited to write to the publishers, so that a full acknowledgement may be included in subsequent editions of the work.

Designed and typeset by Design 23

Printed and bound in Great Britain by CPI Cox & Wyman, Reading, RG1 8EX

CONTENTS

It was a cold, bright day in November and the clock was striking thirteen.

'You prat!' I shouted.

'No one'll notice,' came the reply.

'Really?' I said, 'Every single kid in the world knows the clock strikes *twelve* times!'

I was directing a pantomime, *Cinderella*, and the drummer was imitating the chimes of the Palace Ballroom clock. Pantomime has been an obsession of mine since I sat with my Gran in the gallery of the Croydon Empire watching my first. It must have been *Dick Whittington*, because the Cat made a huge impression on me. In fact, for the following fortnight I asked Gran to serve all my food – and saucers of milk – on the floor. Just how important this lady was in my life you can guess from her not batting an eyelid at this request. She plonked the plates on the floor and carried on singing and cleaning up the house. 'It's just a phase,' she said to amazed aunties watching me trying to lick my backside. Little did she realize that it's a phase I am still going through … not the backside bit, but wanting to be something I'm not.

All my life I have been, and still am, looking for things new, different ways of escaping being stereotyped. I didn't want to be the child who was a swot, a goodie-goodie, but I didn't want to be a complete tearaway either. Perhaps a child who swotted up on how to be a tearaway! I didn't want to be a rebellious teenager but I didn't want to be in the Scouts or the Church Lads' Brigade either. I wanted to be an actor, but I wanted to be a stand-up comic, a researcher, a singer and a variety turn too. Still do. I wanted to be married but play the field an' all. I want to be a dear, lovable old grandad and a rakish roué as well.

Those are the reasons why this book is called *A Fart in a Colander*. The phrase was just one of many memorable ones used by my Gran, Alice Mary Barham. She was the lady who was lumbered with bringing me up, for all sorts of reasons. No one could have had a better bringing up, and I have to say, given the choice, everyone should be brought up by their grans. She knew exactly when to quote from her years of experience, when to defend me and when to give me a real ear'ole bashing *and* she had the unique ability to make her point and then, without even pausing, make you laugh. I do love women who make me laugh.

From the earliest days of our relationship I was always trying different routes out of the mundane, always noisily enthusiastic, animated and never sitting still. One evening, after a particular burst of exhibitionism, she said, 'For Gawd's sake stop it. You're like a fart in a colander!'

This did stop me. I'd never heard her say 'fart' before and, even today, it is the one word guaranteed to get a laugh out of most children – from two to ninety-two. It got a laugh out of me, but it did nothing to cure my constant search for a different way out.

The following words will, I hope, chart in an amusing and entertaining way, my adventures in the colander.

CHAPTER ONE

'I'm writing this letter slow because
I know you can't read fast ...'

I remember hearing a radio programme about memory and the person who could go back the furthest was Sir Compton Mackenzie, who had memories of his life when he was one year old. I thought, 'I can top that.' My earliest memory was of being held up above my aunt's head – *à la Roots* – and being told, 'Now look at this – it's something you'll never forget.' Then being taken to the bedroom window, at 5 Neville Road in Croydon, Surrey, to see a huge red glow in the sky. It was November 1936, and the red glow was the Crystal Palace burning down. I was six months old and I've never forgotten it.

But do I remember it *actually* happening, or do I just remember being told about it? The event certainly always comes back to me whenever I play in *Cinderella*. There's an obligatory line in the scene where the Ugly Sisters are trying on the slipper. One of them shouts, 'Me! Me! I'll get my foot into the crystal slipper!' To which her sister replies, 'You couldn't get your foot into the Crystal Palace!' So many directors, quite correctly, insist that gag is included. Today's kids haven't a clue what it means, nor have many of the grown-ups, but it was a great topical gag in the 1850s.

I do like the pantomimes that obey these old traditions: never speak the last two lines of the goodnight doggerel until the first performance; always ensure that the goodie enters from stage right (God's right hand) and the baddie from the opposite side.

But back to World War Two. I definitely *do* remember it breaking out, and the first air raids. I had a little three-wheeler Mickey Mouse tricycle and I remember my Mum calling me back home – I could hear her from two streets away, even with the siren going full blast! I pedalled furiously homeward and turned the corner of our road so fast I rounded it on just one wheel. I loved it. So much so that I went back and did it again, while Mum shouted even louder, 'Roy! Come and get down the shelter!'

We had an Anderson shelter in our garden and this was a magical place to me. To be in there, in the candlelit gloom, with the sirens wailing as Evalina, my mum, tried to calm me while at the same time frightening Gran with gory ghost stories, is a very special memory. How all kids love to be frightened – and how they love to see old 'uns frightened. The first stirrings of acting, I suppose, made me pretend to Gran that I wasn't the least bit scared and that *I* would see she came to no harm. I was four.

Dad, Harry Hudd, was a carpenter and joiner, but we didn't see that much of him. It was rumoured that he spent most of his time at the billiard hall in Katherine Street in Croydon.

My Mum was always called Evie by her sisters and family, and it was only recently that I found out her name was Evalina. Where did Gran find that one? Probably the same place she found her youngest girl's name: Snowdrop! I always used to say to her that Grandad must have been sloshed when the vicar asked the child's name.

'I dunno, do I? *Lovely* flowers in the churchyard ... Oops, I must wipe my nose. Dewdrop! No, we can't call her that ... I know – yes that's it – Snowdrop! That'll do.'

Gran used to enjoy me doing that routine – as a five-year-old drunk.

Mum has always been a bit of a mystery to me. She died when I was seven, and why and under what circumstances I only learned when I started to write this book. I will tell all at the right time. She was, according to aunts, uncles and chums, a character. She was a good impressionist. I wish I'd inherited that. But most of her impressions were, apparently, like those of my wife, Debbie. Debbie's are brilliant, deadly accurate take-offs of people no one knows – except us. Evie was good at doing managers, shopkeepers and friends.

When my brother, Peter, was born in 1942, Gran and I walked to the maternity hospital to bring Evie and the new arrival home. The closer we got to the hospital, the more jealous I became: jealous of the new baby who, I thought, had supplanted me in Mum's affections. I can see her now, pushing the pushchair full of Peter through the hospital gate. I let go of Gran's hand and dashed towards *my* Mum. Evie was as clever as Gran, and left the pram-pushing to Gran while she gathered me up and sang to me our favourite song, 'You Are My Sunshine'. Ah! I was still number one.

Number two – aka Peter – shouldn't really be with us now. Thankfully he is. The old cliché is you can choose your friends but not your relatives. If my brother hadn't been a relative I'd have chosen him as a friend anyway.

Mum shared a bed with baby Peter in the front room.

Mum was a fatalist and always believed she and Peter were leading a charmed life – to which Gran would say, 'You may believe so, Evie, but nobody's told Hitler!' So when the sirens wailed and we really should have been running for the shelter, she'd stay in bed until Gran and me dragged her and Peter down there. One particular night we'd all just got to safety when a terrific wallop sounded outside. The closest we ever came to a direct hit. When the all-clear came, we went back into the house. The front room wall had disappeared completely and embedded in the headboard of Mum and Peter's bed were great long shards of glass from the broken windows.

While Mum risked life and limb sleeping with Peter, I shared a bed with Gran. This suited me well as she would tell me stories of when she was a girl and, best of all, sing and teach me the songs of her childhood. Of course they were mostly music hall songs. Other kids had cheesy pop songs to send them to sleep, but I had 'The Hole in the Elephant's Bottom'. About forty years later I recorded it on an LP (oops, CD now) – and it was that song that sold more copies of the record than anything else. And still does.

When Mum complained that our laughing and singing was keeping her and my brother awake, Gran and I had to think of something musical yet silent. I solved this by patting out the rhythm of a song on Gran's arm. Once she'd guessed what it was, she would do the same thing to me. It worked beautifully, until she patted the rhythm of 'The Hole in the Elephant's Bottom' on my arm and the pair of us burst out laughing. Mum was not amused – simply because she wasn't in on the joke. Once she knew what we were up to she'd make sure Peter was asleep and then join us. Her

'Flight of the Bumblebee' was a sensation. I finished up black and blue.

Gran would also tell me stories of her early life. Her father was a railway signalman, and I still have a letter from the company he worked for enclosing a guinea for 'Saving many lives by thinking quickly'. Apparently he managed to change the points just in time to divert an engine that was heading for a commuter train. I can't find the guinea though.

Gran also told me of her husband, Tom Barham, the grandad I never met. He went off to Canada to make a new life for Gran and their four daughters – Ivy, Elsa, Snowdrop and Evalina. Before she had even met Tom, Gran had had a son who, from the sketchy details my aunties gave me, was illegitimate. I never found out who his dad was. Ernie (another railwayman) was a big, jolly man, a smashing bloke. Anyone who pressed a half-crown into my hand when saying goodbye was a smashing bloke to me.

Gran had a few letters from her husband in Canada. She read some of them to me. They were full of hope of a new life for the family over there. It never happened. The letters stopped and not even all the resources of the Salvation Army who were, in those days, the great missing-person-finders, could trace him.

So, Gran was left to raise my aunts and my mum on her own. And then, just when she'd finally married off the quartet, she got lumbered with yours truly – yet again, with no support from anywhere.

How ever she managed to raise the four girls and hold down all sorts of jobs I'll never know – but she did. She worked in the household of Derek McCulloch (Uncle Mac of radio's *Children's Hour*: 'Goodnight children – everywhere'), and she was the manageress of Wilson's Tea Shop in Croydon (where she got three of her girls jobs as waitresses). Auntie Ivy told me of the time when Gran was about to hand in her notice because one of the customers had called her a donkey. She withdrew it after the boss had explained the customer was German and was saying thank you – *danke*.

We had a photograph, sadly gone, of Gran as a waitress, at the opening of the Davis Theatre in Croydon, which was the largest cinema in the UK for a while. She was standing next to Rudolph Valentino, of whom she said, 'He was only a little squirt.'

By the time I started going to the pictures, the Davis Theatre was a shadow of its thirties splendour. The restaurant was still there but the shops in the foyer had all closed and its two thousand seats were rarely more than two per cent full. Only the Sunday concerts filled the place – big band shows from Ted Heath, Vic Lewis and Stan Kenton and occasional ballet and opera. The first time I ever saw Max Wall was at the Davis. He compèred a show headlined by Eartha Kitt. Max did the rudest bit of business I'd ever seen – up till then. He held a felt hat in his left hand and with a swipe of his right hand put a vertical crease in the hat. His comment: 'Not very clever, but some people like it.'

I do recall being ejected from the Davis during a production of *La bohème*. It was an Italian Opera Company and Mimi was a huge lady. I started to titter when 'Your Tiny Hand is Frozen' was sung to her, but when she rose from her deathbed to sing an encore I was gone – and slung out.

Gran used to dread Jack Hylton's Band working at the Davis. They would come into the restaurant for tea and then, over the heads of the arriving audience, skim silver trays across the foyer. They all flirted with her and I'm just sorry she didn't take up with one of them. I might have got my band parts for nothing.

My first school was the little infants' school in Maidford, Northamptonshire, the village to which we were evacuated as soon as Gran and I could get away from Croydon. I loved village life: the fields and the folk. Long hot summer days and short frosty winter ones. I loved them all – doing nowt but living the life of a dog. Going where I wanted, doing what I wanted with whoever I wanted to be with.

Our home throughout the war was one of a row of four already condemned dwellings. Gran and I were in one, Auntie Snowie, Uncle Len and Peter in another, and Auntie Elsa and my cousins Pat, Mavis, Dennis, Valerie and the youngest, Alma in the last two. They were all in just one room downstairs, on the flat earth with a wooden ladder to the one room upstairs. The village blacksmith and his missus were supposed to have raised thirteen kids in our two rooms – so we had bags of room.

My cousins were a lovely lot. Sadly Pat and Mavis are no longer with us, and we hardly knew poor Valerie as she spent most of her early years in and out of hospital. Dennis married a Canadian lass and lives out there now (in fact we met up again when I played Fagin in *Oliver!* in Toronto, of which more later). Whisper it, but Alma was my favourite – and still is. She makes me laugh and that'll do for me.

Then came the day I dreaded: education commence! Gran marched me along to school to meet Miss Chambers, the only teacher, from what I can remember (who, I might add, was still alive a couple of years ago). Miss C looked me up and down in a, quite rightly, suspicious manner (well, I was from down south). As soon as the lady turned her back I was gone! I galloped home, passing Gran on the way.

She, of course, dragged me back, and that's about all I can remember of my first academy. I do recall nicknaming her 'Potty' Chambers. It took a long time for some of them to work that one out.

The school was next door to the church, a place I frequented every Sunday for Sunday school and sometimes the morning and evening services too – depending on whether Gran and I were getting along. If we weren't, I got a snappy 'Get off to church, you!'

The big thrill at church was working the bellows for the organ. You sat in an extremely narrow cubby hole – nose practically wedged against the wall you were facing. The pumping was done with a big wooden lever and you knew when to pump by watching a little lead weight, which had to be kept between two pencil lines, one above it, one below. I loved this and was always the first to put up my hand when volunteer pumpers were required. In my usual crafty manner the first few times I did the job I did it immaculately. 'What a *dear* little evacuee,' the village ladies thought. I was, of course, lulling them into a false sense of security: I'd discovered that if the lead weight fell *below* the bottom pencil line, the organ would make the strangest wheezes and groans. I rehearsed this and, after a few minor weird sounds from the instrument, which I explained away with tearful countenance as 'The weight just wouldn't respond,' I was set for the big one.

As the organ thundered 'Onward Christian Soldiers', I let the weight fall – then rapidly pumped it up to the top – and beyond. I happily hurled myself around the cubby hole, as the organist gave an unintended, and never heard before (or since), Stockhausen recital. I was so carried away with my creativity I didn't hear the cubby hole door being flung open. I only knew that the vicar didn't approve as he dragged me, by the ear, out of the pump room, down the aisle and into the graveyard. I was never asked to pump again but I didn't mind – for weeks villagers pointed me out in the street. I started to realize how much I liked being recognized.

I eventually became a regular at the village school, but it was the freedom once we were out that I loved the most. I enjoyed listening to my country classmates as we sat with our backs against the baker's oven wall. That lovely smell of baking bread, and the not so lovely one of sweaty shirts drying out. They were a shy lot, but us townies showed them how to run amok and they taught us how to hide quietly to watch deer, rabbits, badgers and courting couples.

What I liked best of all was 'helping' on the Thomas family farm, just down the road. There were two big horses, Rose and Star, to pull carts and ploughs. The first time I was told to lead Star around the field was a big day indeed. I had to hold her still every few yards while the pickers threw potatoes into the cart. Just like I am today, I was very anxious to appear part of the scene, to look as if I knew what I was doing and wasn't an evacuee. Every time Star stopped she stood on my foot. The pain was excruciating. Of course I didn't say a word: I couldn't let them know what a twit I was. The field was eventually shorn of spuds and I could give Star a butch smack on the rump before I limped behind the barn and cried my eyes out. Even today, when we have new potatoes, the right foot gives me a twinge.

My aunts, Elsa and Snowie, had a ball. Particularly Snowie. She learned to drive a tractor, milk a cow and do everything that was required on the Thomases' farm. Whether she had a bit of a do with the farmer, Eugene Thomas, I never found out, but she was a real stunner and Gene was always very nice to me. The Thomases had an Italian prisoner of war working on their farm and he would show us all much-thumbed photographs of his wife and children, a tear trickling down his cheek. I, the man who still cries at *Bambi*, was the only one to cry with him.

At harvest time I used to love sitting in the hedge with Gene, the weepy Italian and my beautiful suntanned aunt, as she shared her cheese sandwiches and tea from a metal jug with me. I think she liked it too. For many years after we'd all come back to the smoke, she would drift off into her very own *Cider With Snowie* world. Her husband, my Uncle Len, was there with us. He was a butcher and so he was exempt from military service.

Later on he and Auntie Snowie adopted my brother Peter, and a great job they made of raising him. I have a photograph of Peter and me outside the cottage that Gran and I lived in. I'm looking smug and know-all, and he is looking jolly and carefree in a pram. It's a photograph with a tale. Directly after Uncle Len had taken the picture I pushed Peter and the pram into the cottage. Suddenly a great roaring sound followed us in and a vile smelling, dust-clouded pile of mice (alive and dead), old birds' nests and rotting straw covered the spot where we had posed. The entire thatched roof had slid off its rafters. It was the second time Peter had missed death by a hairsbreadth.

Gran wasn't a great frequenter of pubs, though one of the first 'jokes' I remember her telling me, was on a trip into Croydon High Street.

'Do you know where the nearest boozer is?'

'No.'

'You're looking at her!'

I still use it …

The only drink I ever saw her tackle during those years in Maidford was a Guinness. But not an ordinary one. She'd fill her glass with the stuff and then plunge a red-hot poker into it. This strange warmish mixture was her number one tipple.

She couldn't bear mice and you can imagine our condemned old cottage was a positive Hilton hotel for them. She managed to keep most of them out of the room we lived in by setting dozens of traps. To me, upstairs in bed, the sound of them being set off was like being on the front line. She'd call me down to unload the victims and set the traps again: 'Only use the rind – not the proper cheese!'

There was a hole by the side of the fireplace and it was used by a supermouse who was never daft enough to go for second-rate cheese rind. The war between Gran and that mouse went on all through the evacuation years. She would prepare her noxious brew – the warm Guinness – and seat herself by the fire. She would then drink and knit. At one side of the mouse hole was a big flat iron. This was stopped from falling flat by being attached to a piece of string, which was kept taut by being under Gran's foot. She would sit perfectly still and quiet, save for the soft clicking of her knitting needles. Eventually, the daring fella would emerge from his hole and then, with a cry of triumph, Gran would take her foot off the string and down would come the iron. Never once, in dozens of attempts, did she even catch his tail, and she always blamed me for frightening him away. 'I didn't make a sound!' I used to say. 'He saw the look in your eyes,' she'd say, as she loaded the futile ambush yet again.

I was about five or six when I had my first sexual experience – in a disused pigsty. Sorry, but it was no *Far From the Madding Crowd* moment. Myself and a chubby little village maiden – an older woman, six and a half – had crawled into the porker's retreat to play – yes you're right – Mothers and Fathers. We had, according to music hall tradition, a bit of a fight, a few rows, and some kisses to make up. Suddenly the lady said, 'I'll show you mine if you'll show me yours.'

'My what?' asked the innocent townie.

'Your winkie,' she said.

'My *what?*'

'Your winkie,' she repeated, eyeing the middle of my grey flannel shorts.

'Oh,' I said, 'My *willie!*'

'Yes,' she giggled. I duly undid the fifteen buttons and showed her. She, the rotten cow, laughed out loud and ran home. I wish I had a pound for every time it's happened to me since.

Harvest time was exciting. All us lads stood around the edge of the field as the combine harvester ate away at the corn and the area of the crop got smaller. Once a square of about twenty feet by twenty was left, we tightened our grips on our wooden clubs. This was when the rabbits ran out of the corn. To much shouting and whooping and barking of dogs, we chased them everywhere. Throughout the whole of the war I never saw a single rabbit clubbed.

The slaughtering of the pig was another big deal. Nowadays, I start to feel queasy if I see an uncooked kidney but back then ... I suppose after a couple of months in the country you realized it was all part of country life. You could hear the ghastly porcine screams half a mile away, and that was our cue to get to the slaughtering place double quick. The eventually dead pig was hung on a hook and the slaughterer got to work. We were only waiting, as surely country children had waited for hundreds of years, for the pig's bladder. Inflated it was a unique plaything. It was the only balloon any of us saw until VE Day.

Talking of ghastly screams, I heard some human ones too. They were from my cousin Dennis who was pushed, by a local lad, into a phone box. The glass shattered and left Den with bad cuts. So deep were the wounds that they had to be repaired with stitches, a job the local doctor did on the kitchen table – without anaesthetic. Dennis's sisters and I ran into the next field and we could still hear him shouting and crying.

We did hear the occasional plane on its way to bomb my mum back in Croydon, and though us townies pooh-poohed the bombing terrors – seen it all before, hadn't we? – we nevertheless made sure we were under the table when the ominous engine sound came within earshot. When you're that scared a laugh is often a great salver and we had a sure-fire way of getting one. As soon as the trouble started we would, with shouts of 'We'll get her!' and 'Poor old soul!', run down to Mary Billingham's cottage. Miss Billingham was a tiny ancient villager who seemed to us to have been spun by a spider. She seemed all hair, from her cottage loaf-shaped topknot, to her chin, to her shawl and skirt, down to her fraying bedroom slippers. Poor Mary would collapse into a gibbering heap at almost any sound – but particularly at that of the Jerry bombers. We'd drag her back to our place and sit her in a chair, and Gran would give her a cup of sweet tea. Mary would get so upset. Her hands wouldn't stop shaking and the sound of the cup rattling in the saucer would start us off. This, coupled with the animated behaviour of her bristly chin and the anti-Hitler curses she spat out, really made our day. We used to look forward to the bombers coming over.

Away from the raids, Mary would often shout for me, 'Oi! Townie!', and I'd be given a list of stuff to get from the village shop. When I returned, without fail she would give me a farthing. A farthing was a quarter of an old penny.

Mary was someone we all liked, but there was one old boy we didn't. He treated us Londoners as if we were all members of Fagin's gang, as if we'd make off with his cows, wife and daughters while he wasn't looking. He called us 'damned furriners' – even my Gran, who told him, as only she could, 'We are on the same side you know!' He wore a deaf aid and I suppose he had every right to hate us because we never stopped doing the same gag on him. We would start by miming a few words to him. He'd turn up the hearing aid, we'd mime a few more, and he'd turn it up some more. This continued till the receiver could be turned up no further. The next few words weren't mimed. They were shouted into the hearing aid. The poor old sod would be practically blown over. When he came round from this terrifying ear'ole bashing, he'd get to his feet, shake his fist and give us a right mouthful – but we were gone.

My mum wasn't there with us. I remember when we all first moved into the cottages I did get letters from her. They were smashing letters, always printed so I could stagger through them. They were full of fun and jokes. Of course she included the old gag – 'I'm writing this letter slow because I know you can't read fast.' Jimmy Cricket is still using it! The letter I really liked was one included in a parcel that contained my overcoat. The letter read:

> *'I'm sending you your best coat. The postage was rather a lot as it's a heavy winter one. To save money I have cut the buttons off.*
>
> *Lots of love,*
>
> *Mum.*
>
> *PS: You'll find the buttons in the right-hand pocket of the coat.'*

The other side of the letter had no words on it, just row after row of kisses.

How I longed for her to join us in Maidford, but Gran always told me, 'She'll come when she can. She's very busy in London.' I did sometimes see Gran blow her nose after she'd told me that, but I didn't suspect a thing.

CHAPTER TWO

'Oi, Harry! You forgot the piss pot!'

When Spike Milligan finally caused Hitler's downfall, it was time for all the family to return to town. I cried for three days. The country life was so perfect and it's only now, nearly seventy years later, that I'm getting the same feelings. My wife Debbie and I moved to a village in Suffolk about six years back and it is a bit good to hear the birds singing in the morning instead of coughing. For years Percy Edwards, the naturalist and bird and animal impersonator, used to look at me in his funny old country way and say, 'You've got to move to Suffolk, boy. It's made for you.' He was right. But more of the Suffolk idyll later. Right now I've just made my tearful return to Croydon.

Over the years we'd been in Northamptonshire, the letters from Mum had dried up and to be honest I'd almost forgotten her. The house where I had last seen her was 5 Neville Road in Croydon, to where Gran and I returned. I was knocked out to see the Anderson shelter was still in the garden and it was memories of the fun we had in there that made me enquire vaguely as to where Mum was living. But my enquiries were always brushed aside.

Then, one afternoon, Gran was taken unawares. She was pottering about her garden – the four feet all round the

Anderson shelter – when I asked outright, 'When am I going to see Mum?'

'Your Mum's dead,' Gran replied, in a totally untypical short way, adding the oddest postscript ever, 'and there's no Father Christmas.' A terrible double whammy. I fled into the house, threw myself onto my bed and bawled my eyes out. I'm ashamed to say I'm still not sure what upset me most – losing Mum or losing a Christmas stocking.

It was many years later – recently in fact – that I found out just how sad my Mum's death was. Neither my gran or any of my aunties ever mentioned it and I was too scared to enquire – in case I might hear something awful. There was definitely something a bit dodgy about it. Coming back to Croydon after the War, some of the kids in the street would shout out, 'Your mum – put her head in the gas oven, didn't she?' I would run away – I didn't want to think she had.

My brother Peter knew no more than me, though Auntie Snowie did once say to him, 'Your mum used to get headaches', and then, before he could ask, 'Why?', she shut up like a clam.

When I began to write this book I had to find out more about the lady whose jokes and love I do, just, remember.

I went to the British Newspaper Library at Colindale, and the staff there found a copy of the *Croydon Advertiser* for 15 October 1943, which included a report headlined: WOMAN'S DELUSION.

It told a sad story. My gran had found my mum, dead in a gas-filled bedroom. On going to bed the night before, Mum had jammed the gas tap so that it couldn't be turned off. The report went on to say that Mum was convinced she was pregnant, although local doctors had assured her she wasn't. She had been a voluntary patient at the Warlingham Park Hospital (for mental problems). The 'headaches' she herself had described to a neighbour as 'a living death' could have been a brain tumour and, if so, I think what she did was perfectly understandable.

I also understood why the family were so tight-lipped about the whole affair. They all came from a generation in which suicide was considered an unforgivable and disgraceful act, even for someone who was obviously suffering great pain and was in the deepest despair.

Gran, obviously thinking she had been a bit too bald with the information, did what she felt would make me feel better – she bought me a hamster.

This hamster, the first of many, wasn't with us for long. I kept it in a cardboard box, and by the next morning it had chewed its way out and was gone.

The second, Herbert, housed in an adapted biscuit tin, I discovered a couple of weeks after its arrival lying on its back, legs in the air, stiff as a board and cold as yesterday's rice pudden. Peter was visiting us with his adopted parents, Auntie Snowie and Uncle Len, and was honoured by being appointed chief mourner at Herbert's funeral. I, of course, was the funeral director. An elaborate ritual involving a Typhoo tea packet coffin, a wreath of one of Gran's alyssum plants, and a kazoo version of 'Ain't It Grand To Be Bloomin' Well Dead', ended in the rigid rodent being lowered into his grave and buried. A few pebbles were scattered on top and 'RIP Herbert' captioned on two ice lolly sticks formed a cross at its head. It was, I have to say, almost as good a job as when I did a bit of burying years later as Archie

Shuttleworth in *Coronation Street*. Peter was greatly moved.

The next morning I went into the garden shed to feed my pet mice and there, sitting outside his biscuit-tin home, was Herbert. I ran indoors and, pulling Gran towards the shed, I whispered, 'The ghost of Herbert is in the shed!' She was used to my fantastical imaginings but still, sighingly, came with me. Sure enough, there was the phantom, cleaning his whiskers and longing to get back into his wheel.

'You sure it's him?' Gran asked.

I reached towards him and he returned my concern with his usual vicious bite. 'It's definitely Herbert,' I said, and hustled him back into his cage.

That morning I found out, from a pet-loving schoolmate, that hamsters could actually sort of hibernate, go into a death-like trance but then come round. No wonder Herbert bit me – I'd buried him alive. He lived for more than a year after he'd survived his Edgar Allan Poe nightmare.

The return from Northamptonshire wasn't the great homecoming I'd imagined. I'd picked up a real country accent over the preceding four years, so much so that my school friends and our neighbours christened me 'Swede'.

'Count up to ten for us, Swede!' they'd say and I'd try: 'Wun, too, feree, forwar, foive.' Long before I'd got to 'foive' they be cackling away and doing cow and sheep impersonations. I hated them for it. All you want at eight years of age is to be just like everyone else, and I wasn't.

But I soon set about changing that. Within a month 'Swede' was no more. I really worked on the accent and tried out all sorts. I could have been called anything from 'Taffy' to 'Mick' to 'Jock', to any of the characters in Tommy Handley's radio show, *ITMA (It's That Man Again)*. Gran used to enjoy my Colonel Chinstrap and my Chief Bigga Banga.

One big lad didn't enjoy my voices at all. He insisted on still calling me 'Swede'. I've never been very good at any form of sport that involves throwing, but I have one great memory of doing it right. The big lad had just clouted me round the ear'ole and run off, shouting back, 'Go and dig us some spuds – Swede!'

I'd had enough and reaching into the gutter I found a quarter brick – I threw it, hard, at his disappearing back. I couldn't believe it. It landed smack on the back of his head and he practically somersaulted backwards. What a shot! But, oh dear! He didn't get up. I ran over to him and would have given him the kiss of life if he hadn't been so ugly. Thankfully he opened his eyes – and spat into mine. He ran off, promising what he'd do to me the next time we met. We did meet lots more times, but he never called me 'Swede' again.

After the War I only remember my Dad coming back to Neville Road once. He came to collect all sorts of bits and pieces of furniture that he and my Mum had shared, but now he took it away with him. I remember that day well: it makes me smile to think of it even now. As he loaded all the swag into a car, Gran, who never had a single good word to say to or about him, opened a bedroom window and, waving a chamber, yelled, 'Oi, Harry! You forgot the piss pot!'

He drove off double quick, while the neighbours gave a round of applause and I, who loved every minute of it, got a clip round the ear'ole for laughing.

Gran, as I never tire of telling people, looked after the both of us on her Old Age Pension. Just how the following adventure came about I don't really know, but I suspect that someone had told Gran she ought to have a few bob off my Dad towards my keep. Anyway, in the summer of 1947 I was sent to stay in Birchington, Kent, with Dad (Harry), his new wife, Dorothy, and her two girls from a previous marriage. I thought I was there for a bit of a holiday and that was OK.

Then one day, while going to the shop on an errand for Dorothy, I noticed in my ration book that my Croydon address had been crossed out and a new permanent address written in: Quex View Road, Birchington. This hit me like a thunderbolt. I stopped in the middle of the road and realized I wouldn't be going back to Gran. I worked out that Harry, rather than pay for my upkeep, had taken me into his new family. Fair enough, I suppose, but at ten years of age I was heartbroken. Not see Gran again, nor Peter nor Auntie Snowie nor Uncle Len? No way.

I wrote dozens of over-the-top letters to Gran explaining how I was being kept against my will and pouring out my love and longing for the company of her, Peter, Auntie and Uncle and the people who lived next door – even their cats and dogs. I can't now believe I was such an unloved, ill-treated prisoner, but my letters, which I found in my Gran's papers after she died, are so melodramatic and real – perhaps I should have been a writer full time.

The outcome was that one glorious day my family arrived in Kent, mob handed. Led by the Good Gran, they returned to London with yours truly. Whatever they sorted out, I was blissfully happy to be back.

I did hear from Harry again in 1950 – he sent me five bob – but it was many years before I actually saw him again. The story of our bizarre reunion is well worth reading – and later in the book, you will.

All I knew was that, once again, it was great to be back home in Neville Road and to resume normal life. Strange for someone like me, who later really did become the life and soul of the party, that my years from about the age of seven until I discovered the concert party, were spent inventing worlds of my own. I needed no one else when I was in those worlds. The hangover from my days as an evacuee in Northamptonshire was that I created my own farmyard. I would spend hours on the living-room carpet, laying out fields and shifting toy animals from one field to another.

One or two trips to Selhurst Park, the home of Crystal Palace FC turned me on to football. Not playing it. No – managing was my thing. Managing a whole world of football. I found a board game (where it came from I don't know). It was a pitch laid out on card with dots for the playing positions. It was all brought to life by the throwing of a dice, which determined where the 'ball', a simple tiddly wink counter, would go next. Again, like my obsession with the farmyard, I would spend hours in my new world. I invented teams, players and leagues. I produced my own football newspaper with portraits of the stars and all the results of the matches that I had played – against myself! I had favourites and would go to sleep some nights totally ashamed because I had cheated to allow them to score. I remember that board game was a good one: I'd love to find another copy but I can't remember what it was called. It was nowhere near as physically exhausting as Subbuteo – all that finger flicking, not for me.

The final lone hobby was writing and drawing strip cartoon versions of favourite films. I still have my version of the Ealing comedy *The Lavender Hill Mob* and it's not bad. It led me away from what I suppose I should have done – technical drawing.

I was a strange little lad. Nervy, myopic, dead skinny and totally unathletic. I was quite good at drawing and, looking through my papers, I found some worthy essays in a couple of old exercise books.

I read everything I could lay my eyes on. Gran used to complain, 'When he sits down to eat he even has to read the labels on the sauce bottles.' I remember making up an involved story based on the Camp Coffee bottle. I'd noticed that the illustration on the label showed an Indian servant holding a tray, about to serve coffee to a British army officer. On the tray, of course, was a bottle of Camp Coffee. And on the bottle of Camp Coffee in the drawing was a drawing of the previous drawing. I tried to weave a story round this. Gran's comment? 'You know, you worry me sometimes. You really do.'

I was a bit of an odd 'un. I kept a diary and searched some out when I was writing this book. It always makes me laugh to see how a kid's mind works. My entry for Wednesday, 6 February 1952 reads 'It was announced at school today that King George VI died early this morning.' Followed by, 'Cleaned out my mice.' The entry for Thursday, 4 September 1952 was 'Went to the Earl's Court Radio Show. Had voice recorded. Saw myself on TV – urgh!'

I was always looking for something, apart from books, to spark my imagination. Then one day, something wonderful happened.

Exactly when Gran first took me to the Croydon Empire I can't recall but oh did I want to go again. I never tired of the whole experience. The ritual began as we took our seats in the gallery for the 6.15 show. I remember the almost sexual thrill as the house lights went slowly out, leaving just the footlights shining onto the bottom of the front curtains and the little lights on the musicians' music stands; the conductor entering to desultory applause; the start of the overture … Now we were in for some fun.

How she managed to afford an almost weekly visit I never knew. But now I understand her values better and, of course, she thought two hours with pretty, handsome, graceful, smiling people doing amazing things, singing songs she liked and, very best of all, making her laugh, was well worth missing a meal for. She was so right.

I can never remember her and me sitting anywhere except right up in the gallery, just under the roof, the 'gods'. An oft-repeated line of hers, as we climbed up the (to me) *hundreds* of stairs to our destination, was, 'Gawd! Any higher and I'll get a nosebleed!' She liked it when fellow gallery-ites heard her and laughed.

Exactly how it happened I don't know, but I always came out at the end of the show with whitewash marks on the back of my shoes. So did all the kids who went up there. Just before we got into the street at the end of the show Gran would make me stand still and turn round. She'd get out her handkerchief, spit on it and wipe the chalk marks off the back of my shoes. 'That's it,' she'd say. 'I don't want people thinking I can only afford the gods!'

When she couldn't even afford the gods, she'd say 'Never mind. Let's go down to the theatre and see them come out.' Yes, she was stage-struck and she made me so too. We'd stand at the end of the alley and watch the procession of beautiful, heavily made-up ladies and handsome camel-hair overcoated, brown trilby-hatted men come out of the stage door and nip across to the pub.

We always liked the 'lads' from the drag shows. 'He always wears lovely clothes,' Gran would say, as 'he' and his pals would argue their way to the boozer for a between-houses drink.

When we were able to get into the theatre, Gran was in her element and her favourites were those who made her laugh. She was a good judge of comics and good at spotting embryo talent. She told me (and whoever was sitting near us) that Max Bygraves, Frankie Howerd and Harry Secombe would make it. Her greatest praise for a performer who made her laugh was: 'Oh he's a silly bugger!'

The one singer she was mad about was the Irish tenor Josef Locke (for younger readers there was a smashing, fairly recent, film about him called *Hear My Song*). Gran wasn't an autograph collector, but Josef Locke was the only person she ever wanted a signature from. As I write this, I am looking at a tiny photograph of the man, which I gave to my gran. Let me explain.

She dragged me to the stage door to get an autograph. There was a fair crowd there. Josef Locke didn't come out but suddenly a window was opened and there he was: a larger-than-life, real showman. He gave us a burst of one of his hits, 'Hear My Song Violetta', and then as he sang another, 'I'll Take You Home Again, Kathleen', he threw these little photographs out to his fans. Gran had her hand trodden on trying to get one and came away disappointed. As we walked home, I handed her the signed picture. I was a damn sight quicker than most of his middle-aged fans. She stopped in the middle of crossing the road and gave me a big kiss. I wasn't mad about the kiss but the two penn'orth of chips' reward was well worth having.

My Saturdays then were terrific. Saturday morning pictures at the Croydon Hippodrome. The preliminaries before the actual films were a pain in the neck. An old bloke with a bald head would 'uncle' on before the screen and lead us all in community singing. They weren't the songs my gran sang, but dreary parodies of things like 'Men of Harlech'. No laughs, they were full of good, sound, sensible advice about crossing the road and helping people. The roar from us kids when he scarpered, the lights went down and we heard the notes of that piping little tune, must have told him we didn't like singing his soppy songs. The roar doubled when onto the screen came those two bowler hats – bugger helping people now we were in for some fun with Laurel and Hardy. Oddly enough, in those days Ollie was the one who made me laugh the most. I think it was him addressing the camera that turned me on. Although, as I learned more about what made people laugh, Stan became my favourite. He was a comedy craftsman par excellence.

Looking through childhood diaries I'm amazed how much time I spent at the cinema or how I managed to afford it. A favourite bug hutch (as we called the tatty old picture houses) was in Thornton Heath. I remember sitting at the back there with just half a dozen others. On the very front row, just two seats were occupied – one at each end of the row. Suddenly there was a loud bang and the exit door next to the screen was kicked open, from inside. Silhouetted in front of the screen were the two occupants of the front row carrying the entire row of seats! The manager came running down the aisle but too late. The seats, and their new owners, were way down the high street and into a waiting lorry.

Years later, in 1981, I told that story on a film programme I did for Anglia TV called *Movie Memories*. A couple of days after transmission a letter arrived at the studio from one of the two seat nickers. He confessed but didn't give his name or address.

The Croydon Hippodrome had been, before my time, a theatre. Gran had seen the famous Tod Slaughter there in many of his lurid melodramas: *Maria Martin, Spring Heeled Jack,* and *The Grip of Iron.* In this one, so Gran said, 'He ground his teeth and you could hear it at the back of the gallery!'

Tod Slaughter's most famous role was Sweeney Todd in *The Demon Barber of Fleet Street.* I saw him play the part at the Croydon Empire. It was yet another occasion that only 'live' theatre can give you.

Tod had a great opening to the play. Down the centre aisle would run a girl, screaming, being pursued by the Demon Barber who, in turn, was being chased by a gaggle of Bow Street Runners. On this evening someone in an aisle seat stuck out his foot as the Runners ran after Tod. The police force collapsed in a heap – to the audience's delight and Tod's fury. He came running back and enquired, 'Who did that?' Such was his command that quite a few people pointed towards the tripper. Tod yanked the culprit out of his seat and propelled him to the back of the hall and out. Wiping his hands on his apron he advised us, 'Now we'll get on with the play!' and exited backstage to a generous round of applause.

Neighbours told me that, between entrances, he would

nip across to the pub wearing the bloodstained apron. Having spotted the gory prop, after he'd left the pub all the customers would ask who he was. That's what you call publicity.

I was now a pupil at Tavistock Secondary Modern School in Croydon, where I met and made friends with a lad who was quite an influence on my life: Ron Thoroughgood. He was the son of a market trader – and a son of a gun, too. His offbeat flights of fancy made me laugh. I spent all my spare time with Ron.

Saturdays in Croydon never varied. First the children's film show at the Hippodrome and then a trip to the library with Ron who, believe it or not, at the age of thirteen introduced me to Evelyn Waugh, George Orwell, J.D. Salinger, F. Scott Fitzgerald and, not in the library, the naughty writings of Mickey Spillane (all full of gangsters and their molls – 'she wore a dress so tight I could hardly breathe!').

In the afternoon, we 'helped' Ron's dad on his stall in Surrey Street Market. The market was a magical place for a kid, apart from all the fruit and veg stalls, which held no interest at all. There was a stall that sold sweets; a fabulous pet stall that even sold monkeys and parrots; and one that dealt in 78s – no LPs or CDs then. A list of the top twenty records was chalked up on a blackboard and the lady who ran the stall was the epitome of 'hip' to me, even though she kept her money in a leather apron just like the fruit and veg sellers did. I fancied her.

The smell of naphtha lamps and paregoric and the sound of Frankie Laine, Teresa Brewer and David Whitfield – ah, lovely.

Several stalls were owned by the Hart family. Mark Hart was a well-known boxer and we'd hide behind his stall just to get a glimpse of the great man. At one end of the market were the Scarbrook Baths, and I'd try and sneak in to stand at the back whenever boxing was on. It was there I first saw the legendary 'Nosher' Powell. Nosher, I'm told, was usually last on the bill and, if the previous fights finished too early, boxing promoter Jack Solomons relied on him to give the customers value for money.

I remember one night Nosher was getting a bit of a seeing to and was ready to quit. Mr Solomons banged his fists on the ring floor, pointed at his watch and said, 'Come on, Nosh! They haven't had their money's worth!' Nosher pulled himself together and went another three rounds.

Nosher was a big Joe Palooka-like figure, and was one of my first heroes. Even in the boxing ring he'd get laughs and I longed to get to know him. Much, much later – in the mid-1960s – he did stunts and played parts in my TV series, *The Illustrated Weekly Hudd*. An ambition realized.

Ron Thoroughgood's dad was a character. He sold only tomatoes and cucumbers, with plastic pegs pushed into them saying 'Worthing grown' and 'We lead others follow'. A gambler on the horses, he was always called Charlie because of his resemblance to a well-known jockey, Charlie Smirke. What his real name was I never knew – I don't think Ron did either. His other nickname was 'Wagger' – I didn't pry. He always gave us a couple of bob at the end of the day before he repaired to The Drum and Monkey for an evening of boozing and post-mortems re dead certs that had let him down.

Both Ron and I were interested in theatre, and I found a

booklet I had put together when I was eleven entitled, 'The Double R Theatre Notebook by Roy Hudd. Illustrated by the author'. This set out exactly how we were going to start our own company. One page, headed 'How it Began', told how we were inspired to think about our own theatre through listening to a radio serial (I think it was Noel Streatfeild's *The Swish of the Curtain* on *Children's Hour*). It went on to say that we started making our 'temporary' theatre on Wednesday, 28 January 1948, and, 'a show followed the next day. The show consisted of a song, two comedians and a play. The End.'

The notebook must have been written before we produced our first play because it was rapidly forgotten after that one performance. We were both fans of the Arthur Ransome books: *Swallows and Amazons, Picts and Martyrs, The Coot Club*. All these and Evelyn Waugh! We were an odd pair.

I remember that first show very well. Not for the content but for the 'scenery'. The 'temporary' theatre was our spare bedroom, which accommodated a row of three seats containing Gran, Auntie Snowie and brother Peter. They faced a curtain we had somehow rigged up. The 'two comedians', me and Ron, did our stuff in front of the curtain. Then came the play – a total rip-off of a scene from an Arthur Ransome, 'written by R. Thoroughgood. Produced by R. Hudd.' Behind the curtains was our big spectacular backcloth: on board a ship against an azure sky, flocks of seagulls and assorted other ships. As the curtains opened to reveal 'The Swallow' sailing ship, Gran gave a howl and said, 'Gawd help us! What have you done?' We didn't have a backcloth so I'd painted the scene directly on to the bedroom wall. Peter and Auntie Snowie laughed and Gran chased us downstairs.

That was the Double R Theatre Company's opening and farewell performance.

My next venture into production was a much more modest affair: puppets. I'd read a book from the library, *The Peep Show*, a true story, by Walter Wilkinson (who, years later, I played in a Channel 4 series *The Puppet Man*). It was basically about the author's escape from the rat race by building a puppet show and walking across the West Country, living on what he could collect from customers. It was the only book I could find that told you how to make glove puppets and a Punch and Judy type booth. I made the booth and the complete cast of *Treasure Island*, inspired, I would guess, by the Disney film and Robert Newton's Long John Silver. I don't remember actually ever giving a show. Being in charge of the theatre and all the actors was enough for me.

But that wasn't my first brush with show business. Oh no. I only heard this story a few years back when I was in a TV series called *As Common as Muck*. It was about a gang of dustbin men and starred Edward Woodward. One day during a break in filming, Ted called me into his caravan for a cup of tea.

'You come from Croydon, don't you?' he asked. 'Well, so do I. You were brought up by your Gran, Alice?'

'Yes,' said I.

'And she had a mate called Daisy?'

'Yes, I used to call her Aunt Daisy.'

'Well, she was my real Aunt Daisy and when Alice and Daisy went shopping I used to babysit you!'

It was all true. I've dined out many a time since on having The Equalizer as a babysitter.

Around this period I remember finding out people could actually die, especially old grans. So, at the end of an afternoon on Ron's dad's stall, I just had time to get to Woolworths (how I mourned its passing, like so many others of my vintage) to buy something for Gran. I tried to show her how much I loved her – and make amends for my bad behaviour – by lashing out on little presents for her, like a pencil, a ball of string or, once, a couple of sticks of liquorice wood.

'What!' said she, 'With my teeth?'

I hope by now you're beginning to see just exactly why she meant so much to me. From the age of seven to seventeen she was my guide, mentor, explainer of what, to her, was justice, what was of value and what wasn't, teacher of songs and disperser of the blues. She fed and clothed me, paid the rent and introduced me to the love of my life – show business. She did all this on an Old Age Pension. How she did it I'll never know, but she had had good practice raising her four daughters in even worse circumstances. I never, ever, felt deprived, only gratitude that she liked me enough to let me stay with her.

CHAPTER THREE

'You silly bugger!'

I passed the eleven plus and, how I've regretted it, didn't take up the offer of a place at a grammar school. It would have been so useful to have had that sort of education and perhaps have gone to university. I know I would have enjoyed the atmosphere and made friends and I'm sure the whole experience would have served me well in later life. When I first worked in BBC Radio nearly everyone involved with light entertainment was from Oxford or Cambridge – the comics I knew called them the Oxbridge Mafia.

I settled for staying on at Tavistock till I could go to Croydon Secondary Technical School – the School of Building. Nearly all the lads of my vintage were advised to 'get a trade', and that's what I, and Gran, thought would be best for me. At the School of Building we were taught terrific (to other people) things: bricklaying, carpentry, plumbing and technical drawing. I wasn't bad at any of these, but none of them set me alight. Maybe technical drawing was a touch more appealing than Dutch bond, Queen closures and bossing lead, but I soon lost the trust of the specialist teachers. I was quickly bored. Boredom is still fatal for me. I always start looking for something to distract me, and anyone else I'm with – certainly I've lost quite a few jobs by being a distraction. Even all those years ago, the saving grace for me was being able to make people laugh. Maybe that was the start of it all.

I was a disappointment to most of my teachers. I disappointed Mr Sheridan by arranging walls and arches that, with the removal of just one brick, were reduced to debris. I disappointed Mr Griffin by producing a beautiful pair of drumsticks instead of a useful mortice and tenon joint. I infuriated Mr Quirk by coming top in the plumbing written exam. He knew I knew nothing about the subject and hated getting my hands dirty handling pipes and spanners. The night before the written exam I looked through the theory exercise books. There was just one detailed diagram: the cross-section of a hot water system. I convinced myself it would be asked for the next day and so I practised drawing every detail of it. Well, what d'you know, came the exam and it was the first question! My effort was a masterpiece, immaculately drawn, in colour, complete with all the un-understood figures and measurements, which I'd learned parrot fashion. I came top. Which proved how right I was, and still am, to dismiss one-off examinations. Surely being judged by work over a period of time has got to be better? I came top and both I, and Mr Quirk and every single one of my classmates, knew I was a lousy, ill-educated, uninterested plumber.

Mr Macadam liked me. I was a fair draughtsman – and keen.

Alas my designing posters for my favourite films in technical drawing classes soon disillusioned him.

We had a history teacher, Mr Smith, who could have been cast as the archetypal teacher: corduroy jacket with the leather elbows, top pocket full of pens, and a barely controlled crop of red hair. His one distinguishing difference? He spoke very beautifully – and very carefully. He was the very meaning of Received Pronunciation (BBC spoken English). All our class were very impressed with his posh delivery but I was sure I could spot a slightly north of Watford accent in there. I took bets that I could get him to speak in his native tongue.

At his next class I did my distracting worse. I started by simply, and constantly, dropping pens, rulers, etc. I then questioned every fact he gave us and even illustrated some of my aggravating enquiries with bursts of 'I'm 'Enery the Eighth I Am' and 'One of the Ruins That Cromwell Knocked About a Bit'. Finally, after a couple of missile-like bits of chalk had headed my way, 'Smudger' Smith could stand it no longer. His face changed colour so you couldn't see where the skin finished and the hair began.

Throwing down his blackboard cleaner, he roared at me, 'Hood! Wun more peep out of thee and you'll measure thy length ont floo-er!' I won a few bob and Mr Smith stopped 'putting it on' from that moment onwards.

I'm convinced that good teachers are the people who shape your life, and I had one good 'un at the School of Building. Our English teacher was Tom Gibson, a chunky, fairly old (to us), one-off. On a Friday afternoon, we'd have 'free reading' periods. They were a pain as the teacher would supply the books to read and they were never the ones we liked. Tom's free periods were different. He made it clear that he didn't mind what we read and told us to bring our own reading matter. This was heaven to the lads, and the desks were littered with issues of *Wizard*, *Hotspur* American super-hero comics, even *The Beano* and *The Dandy*.

Tom would wander round the classroom, looking over shoulders and, his masterstroke, ask what it was in what we were reading that we liked. He would follow this by saying he had a book like that. He'd then produce it and read us scenes. He was good. He could have made the Telephone Directory exciting. I still remember him doing the arrival of Blind Pew at *Treasure Island*'s Admiral Benbow Inn. Within two terms he'd turned us all on to good stuff. Clever.

Tom was a Communist and, indeed, was a football correspondent for the *Daily Worker*. Yet again, my distraction techniques bore fruit. Whenever he attempted to get heavy with us and started on syntax and iambic pentameter, my classmates would give me the nod and I'd put my hand up.

'Excuse me, sir, but I was reading the *Daily Mail* this morning and I do think that, as far as the unions are concerned, the Conservatives have got it right.' That was all that was needed. The rules of grammar were immediately forgotten as Tom steamed into a violent dismissal of the Tories and an explanation of the absolute joy of following Karl Marx.

All it required was the occasional, 'Could you explain, sir?' or, even better, 'I don't agree, sir!' and we'd escaped.

So many silly people these days kick up a fuss about teachers being able to brainwash their pupils. I don't believe it. Kids today are surely just as sharp as we were all those years ago. We knew exactly what we were up to. And I think Tom did too. He was an enthusiast, an inspirer, a larger-than-life entertainer and an informer par excellence. He had, though we'd never heard of the word at the time, true charisma.

I wrote a piece for an article on 'Teachers I remember', and raved about Tom Gibson. I wasn't his only fan. I had dozens of letters from ex-pupils on whom he'd worked his magic, and four from folk who became teachers themselves because of the effect he'd had on them.

I've said I was unathletic, which is true, but there was one sport I fancied: table tennis. I'd seen it on television and it didn't look too energy sapping – and I could see myself in the T-shirt and shorts. In a shop window, on a Roneo'd sheet of A4, was the message: 'If you'd like to play table tennis, come and join us at The Sir Philip Game Boys' Club.'

In the early 1950s, Croydon was a trouble spot. The front page of one national newspaper had a photograph of a group of Teddy boys, most of whom I knew, looking hard as they walked down Croydon High Street under a headline, 'THE MOST DANGEROUS TOWN IN ENGLAND'. The police were doing their best to get the lads interested in something other than trouble by starting a club. Sir Philip Game himself was an ex-commissioner of the Metropolitan Police.

So I went to the club that same evening with my pal, Ron, and we happily signed up for the sport. However, the crafty coppers insisted you also signed up for another activity – an 'improving' one. I looked down a list that, to me, was just boring: metalwork, woodwork, car maintenance, judo. 'You've got to do one,' I was told. The very last activity on the list was concert party.

'What's that?' I asked the man who was signing us on.

'It's a group who put on shows, pantomimes and that. Amateur dramatics.'

'That should be all right,' said Ron. 'They won't be trying to teach us anything.'

'Okay,' I agreed, and ticked the concert party box.

The best day's work I ever did.

Ron and I turned up for the meeting of the concert party to be greeted by the producer of the shows, Tom Cooper. Quite a few others joined with us and Tom put us all in a line and went along it, casting as he went.

Ron was down for sketches and my destiny was sealed with five unforgettable words: 'You can be a comic.' Years later, Tom told me it was my having a funny face that made him catapult me into what I've been doing ever since.

Talk about falling on your feet. Tom Cooper was an ex-performer and ex-'Sand Rat' (the name for those who had been in concert parties at the seaside, who played directly on the beach). These groups didn't charge you to watch them. At the end of their show they took a collection, which was shared between the performers. This collecting was called 'bottling'. All the team had to do it, and a really good bottler was worth his weight in gold. I eventually found out, from another old performer, why it was called that. Some members of the concert party were not only ace at getting money out of their audience, they were just as good at helping themselves to a bit of it. The solution was to issue each of the collectors with a bottle. The money, once put into the bottle, was safe from any would-be syphoners: they couldn't get their hands in. The bottles were solemnly broken open and the contents equally shared in full view of the entire company.

Tom, a light comedian and dancer, had done all this and married a girl who could play the piano, Doris. When he finally became too long in the tooth to keep his legs moving (that must be the strangest sentence I've ever written!) he became a commercial traveller, and a good one. Well, he had all the old patter, didn't he?

He was the perfect example of show business being like a drug. His love of it was still in his bloodstream and at the club he was passing on what he knew to youngsters. He was the dealer who turned me into a show business junkie.

Doris got the content of the shows together and Tom put in the comedy and directed.

The first show I did was a pantomime, *Aladdin*, in 1952. I played, in drag, Fatima, an elbowed in part, the friend of Widow Twankey. The Widow was someone who soon became a friend – out of drag – Eddie Cunningham. Eddie was a terrific dame and I would watch him like a hawk. I still can't take my eyes off anyone who is good at the job.

Eddie and I had one scene together – a sort of Les Dawson and Roy Barraclough 'Sissy and Ada'-type chat at a tea table. I had an idea. If I could somehow have a bottomless teacup on the table, Eddie could pour the entire contents of a huge teapot into the cup, while we were talking.

'Good idea!' said Tom. 'Can you make the prop?'

'Of course,' I said, desperate to please the master.

I had no idea how I could make it work, but I tried and tried. I knew nothing about drilling holes in crockery but I managed, after a stack of failures, to make a tiny hole through the bottom of the mug we were going to use. My next Heath Robinson-inspired bit of magic was to fit a bit of garden hose into the bottom of the mug, which would direct the 'tea' into a bucket under the table. Making the tiny hole big enough to accept the hose was the problem, and I spent weeks with a series of round files enlarging the hole. I spent my every spare minute filing away.

Finally it was done – and it worked! Came the first night of the show and Eddie and I took our places either side of Twankey's tea table. The patter was going quite well and the never-ending pouring laugh got bigger the longer it went on. At the end of the piece, Eddie gave me a wink and I was on cloud nine. Even Tom, desperately trying to get everyone onstage at the right time, gave me the thumbs up. We ran for a week and the patter improved every night.

Oh, the sound of those laughs. I'm sure I've heard bigger ones, but none sweeter. The night before the last, I dragged Gran along.

'What is it?' she asked.

'A pantomime, and I'm in it.'

'Git out of it!'

'It's good.'

'Really,' said she who had seen it all. 'I'll let you know!'

The scene went great, as did the whole panto, and as we walked home her chuckling told me she'd had a good time.

'What did you think, Gran?' I asked her.

'It was all right,' she said.

'Did you like my bit?'

She smiled a big smile and said, 'I did – you silly bugger!' That was the moment – the rockets shot into the sky, the orchestra swelled, and waves crashed onto the rocks. 'SILLY BUGGER!' She had given me her greatest compliment and I skipped the rest of the way home. Never mind about not ever forgetting where you were when Kennedy was assassinated or Obama was made president. I know *exactly* where I was when I thought show business was for me: on the corner of Morland Avenue and Whitehorse Road, Croydon.

I made lots of friends through the Boys' Club concert party – lads and lasses I'm still in touch with now. Ray and Veronica Jones-Davies, Tim and Marion Attewell and, of course, Eddie. Most of them still have their interest in concert party and drama – inspired and nurtured by Tom and Doris.

Every year, at the Streatham Hill Theatre, the Croydon police put together a big charity show to raise funds for the club. Our concert party used to kick off the show with a snappy ten minutes of gags and songs. One year I had a little solo bit to do and, as we came off, the next turn on grabbed my arm. He said, 'That was funny. You ought to do it for a living.' He was Michael Bentine. Years later I told him this story and he said, 'Oh yes, well, keep it to yourself. I don't want thousands and thousands of people blaming me!'

I was all set, on leaving the School of Building in March 1952, to become a draughtsman and then, at the last minute, I thought I'd like commercial art. Yes, my love of illustrating my favourite films had won the day. I got a job in a little advertising agency on The Strand. They took me on because of my lettering. I thought I'd be used in their studio for that, but no. I was mostly employed as a messenger, delivering artwork to the newspaper offices along Fleet Street.

In the early fifties, Fleet Street was still the hub of the newspaper business. There were dozens of 'London offices' up little alleyways and courts. They were the London offices of provincial newspapers like *The Black Country Bugle* and *The Redruth Packet*. I climbed so many narrow staircases to attic rooms where, straight from Dickens, old boys still sat on tall stools and, if I'd have really looked, were probably doing their business with real ink and quill pens. The agency allowed me bus fares, so I supplemented my two pounds fifteen shillings (£2.75) wage by walking everywhere.

I can't begin to describe the feeling of bringing home my first week's wages. I remember sitting at the kitchen table with Gran and letting her open my wage packet. She took a pound and gave me the rest. 'Right!' she said, 'That'll do.' The next day's lunch was two big steak and chips with all the trimmings. I'm sure it cost her more than a quid.

When I wasn't marching all over the City, and pocketing at least a shilling (5p) a day, I was back in the studio, being encouraged by our studio manager, John Morton, to be a proper lettering and layout artist.

There were two, to me, very sophisticated lady artists working with John.

Gill Pickles, sister of the actress Vivienne, and Phyllida Legge, a very offbeat, likeable and funny girl. Though never spoken, I did carry a torch for her: yet another witty girl who turned me on.

Someone else who was far too far above me was the telephone operator, Yvonne. She, when a little girl, had been a dancer in an amateur children's show and I still remember her singing to me their signature tune (to 'Happy Days are Here Again'):

HAPPY DAYS ARE HERE AGAIN
THE MORGAN JUVENILES ARE HERE AGAIN...

Yvonne and another would-be advertising giant, Peter Newsome, would occasionally join me for a lunchtime session of jazz at the Fleet Street Jazz Club. Some of the very best bands and soloists in the world were blackmailed into playing there. The jazz club organizers made it known that if they played Fleet Street they were ensured good publicity for upcoming tours, etc. If they didn't, well . . .

It was there, one Friday lunchtime, that the hugely popular New Orleans revival trad band of Chris Barber were the attraction. To break up the concerted items, he introduced his banjo player to sing what he called a skiffle number. The number was 'Rock Island Line' and the singer was Lonnie Donegan. He paralysed that tough, know-all crowd, and his one number became a recital of dozens of American folk songs that Lonnie knew. How long he went on for I can't guess, but no one left and, when we did get back to the office, the boss gave us a hell of a telling-off. Unusual for him as he rarely came out of his office.

He was a chubby rogue who chased all the girls in his employ around his desk. I think he caught some, as so many would emerge from his inner sanctum with red faces and slightly perspiring brows. The boss's partner was a lovely bloke, Ken Curtis. He was on my side and arranged for me to have time off to go to the London School of Printing and Graphic Arts. He also organized for me to go to the Regent Street Poly for an evening class. And there I was again lucky enough to have an inspiring teacher. A big, gentle man with a sense of humour who talked sense – especially as far as graphic design was concerned. His name was Harry Beck. He was, wait for this, the man who designed the London Underground map in 1932. Since then, all sorts of changes were tried but Harry's original has won through every time. They always go back to the best.

When you think of the brief he was given – to simplify an existing map where all the stations were placed geographically – where did he start? The use of different colours for the different lines was a masterstroke, as was the laying-out of the network in a simple form. Totally unrealistic, but so easy to follow. Mr Beck's map is accepted as a masterpiece of design all over the world. His name, H. C. Beck, was dropped from the bottom right-hand corner of the map for a few years, but now, quite rightly, it is back again. Have a look.

Harry Beck knew the illustrator, sculptor and designer of alphabets, the notorious Eric Gill. Gill designed and sculpted the figures of Prospero and Ariel above the entrance to BBC Broadcasting House. Harry remembered that Gill had done most of the work on the figures in his studio but finished the job with them *in situ*. As was his wont, Gill sculpted wearing a sort of cassock that didn't in the slightest hide his meat and two veg. Harry said, 'We'd never seen so many secretaries going in and out of Broadcasting House, constantly checking cloud formations!' Harry Beck: yet another master craftsman I had the pleasure of being taught by.

Things couldn't have been better. A proper job that I enjoyed, shows at the Boy's Club and a few bob on the kitchen table that Gran and I could squander on a couple of ice creams at the Empire on Carnival Night. We were in clover.

Sadly, as happens so often – as one door opens, another swings back and smacks you in the whatsits. Our good fortune came to a devastating halt.

I'd only been at work a few weeks when, on a Monday evening – and looking forward to Carnival Night on the Tuesday – I came home and, noisily, let myself into the house. It was silent. No 'What Ho, Huddy!' No 'Picasso's back!' No burst of a music hall song. No note of explanation. I really did feel the cold sweat of fear as I went upstairs.

She was in my bedroom, lying on the floor next to an upturned chair with a chamois leather in her hand. She was very still, but not dead. 'God,' I thought. 'How long has she been lying there?' She'd said she was going to clean the windows when I'd left for work that morning, about half past seven.

I carried her to her bedroom and there she stayed for another two days. I sat by the side of the bed and only once did she say anything. At the end of the second day she suddenly jumped out of bed and, with a shout of, 'Come on, love! You'll miss the train!' started getting dressed. My heart leapt, but there was no miraculous recovery. She died within an hour.

I was desolate. I could rely no longer on someone who'd been not only my gran but my mum and dad as well.

Whatever sort of discussion took place as to which of my aunts would get lumbered with yours truly I have no idea, but there was really only one who had room, Auntie Ivy. Auntie Elsa and Uncle Jim already had five kids and Auntie Snow and Uncle Len had brother Peter. I honestly didn't care where I went. I was totally devastated. I did have the Boys' Club concert party to think about and, through that, what should have been a treasured moment in my teenage life – but wasn't.

We did have a few girls in the shows and one of them, feeling sorry for me losing Gran I suppose, forced me to desert my virginal couch. It was completely unromantic and not nice at all. I was told exactly what to do and, shaking like a leaf, did my best to comply. I didn't know whether either of us liked it very much.

I did know that this was a huge turning point in my life and, in effect, it was the much-maligned National Service that pointed me in a new direction. I'd had a year's deferment to complete my art training but now, at nineteen, it was time to join up.

In 1955, National Service meant two years' compulsory service in the Army, Navy or Air Force. I plumped for the RAF, mainly because I liked the colour of the uniform and it did seem a bit more dashing and devil-may-care than the other two. They did ask you what trade you would like to follow once you were in. I, on advice from Boys' Club chums who were already in, put down PBX operator, which meant manning the telephone switchboard. Apparently, no one ever actually chose this job, so you stood a good chance of getting it. The attraction was it took about half an hour to learn the job and promotion came very quickly. As you got a few more bob for being a senior aircraftman (SAC) rather than an aircraftman (AC) it was a good choice.

After being kitted out and given my service number (which you never forget: mine was 2765225 and I still use it if I have to quote a telephone number in a play), I was sent to West Kirby for six weeks' square-bashing. This was the part all of us dreaded. For most, it was the first time they'd been away from home: 'But my mum always cleans my shoes!' It was interesting to me that all the hard men, the ones who swore they'd sort out the Air Force, were the ones who cried themselves to sleep.

Our sergeant was a big Irishman, ex-army, with a face like the bulldog friend of Tom and Jerry. Terrifying? No. He was coming to the end of his career and just wanted peace and an easy ride to retirement. He was alone among the NCOs in quite liking the National Servicemen. The corporals were very different. They strutted about doing what they were supposed to do, shouting, never speaking, and being ludicrously horrible to us all. They used to put chains in their trousers, just above the boots, to make them hang beautifully. I still jump if I ever hear anything like the quiet chinking sound they made as they approached.

I quite liked the National Service life. I didn't miss home at all – there was nothing to go back for. I liked sharing a billet with twenty-nine others too. I'd never been much of a gang member before, and now I was. We were all in it together and there were a few laughs to be had.

There was one chore that no one enjoyed: kitchen duty. This meant reporting to the cookhouse at about 06.30 – to do whatever the cooks wanted you to do. One of the lads in our billet was a great sleeper. In bed hours before everyone else and asleep as soon as his head touched the bolster. Came the day when our lad was down for this duty the following morning, so he was tucked up and away with the fairies by 21.00. My friend, Terry Key, had an idea and, after whispered instructions, we went into action. The plan was to act as if it was the next morning and send the sleeper off to the cookhouse.

I did my bit, changing his watch to 07.00, while the rest of the lads gave an exhibition of some of the very worst 'I've-just-woken-up-and-am-getting-ready-to-start-the-day' acting imaginable. Some came from the showers with their towels and washbags; some dressed for parade; and some walked about with shaving cream on their faces.

In the midst of this scene from *Carry On National Servicemen*, someone shook the sleeper awake.

'Come on, mate! You're on cookhouse duty and it's seven o'clock!'

'Shit!' cried the sleeper, checking his watch as he struggled into his shirt, tie, trousers, tunic, socks and boots. As he dashed into the night, someone thoughtfully threw his beret after him.

'Don't turn up unsuitably dressed!'

Then we all, very quietly, turned out all the lights and got back into our beds. I lay there practically bursting. I'm never any good in those sort of situations – I always laugh.

We all heard the sound of boots hurrying across the gravel outside and then the door was thrown open to a shout of 'You bastards!'

The howl of laughter that greeted this was music to my ears. On went the lights and the sleeper ran through the billet tipping people out of bed, kicking boots, socks and uniforms everywhere while we all, helpless with laughter, could only cling to each other.

The sleeper had gone across to the cookhouse, which, of course, was deserted, and only a very unfriendly patrolling RAF policeman had told him to, 'Get back to your billet. It's ten o'clock at night – you poxy little freak!'

But even the sleeper had to admit it was a good 'un – until he was put on a charge for being out of bounds in the middle of the night!

He also missed the infamous VD film. Everyone thought this would be a naughty treat, but no. It was shown in order to put us all off sex. It was a real Mr Cholmondley-Warner job, with highly coloured close-ups of all sorts of revolting, rotting things. I lasted about four minutes before I joined the other sensitive souls who were throwing up outside the cinema.

Our sergeant, in former times, would have roasted us all for the slightest misdemeanour but, as we were his last lot, he was quite laid back about our behaviour.

My leaves during National Service were mostly spent at my Auntie Ivy and Uncle Bill's place in Coulsdon. Well, I had a bed there. But the Boys' Club shows still took precedence and I was always either at the club or with my pal Eddie. Ivy and Bill were good enough to let me have a room with them, but they weren't very happy about it. Who can blame them? Being lumbered with a troublesome, didn't know what the hell he wanted to do, just beginning to feel his oats, nineteen-year-old.

If I wasn't with the Boys' Club gang or with Eddie, I could be found with my first girlfriend, Ann Conroy, the sister of a club member. Ann was in our shows and lived just round the corner from the club. Very handy. She put up with all my hopes and dreams and encouraged me. Well, encouraged the hopes and dreams, but not much else. Ann and her family were staunch Catholics, so there was no chance of the ultimate naughtiness. Kissing? Yes – but a hand on a knee brought a swift smack round the ear.

We eventually broke up after seeing Audrey Hepburn in *The Nun's Story*. I couldn't bear the thought of the beautiful Audrey being subjected to life in a Catholic nunnery and we had a stand-up row in the street outside the cinema. Ann later married my mate Eddie and they had two smashing kids. He always was a lucky boy.

I would often get back to Coulsdon lateish, but Ivy and

Bill, who never let me have a key, would go to bed, locking the back door from the inside. I spent many an uncomfortable night sleeping on the back doorstep. Actually, although I didn't enjoy it, I did feel a bit like Chaplin – and that I *did* like.

Ivy was a fairly jolly white-haired lady, but she was nothing like her mum. I guess that all those years with Bill had made her as uptight as he was.

I quite liked Uncle Bill. He was a hairdresser and a bit of a know-all. He would insist we watched anything vaguely classical on the telly – especially Shakespeare. He would look very interested and knowing for the first half-hour, and then fall asleep. When he woke up he'd always insist he'd closed his eyes to appreciate 'the golden words' – oh yeah!

In his spare time he was a football referee, which probably accounts for his pedantic approach to everything. He was a great fan of Crystal Palace Football Club, as was I. The times Uncle Bill and I spent watching our team were the best things we did together. It was always just us two – Ivy would never come. I kept on trying to persuade her how different it was 'live', how exciting it was being in the crowd, not knowing just how it was going to develop and all that.

Finally, one Saturday she gave in and agreed to come with us. We stood in what was called the 'enclosure'. The standing wasn't a good start. At the kick-off our centre forward passed the ball back to Alfie Noakes and, with the rest of the forward line, belted up the field into the opponents' penalty box. It was one of our classic moves. Alfie stopped the ball and whacked it upfield. Alas, as so often happened, the ball came off the side of his boot and whistled towards the enclosure. It hit Ivy right in the moosh and knocked her out.

With the help of the St John's Ambulance men we carried her back to the car – Uncle Bill looking over his shoulder towards the pitch all the way.

Once home, Ivy moaned her way up to bed, while Bill and I complained about missing the match. He did come out with the occasional one-liner and this time he had a good 'un: 'They should be thankful she wasn't talking at the time or they'd never have got the ball back!'

From upstairs came a swollen-lipped, 'I 'eard that!'

When leave was over, it was back to square-bashing, which, believe it or not, I enjoyed. Because I had a loud voice as well, it was suggested I went on to be an instructor. This interest was never shown again after the rehearsal for our passing-out parade. The order was 'tallest on the right – shortest on the left – form threes!' I, in front of the entire camp, formed a fourth. That was it. I was sent off the parade ground and ordered not to take part in the passing-out ceremony.

The RAF beret was the garment we all wrestled with to make look trendy. The usual method was to soak it in water and, as it shrank, mould it into a streamlined head-hugging shape. Mine wouldn't shrink and remained this big flat thing that extended out sideways and downwards over one eye. Our sergeant was obviously a film fan and those of a certain vintage will get the perfect picture of just how the beret looked when I tell you the first time he saw me in it he did a double take and growled, 'Cor, dear – fuckin' Veronica Lake!'

Despite the constant threats of being reflighted (sent back to begin the whole six-week course from the beginning) we, without exception, finished at West Kirby and were posted to wherever we could do the least damage.

So, in late 1955, I was sent to RAF Waterbeach in Cambridgeshire, where I spent the rest of my two years. I loved it. Waterbeach was a small village with an RAF station containing three squadrons of Hawker Hunter aircraft and three thousand blokes to keep them flying.

I started work in the telephone exchange. It took our corporal, Pete Godfrey, about an hour and a half to teach me all I needed to know. Then I, naturally as always, started to look for distractions.

I found a few like-minded souls: Frank Jervois, an ex-public schoolboy who introduced me to two of my favourite humorists, James Thurber and Stephen Leacock; Alan Mills, a Geordie who had done the working-men's clubs up there; Derek Gray, who had done a bit of amateur comicking; and Mick Pickering a left-wing rogue who I worshipped. We put together a revue, *The Rafter Show*, and played it in the NAAFI. The lads liked it – especially my impression, in drag, of Lita Rosa (a popular vocalist with the Ted Heath Orchestra).

I knew no fear in those days. During the song I naturally went into the audience and sat on the lap of fiery old Wing Commander Morris. The day after the show I was walking from the canteen when, coming towards me, was the Wing Commander himself. Half hiding my face I threw him a salute. He called me back and, as I stood stock still he walked all round me and observed, 'Yes. Hudd. Hmm. Funny bugger!'

'Funny' now, as well as Gran's 'Silly' – I was getting there.

We started to put together another show and I noticed a lad called Bernie Fountain going into a back room of the

NAAFI with a trumpet case. He was joined by another lad, Geoff Hull, with a trombone, and a third, Dave Layfield, with a clarinet. Ever on the lookout for new items, I tackled Bernie about doing a spot in the next revue. He explained there were only the three of them. A drummer came along from my billet, Les Wilkinson, and we were almost there. Bernie said they needed a banjo player – and I immediately volunteered. I'd never even picked up a banjo, but Bernie wrote out a few basic chord shapes for me and I borrowed, and eventually was given, the padre's banjo. We had a band.

The three front men were fine, Les was OK, while I, hiding at the back, my face buried in the book of chords, plonked away and tried to keep the balls in the air. We did *The Rafter Show* and played local RAF camps. I have a receipt dated 4 March 1957 from the Newmarket Jazz Club, for £7.10s. It was the first time I ever got paid for entertaining. We played for four hours. I didn't have a plectrum and at the end of the evening the fingers on my right hand were just blood-soaked sausages. We got just over a quid each.

By now, the man I first saw at the Fleet Street Jazz Club had become a top-of-the-bill performer and I sang all Lonnie's hits and more. The 'mores' came about in a special way.

When I went back to Auntie Ivy and Uncle Bill's on days off, I'd catch a late train back to camp and share a compartment with, mostly American, airmen who were based at one of the many airfields around Cambridge. They'd spot the banjo on the luggage rack (I never left it at Waterbeach) and would play and sing me songs Lonnie didn't do. Songs that I still sing if I'm not stopped:

'Cakewalkin' Babies Back Home', 'Ace in the Hole', 'Hand me Down my Walkin' Cane', 'Blues My Naughty Sweetie Gives to Me', 'Take This Hammer', 'Goodnight Irene' and 'Huggin' and Chalkin''.

My pal Eddie from the Boys' Club used to come up to Waterbeach, where we honed a double act for future use.

I know it's a cliché but I really do think lads miss a lot by not doing National Service. I don't mean in the usual, 'Damn good thing. Give 'em a bit of discipline', way. I remember it as a time when you really had no responsibilities, a few bob in your pocket, somewhere to sleep, clothes to wear, a chance to make lots of friends, and plenty of good grub (we certainly did at Waterbeach – our catering bloke regularly won the Fighter Command Award for his food and we wouldn't let any other station get near him).

Apart from the band and the shows, I still looked around for more distractions. One of the tasks the on-duty telephone operator had to do was broadcast the early morning call to the whole camp. Oh yes. Too good to miss. I started by broadcasting the time in various tentative accents, Scots, Irish, Welsh – and once in a German one. These seemed to amuse the lads, so I went further. Following a chord on the banjo, the lads were treated to my sexy Lita Rosa-type voice announcing: 'Good morning boys. It's now 06.30 hours. Half past six to you. Please stop that and get out of bed!'

Of course, going too far over the top – always a fault of mine. My first seven days' jankers. And certainly not the last.

Night-time on the PBX was a bore. All night in the

exchange with hardly a call to answer, sitting on a hard-bottomed straight-backed chair. We needed something more comfortable to while away the hours on. I came up with a great idea. I smuggled a mattress into the office and, with the help of a couple of other telephone operators, fitted it into a cupboard, which we fixed against a door. Undetectable. The lads did appreciate it: it worked. But then came my chance to use my invention. I locked the exchange door, got the mattress out of its cupboard and horizontally relaxed. Disaster. I still fall asleep like lightning, and once I am I do take some shifting. I eventually awoke to lots of banging on the steel outer door to the PBX. Pretending to be awake I asked, 'Who is it?'

'Flight Sergeant Barkus!' came the reply.

'Oh really?' I said, unbelievingly, thinking it was one of the other operators. 'Put your 1250 (identity card) under the door, please.'

The card slowly came under the door to reveal the unpleasant, red face of Barkus. My second seven days' jankers. I was constantly late presenting myself at the guardroom, which meant the seven days extended to thirty-five – a camp record for one offence. It was worth it. My constant quest to be recognized was nearing fruition. First Lita Rosa and now a jankers record holder.

Everyone has strange stories to tell of their service careers, and here's one that could have been a scene from a film. It was during a Christmas break and I, still on jankers, had to stay on the camp and run the telephone exchange with one other naughty airman. I was walking from my billet to work with an armful of 78rpm records.

I'd managed to get a Dancette record player and my

evening would go much easier listening to Johnny Dodds, Louis Armstrong, George Lewis, Bessie Smith and Leadbelly. The route from billet to PBX was a straight road about half a mile long. As I started to walk I saw at the other end of the road Corporal 'Kit' Carson's Baby Austin coming, very slowly, towards me. We got closer and closer until I moved over to avoid the car. Kit's car did the same, the same way. A bit closer and we both moved the other way. We were now very close and did it again. Finally, very, very slowly, the car knocked me over. The whole business must have taken a good four minutes. It was like a scene from a Jacques Tati movie. Kit and I couldn't stop laughing as we picked up all the records. Not one was broken. Weird.

The fire station, next to the place where we, the signals staff, were housed, produced one glorious slapstick moment. One morning the lads there told us they'd just been delivered a state-of-the-art fire-fighting engine, which they were going to put through its paces later in the afternoon. At the appointed time we all lined up outside to see the great vehicle. The doors of the fire station were, with great ceremony, pushed open and the magnificent machine gently came into view. It was a large, spectacular, gleaming masterpiece of the military vehicle-maker's art. It came towards us and almost immediately took a sharp turn left. It fell over. It lay there like a dead elephant. Red-faced firemen rushed out from the garage, while we all rolled around with helpless laughter. Warrant Officer Sloane, who had laughed louder than anyone, chased us all back to work, and the giant fire engine was never seen again.

I mentioned Mick Pickering, my fellow show deviser, earlier. He was a great big bloke, always arguing with anyone who dared to disagree with anything he said. He was a boozer and, like so many others I've known, highly intelligent. I thought he was wonderful. I can see him now full of Worthington E, his huge black overcoat flying out behind him, careering through the streets of Cambridge looking for fun – and trouble. I would run along behind him knowing something was going to happen. It usually did.

One Friday night we'd both had a few and were weaving our wobbly way to the bus that would take us back to the camp. Mick suddenly spotted an illuminated sign over a door that said, 'The King-Slocombe School of Dance'. Without a word, he burst through the entrance. Half a dozen rather nice couples were staggering their way through a waltz. They stopped and stared in total bewilderment as Pickering, with a terrifying roar, stood in the middle of the dance floor, threw out his arms and declared, in a deep African voice, 'I am de King Slocombe!' Two burly Cambridgeshire heavies threw him out, and me. I met Mick again years later on the front at Brighton where I was filming a scene for a sitcom. He'd become a teacher and I bet he was a damn good 'un.

Yet again, it was being in trouble that led me to my most unforgettable Christmas in the RAF. Because I was confined to camp over the festive season I, with the help of another naughty boy, had to run the telephone exchange. The place was practically deserted as I started my Christmas Eve all-night shift. I sat there dreaming of the stockings Gran used to fill for me and of having a tin of condensed milk all to myself (I was mad about condensed milk at the time). Eventually, I nodded off, only to be woken by a tap, tap, tap on the exchange window. Never the Richard Todd of

Waterbeach, I was petrified. It was about two in the morning and I hid behind the switchboard shouting shakily, but loudly, 'Okay, Hudd. You stay where you are. I, Flight Sergeant Barkus, will deal with this!'

The tapping continued, so I carefully peeped over the top of the board, and there, looking in, was Father Christmas.

It couldn't be him: Gran had told me there wasn't one.

'Can I help you?' I enquired politely.

'Huddy 2765225?' the bringer of goodwill whispered.

'Er, yes.'

'Open the window!'

I did – just six inches – and it caught him on the elbow. From his comment I knew he was an imposter.

'Ho bloody ho!' he cried. 'Do you think I'd forget an 'orrible little hairy man like you? Me and my elves in the guardroom have brought you this.' He passed me what looked like a holly paper-wrapped hand grenade and wended his wobbly way towards the guardroom. I knew him. It was one of the RAF Regiment Corporals in an outfit he'd borrowed from the sergeant's mess. 'Merry Christmas, you poxy little National Serviceman,' he called over his shoulder.

I unwrapped my present. It was a tin of condensed milk.

Who said that RAF police had no hearts?

Despite all the jankers, I became happier the longer I stayed at Waterbeach. I was doing the shows, playing with the band, even contributing to the station newspaper with cartoons and articles. After the sadness of losing Gran, I really felt the RAF were my family. So, just before I was due to be demobbed, I put it about that I might sign on as a regular.

'Tod' Sloane, our kindly, one-of-the-lads Warrant

Officer, called me into his office. He liked me. He knew, of course, of the so-called shame I brought onto the signals section, and didn't mind. It amused him to ask me just how I managed to keep getting into trouble, and he enjoyed my explanations.

'Now then, Hudd,' he said. 'Sit down. I hear you're thinking of joining up full time?' I nodded shyly and he carried on. 'Don't, please. We did all right in the War without you, so please don't go and spoil things.'

After I laughed, he told me how different things could be for a regular airman. 'You like it here. Don't we all. Cambridge just down the road. The only concern is the exciting one of keeping the aircraft flying. No bullshit. No dreary regimented routines. Morale is good and, my son, some of that is down to you. You make the lads laugh. But how will you feel if you're posted away from here to some dangerous arsehole spot? It can happen overnight. Why don't you try show business?'

First Michael Bentine and now W/O Sloane: I took his advice. A couple of months later W/O Sloane was posted to Cyprus and shortly afterwards he and his wife were killed coming out of church.

On 13 November 1957 I made a Chaplin-esque exit from the scene of so much action. I'd learned a terrific lot and, most importantly for someone who is basically a shy person (honestly!), I learned, by sharing a bedroom with twenty-nine other blokes, how to get on with all sorts. It has stood me in good stead in show business ever since.

As I walked out of the camp, past the real Spitfire that stood at the gate, I remember wondering, 'Where the hell am I going?'

I'm still wondering.

Debbie and I went back to see the place a few years ago. The Spitfire was still there, but the army, the Royal Electrical and Mechanical Engineers (REME), were running what was left of the place. Luckily, the guardroom sergeant was a bit of a fan and he let one of his lads show us around. My billet was still there, as was the NAAFI canteen, where I helped kill the trad jazz revival and got a few laughs. Station Headquarters, which included the telephone exchange, was where it always was – the place where my buggering about got me so many days on jankers.

Was it worth it? YES!

CHAPTER FOUR

'Are you as funny as you look?'

While I'd been away, stopping the Russians invading Waterbeach, some swine had invented Letraset, rub-down lettering that anybody could use, so the future for a Harry Beck-trained artist had disappeared down the Swanee.

I was pleased really, because after successes at the Boys' Club and in the RAF I really did want to go into show business. Eddie and I had kept up our double act and felt we now had something to offer, so I wrote to the Nuffield Centre.

Situated just behind St Martin-in-the-Fields in central London, the Nuffield Centre was a sort of 'club' for servicemen. You could get food there, find some company, and you could sometimes get tickets for West End shows. One night I was lucky enough to get a ticket for *The Mousetrap*, and the seat next to me was empty. As now, if people arrived at a show after curtain up they weren't shown to their seat till the first interval. I saw a shadowy figure lurking in the aisle and, come the interval, the seat next to mine was filled. It was Winston Churchill! He didn't have a lot to say.

But back to the Nuffield Centre. Every Tuesday they mounted a variety show and, by lying about our experience (saying we were pros), the guv'nor there, Mary Cook, put us on. Being fresh out of the RAF, I put in all sorts of little bits only a serviceman would understand and we went well. After the show a bloke came round and asked if we'd be interested in working at Butlins for the summer. Would we!

The next day we went to the Butlins office in town and signed contracts for the 1958 season at Clacton Camp in Essex. Come the day we duly arrived, full of bonhomie and enthusiasm. A whole summer as professional entertainers! Now known as 'Hudd and Kay', as we agreed that 'Hudd and Cunningham' sounded more like a firm of solicitors.

We weren't treated like professional entertainers. The first thing we were told to do was sit on a chair to be photographed, holding a number in front of our chests. I made some crack about being convicted criminals and was told by the photographer, 'Shut up! No laughing!'

The jolliness we came in with was rapidly disappearing. We were then sent to another building 'to get your uniforms'. Uniforms? Surely professional entertainers don't wear *uniforms*?

Our uniforms were white trousers, white socks and shoes, white shirt, striped tie and – a red coat! Reading the contracts we had so excitedly signed, we saw we were employed as redcoat entertainers. This meant that, apart from doing our act whenever required, we did all the redcoat duties as well: up at the crack of dawn to shepherd the campers in for early breakfasts (7.30 a.m.); refereeing every sort of competition from football to knobbly knees; dancing with the girls no one else would dance with; taking the kids to the fair; leading pub sing-songs; doing midnight cabaret; and spending twenty-four hours a day smiling. It was very hard work, especially the constant grinning.

Butlins was an odd place. Having just left the RAF I couldn't see a join as far as the staff were concerned. The camps were organized by ex-service personnel and run just the way the army was. However the campers themselves *weren't* treated like conscripts, as so many have suggested they were. The camp at Clacton had everything for every type. All the fun for outgoing folk, and all the quiet places for those who didn't like being hassled. A Butlins holiday was – probably still is – just perfect for couples with kids. There were nurses, children's entertainers and night patrols to look after the offspring, while the mum and dad, often for the first time in years, were able to dance, see shows and have a drink together.

On the back of the identity card we all had to have to get in and out of the camp was a piece written by Billy Butlin himself. It told us how important it was to make the campers' every waking hour wonderful because so many had saved for fifty weeks to go on holiday. Some mornings I'd read this brainwashing tract and think, 'He's right,' and I'd go at it like a good 'un. Other mornings I'd think, 'What a load of bollocks!' and spend the day avoiding punters.

You didn't have to be a fantastic talent to be a redcoat. You just needed to be friendly, always ready to chat, and have a constant smile on your face. It was a place where would-be performers could knock the first rough edges off their talents. I believe it still is.

Another very useful thing you learned: just in case you did become well known in later years, it was good practice for signing autographs. Every redcoat was a star.

Our fellows were either like us – trying to go further – or old hands who had been at it for years. Jimmy Perry, an exredcoat, who wrote *Dad's Army*, got it pretty well right in *Hi-de-Hi*!

We lived on the camp and Eddie and I shared a chalet – a posh name for a five-foot-wide cell with a double bunk and a chair: we took it in turns to sit down. In the chalet next door was an Irish redcoat, Dave O'Mahoney who too did a turn. His was a rather manic routine where he ran all over the stage doing a sort of impression of Jerry Lewis. Years later he scored with a totally different kind of comedy ... under the name Dave Allen.

There were all sorts of bands and musicians to cater for every taste. In the Rock and Roll Ballroom – yes that's what it was called – was a terrific group, The Vic Allen Combo. The trumpet player was John Barry (who later became synonymous with the Bond films). Vic Allen himself became a number one session guitarist under the name Vic Flick. The pianist did all right too. He was Les Reed who wrote 'It's Not Unusual', 'The Last Waltz', 'Delilah', 'Kind of Hush' and loads more.

Halfway through the season, a very young bloke arrived with his own musicians. They were introduced to us as Harry Webb and The Drifters. The kids liked them and they'd made a record that was played on Radio Butlin night and day. The record, 'Move It', made it into the charts and the lads were away as Cliff Richard and the Drifters.

The main attraction for young male campers was the availability of girls. For the redcoats too. Some of them were very good at it and each Saturday (changeover day) at Clacton Station, these redcoated lotharios would be waving goodbye to last week's conquests, while clocking what was just arriving.

When teenage lads, all set for a Rabelaisian vacation, arrived at the camp they were booked in and shown to their chalets by gorgeous girls in red coats. 'Paradise!' they thought, but the 'gorgeous redcoat girls' were the dancers from the professional revue company and after Saturday's shop window they were only ever seen again on stage.

Much as I'd like to be able to tell you I was a lothario – I wasn't.

I was, and still am, a very late developer and I really was far more interested in getting laughs and giggles than giving slaps and tickles. I did have a girlfriend who was just that – a friend. At the height of the season the firm employed lots of students on vacation. This lady student was mad about skiffle and, when Eddie was out of the chalet, I'd sing her my entire repertoire. I sat on the chair while she sat on the top bunk. Never the twain did meet. Sorry. I'll try and think of some raunchier stuff as I go along.

The big event of the week for Eddie and me was *The Redcoat Show*. This was our chance to do our act in a big theatre with a good orchestra. The first performance was a memorable one. We finished our spot and had to come straight back on, wearing plastic macs, for a concerted number, 'Singing in the Rain'. The lighting backstage was lousy and I just managed to find my mac. Eddie – not so lucky. Backstage was now totally black and, with colourful comments he searched, by braille, for his raincoat. 'We're on!' I shouted, and we stepped out to join the others.

Eddie, desperately trying to swing his arms, looked like a giant embryo butterfly. He'd fought his way into a dry cleaning cover. I don't think the campers could work out what he was meant to be.

The campers were really three different types. The young, out for a naughty time, the rum and blackcurrant and pint of cider drinkers; the mum and dad with a bunch of kids; and the OAPs who'd been going to the camps for years. These were the dodgy ones. Some were completely obsessed with Butlins and walked about wearing jackets loaded with dozens of metal badges they'd collected from previous holidays.

Some were on House Committees (placing the campers into four different teams – like the houses we had at school). The worst of these committee members were real Hitler Oldies. I was reported to the Camp Commander several times for unbelievable sins:

'I was walking to the Viennese Ballroom yesterday morning and Redcoat Roy wasn't smiling.'

'A four-year-old girl playfully kicked Redcoat Roy and he told her to stop it!'

'The Beaver Club threw handfuls of mud from the boating pool at Redcoat Roy. There happened to be some stones in one of the handfuls and, quite accidentally, his forehead was cut. He ran off to the medical centre leaving the boating pool unattended!'

Some folk became obsessed with winning points for their House. One time we had a pram race and I had to push a very old lady. We hit a kerb and she went headfirst out of the pram and knocked herself out. I was petrified for her but, when she (thankfully!) came round, her first words were, 'Did we win?'

Just like Paul Shane in *Hi-de-Hi!* we had a camp comic. Not camp *à la* Larry Grayson, but a fella who toured the camp night and day doing comical things. Ours was Don

Cook, a highly inventive chap who could get laughs out of any situation. He knew no fear and would say to me, 'Loosen up! Shout a bit, grab people, do daft things. You could be a camp comic.'

I never could be. I was all right on a stage but not face-to-face, close up, in the street, in *daylight*.

One of Don's whimsicalities, which always caused great merriment, I wish he'd never thought of. At an early breakfast I was welcoming the customers into the dining room when Don ambled in and spotted me. For no reason at all, he picked me up (I was about eight stone when wet then) and hung me on a high-up nail. I hung there about three feet from the ground, too scared to try to get down in case I ripped my jacket. This got such a laugh he did it every time he saw me in the canteen. Why the sight of a skinny, bespectacled, long-haired, grinning twit hanging limply from a nail was funny I don't know. It didn't make *me* laugh, but I did keep smiling.

Billy Butlin himself appeared at the camp – just once. He was greeted by the campers as if it was the Second Coming. He arrived at lunchtime and marched through the dining room, followed by his gang of acolytes. He smiled, shook hands, kissed babies – the lot. At the end of his tour he gave us a nod and commented to the man in charge of the catering, 'The sauce bottle on table 35 had a torn label.'

We all thought, 'Wow! Fancy him noticing that!' Thinking back, I'm convinced the sauce bottle had been planted.

The season finished and Eddie and I were invited to go to a Butlin Hotel for the winter, but we'd had enough. We had big ideas and we'd come a long way since we were spotted at the Nuffield Centre. So what did we do next? We made another huge step forward by doing another showcase spot – at the Nuffield Centre.

But this time our backstage visitor was Morris Aza, a young agent from a very famous show business family. Morris said he'd liked what we'd done and that he'd like to represent us. As soon as he assured us he didn't want us for redcoat entertainers we agreed and he became our agent. In 2009, Morris retired, having been my agent for fifty years.

Morris's dad, Bert Aza, had been an agent, and when he died Morris's mum, Lilian, took over. After a stint in the rag trade and working in films (doing everything from sweeping the cutting-room floor to production managing and casting for commercials), Morris eventually joined Lilian in the agency. Eddie and I were the first performers he signed.

On the surface, Lilian was the most untypical agent. She was a toff. A cuddly white-haired lady who was constantly encouraging, and ready with a chat and char when things weren't so good for you. She was also a highly respected businesswoman – nobody messed with Lilian. One day I went to see Morris in the agency office, which was part of Lilian's house in the Edgware Road. I walked through the front garden and sitting there were Lilian and someone who looked like her clone: it was Gracie Fields, and they were *amazingly* alike.

'Roy,' said Mrs Aza (I never called her anything else), 'This is Grace. Grace, this is Roy Hudd. He's a comic.'

'Oh aye,' said Gracie. 'Are you as funny as you look?'

'Well er . . .' I blushed becomingly.

'Yes he is,' said Lilian.

I am incurably stage-struck and to be there, talking to the

greatest female performer we've ever produced, turned my legs to jelly. How I wished my gran could have been there with me. She, like me, thought Gracie was the very best. I met and watched the great lady perform many times over the following years, and she really did get better as she got older. Even when the magnificent voice aged a bit she could still sell a song, tell its story, better than anyone. For me, only she and Frank Sinatra could make the most ordinary piece of material sound like a classic.

In the year Morris took us on, 1959, variety shows were still holding their own – just about. With all the contacts Lilian had built up through representing Gracie and Stanley Holloway, she managed to get us, Hudd and Kay, a few weeks in the provincial theatres. She did actually get us a spot in a TV talent show for ABC TV called *Bid For Fame* (alas we were outbid).

In an attempt to halt the unstoppable advance of television, lots of theatres tried a rather odd hybrid sort of evening. They renamed the theatres by adding the word 'Continental' – Hull Continental, Chatham Continental and the like. They were just what they'd always been, but tables and chairs replaced the stalls and food was served – famous continental dishes like pie and chips.

Aston Hippodrome was still operating, presenting nude shows – another desperate last throw of the variety dice. Eddie and I worked there – not as strippers but as 'special guest artistes'. The show was called *Striptease Vin Rouge*. We finished the first half – a fairly depressing job – working to an audience of, mostly, raincoat-on-laps businessmen. We got through though and Eddie sensibly suggested we repair to the pub opposite. We did and joined our boss, the stripper

Pauline Penny, at the bar. Pauline, dressed in a beautiful fur coat, was holding court and welcomed us warmly. She bought us a drink. By now the interval was over and Eddie reminded Pauline that she was first turn on in the second half.

'Don't worry, love,' said Pauline. 'I'm all ready.' She opened her coat and had nothing on but three rather sad faded paper roses: two small and one rather big.

We were very wet behind the ears and during the week we ran out of money. We'd paid for our digs in advance. Payday was Friday, so for the whole of Wednesday and Thursday we had nothing to eat – just two big slices of bread pudding. As we collected our wages on Friday morning, Eddie confided to Pauline we hadn't eaten for two days.

'You twerps!' she said. 'I'd have given you a sub!' We were such nice boys we wouldn't have dreamed of asking. We blew the whole week's wage on two walloping great mixed grills.

Our first week's variety in London was at The Metropolitan Music Hall, Edgware Road – the legendary Met. We only got the job because another of Mr Aza's acts – Billy Whitaker and Mimi Law – had to drop out of the show. We duly arrived at the theatre for the band call on the Monday morning.

After finding our dressing room (I got a nosebleed every time we climbed up to it) I wandered around on the ground floor calling out, 'Harry Webb! Where's Harry Webb?' A door opened, a head popped out and whispered, 'It's Cliff Richard now!' He'd done slightly better than us since leaving Butlins and was now topping the bill at The Met. His Elvis-style hair-do and pink jacket were fast becoming famous.

That variety bill was an odd one – a mixture of standard comics, dancers and speciality acts – the sort of stuff we'd seen for years – and, headlining, this boy with a rock group who pulled in a big, very young audience.

Eddie and I were only in our early twenties and, while Cliff's audience were bored to tears with the older performers, we got away with it. The kids liked us because we were different – not very good, but full of enthusiasm.

Every night, outside the stage door, there were dozens of jailbait waiting to catch a glimpse of the top of the bill. One night a girl stopped us and said, ''Ere, give us your autographs!' We were thrilled.

'Certainly, love,' said I, 'Where's your autograph book?'

'Not on me book – on me belly!' she said. Whereupon she pulled up her jumper, displaying all sorts of writing on her flesh. 'What I do, you see,' she told us as we signed, 'is get the signatures, and then a friend of mine goes over them with a tattoo needle.' She pointed out several names – Rory Storm, Vince Eager, Duffy Power, Wee Willie Harris.

'Have you got Cliff's?' Eddie asked politely.

'Not 'arf!' came the reply.

'Where?' I asked.

'Mind your own business!'

I wonder if she's still got the tattoos and if they now read:

R O Y   H U D D   &   E D D I E   K A Y

The best week's variety we did was at the Finsbury Park Empire in 1959. Top of the bill was the immortal (to me and so many people) Max Miller. The first two images I remember seeing on a stage were a man wearing a floral suit with plus-fours, a colourful tie and a white hat (Max's uniform) and another with a long moth-eaten fur coat and a broken boater (Bud Flanagan). Max was a favourite of Gran's and the only time we deserted the Croydon Empire was when he was working at Chelsea Palace or the Met and she'd take me with her to see 'The Cheeky Chappie'.

Neighbours used to complain that Max was a smutty comic and that young lads shouldn't be taken to his shows. To which Gran would reply, 'He doesn't understand what Max is talking about. He likes the way he dresses and his smile.'

Actually I often *did* know what Max was talking about but I wouldn't let on, and Gran never realized I was on to that sort of innuendo until we sat at home one evening listening to a quiz programme, *Have a Go*. It was a simple idea. Wilfred Pickles, a very popular broadcaster, would take himself, his wife, Mabel, his producer Barney Colehan (who eventually invented *The Good Old Days* for BBC TV) and pianist Violet Carson (later to become Ena Sharples) to a village or town hall, where he'd interview local characters. The first guest on this particular show was asked his name.

'John Thomas Hitchcock,' an ancient country voice replied, boldly.

I burst out laughing and so did Gran. She looked at me and blushed. I didn't – and she suddenly knew I was growing up.

But back to our week at Finsbury Park. Max was topping the bill and there with him were two living links with the golden years of the old music hall: G.H. Elliott and Hetty King. G.H. Elliott blacked up and presented himself as a negro. He had a super lyrical voice and was a great soft-shoe dancer. Hetty King was a male impersonator, whose most famous song is still sung today, 'All the Nice Girls Love a Sailor'. Also on the bill were impressionist Peter Cavanagh and a comedienne who became a special pal, Audrey Jeans.

The girls of the Ballet Montparnasse opened the show, and we were on. The conductor was a horrible bloke called Sidney Kaplan who loved it when greenhorns were on the bill. At the rehearsal he would throw their band parts about and offer to write 'proper ones' for a fee. He would also offer 'beautiful' leatherette folders in which to keep your music 'with the name of the act in gold on the front'. Again, they cost. We had been warned about him so turned down his kind offers.

He did laugh at the act – just once. We thought we must have done something better than usual. What could it be? I looked at Eddie, he looked at me, and Kaplan looked at my flies. That's what he was laughing at – they were undone. I've never gone on a stage since without checking.

Our act was an odd little spot which had gone well with the kids at the Met but wasn't really right for the old diehards of variety. We just about got away with it.

One night we were first on and, when I looked into the wings, there was Max Miller watching us. We came off and he was still there. He grabbed us.

'Very good, boys,' he said. 'Original. That's what I like to see. I was once, you know, but now I do what my audience expect. I liked that Shakespeare bit you did.' It was supposed to be a take-off of Noël Coward, but if Max said it was Shakespeare, that was good enough for us.

'Come upstairs, boys,' he said. 'I've got a few ideas that may help. Come on. I'll get you a drink.'

We couldn't believe this. He was notorious for never putting his hand in his pocket. At the Monday rehearsal one of the stagehands said to us, 'Watch this, the mean old bastard. This is the way to get him at it.'

'Any chance of a drink, Max?' the stagehand called out.

'No chance!' Max replied. 'I work hard for my money. I'm not giving it to you lot to piss up the wall!'

But now he said 'I'll get you a drink' to Eddie and me – by golly that was one to tell the rest of show business.

'Come on,' he said, and he took us into the empty bar. All the customers were in the auditorium watching the show. 'Sit down.' We did, and he gave us all sorts of useful advice. Putting the patter in a different order, doing a tiny dance break in one of our songs and suggesting we used a couple of instruments. No sign of the promised drink.

He went on further … still no drink. I looked at Eddy and sighed – he'd caught us. I stood up and asked what he wanted. 'Sit down!' he said, and carried on with ideas and stories of folk he'd worked with.

Now Eddie got up with his hand in his pocket. 'What would you like, Mister Miller?'

'Cor, dear!' said Max. 'I asked *you* up for a drink! Now just sit down for a minute. Relax.'

More help and more stories followed till, eventually, the doors of the bar burst open and in came the punters for the interval. The first bloke in spotted Max and said, 'Blimey! He's here! What will you have, Max?'

'I'll have a large gin and tonic,' Max replied like a flash. 'And what will you have, Roy? And you, Eddy?' He'd waited the entire first half to get us, and himself, a freemans. The master at work.

He might have been a legend for his meanness, but he gave away thousands of pounds, and his house in Brighton, to St Dunstan's, the charity that helps blind ex-servicemen. Come 1960 and variety was more or less over. There were fewer and fewer places left for Eddie and me to close, and he decided to call it a day: 'I may as well starve at home,' he said. I sort of agreed with him and – though it's hard to think of it now – I did think about packing in the game myself. I chatted with Morris about the situation and he pointed out a clause in the contract we'd signed with him. It said, should we split, he would represent us individually.

'Give it a go on your own,' Morris suggested. So I did. Nothing much happened at first, and I had to get some money together somehow. Yet again Tom and Doris Cooper came to my rescue by introducing me to the Cox family – Connie and Stan. Connie was beautiful and must have had a sense of humour to have married Stan, because he was a practical joking rogue. Stan had a little firm making window displays for John Hood, a dry-cleaning company with shops all over South London. Having worked in commercial art, I was quite useful to him and Stan took me on with the proviso that I could leave whenever theatre work came along.

We made the window displays in one tiny room above the dry-cleaning factory. I enjoyed working with Stan. If the phone rang while we were working and the caller wanted to speak to Mr Cox, I was instructed to tell them I'd try and find him.

'He's in the workshop somewhere,' I'd say. Stan would then switch on a couple of machines, while we both ad-libbed all sorts of workshop chat in different voices. On one afternoon there were eight different nationalities working there!

'Sorry, he's not there. I'll try the office.' Stan would then type like mad while I banged a rubber stamp.

'No, sorry, he must be in the canteen.' Stan's cue to clink the two mugs we had together and drop a few spoons, while I assumed the role of the tea lady.

If you'd ever heard me you'd know why I've never played dame: 'No,' said the cross between the Queen and Irene Handl, 'the old b*****d was 'ere but he would keep pinching my bum, so I told him to bugger off!'

'Sorry!' said I to the caller, dropping the voice a couple of octaves. 'Oh, here he is now!'

Stan would pick up the phone saying to me, out the side of his mouth, 'That tea woman's a sex maniac. She kept pinching my bum. Yes, Stan Cox here. Can I help you?'

We spent more time cooking up bits and pieces of fun than we ever did gluing and screwing.

The final trick was to be our masterpiece. Some stuff came into the workshop in a big wooden crate.

'Ah ha!' said Stan. 'I've got an idea.'

I had a girlfriend at the time, and his idea was to put me in the crate and deliver it, and me, to her on her birthday. So, the crate went into the back of his little van, I got into the crate, and Mr Cox sealed it up. We drove off with him chuckling away and encouraging me with 'Be quiet now. Oh boy! Is she in for a surprise.'

The journey did seem a bit longer than it should have been and, when we eventually stopped, the sound of carriage doors being closed, whistles and muffled tannoy announcements, made me suspicious. I panicked and started to bang from inside the crate. The top was opened and the frightened faces of a quartet of BR workers stared at me. I was in the parcels department of East Croydon Station. There was no sign of Cox. I had to explain how I had been tricked. They didn't believe me, not even when I pointed to the labels stuck on the sides of the crate, which said, 'To be called for at Liverpool Lime Street'!

If I hadn't have been in love with show business I'd have been working with the master gagster even now.

I started putting together a few gags, and thought perhaps I should try and get a bit of dancing learnt, so on Eddie's recommendation I went to a dance teacher in Croydon called Joan Rodney-Deane. Joan, I think, clocked she was onto a loser as soon as she saw me shuffle into her studio, so she handed me over to her assistant. I was delighted. Her assistant was Ann Lambert, a very pretty young woman, who was full of personality. Ann struggled with trying to instil into my feet time-steps and shuffle ball changes – and failed. To be honest, I wasn't really concentrating. I was very much taken with Ann. I was in love. I stayed with the classes, dancing less and courting more. I did all I could to ingratiate myself with her. I even helped with the Rodney-Deane School Annual Show.

Ann was marvellous with kids and had good choreographic ideas. One little 'un was an exceptional contortionist and Ann came up with an original way of showing her off, where Ann would play the part of an angler with the little one on the end of her line as a fish. The 'fish' was in a fishing basket and, at the dress rehearsal, had to stay in the basket for a very long time. Just before she was due on, I spotted a telltale run of wee-wee coming from the basket. I opened the basket and, pointing at the evidence, enquired, 'Who did that?' The innocent little face looked at me and lied, 'Miss Ann!'

Joan Rodney-Deane presented cabaret shows for all sorts of people, and 'Miss Ann' and I started to do shows together. I'd do a couple of songs and some gags and Ann used to stop the show with something you rarely see these days – a toe tap routine, tap dancing on top of a rostrum but en point – *à la* ballet.

This was in the early days of our friendship and did I try to press my suit. I remember getting into Joan's estate car coming back from a gig in Brighton. I pushed all the other girls to one side and achieved my goal: sitting next to Ann. After about half an hour I thought I'd take a chance. I put my arm round her shoulder. She didn't shrug it off, so I kept it there. I didn't dare go any further. To move it even slightly would have been too bold but I did keep it there – for the rest of the two-hour journey!

When we arrived back in Croydon Ann happily clambered out, while I limped alongside her with my arm frozen into the 'round her shoulder' position.

Eventually my persistence paid off. I met her mum, Alice, who was a smasher. I started to stay odd nights with them and was a happy man – apart from having no work to go to. I would phone and hustle Morris and often I'd get his mum. I could tell Lilian just how I felt, and how I wanted to give the whole thing up, and she would invite me to her office for a cup of tea and a dollop of sympathy. It worked, and I always came away thinking I could be the greatest comedian Great Britain ever produced.

It was around this time that Morris dropped a bombshell.

'Get yourself down to Richmond Theatre in Surrey and audition for *The Merchant of Venice*.'

'Shakespeare!' I said.

'I believe he did have something to do with it, yes,' said Morris.

'But I know nothing about that sort of stuff, I don't even own a pair of tights!'

'Give it a go,' he said, 'I'm telling you, variety will be all over in a couple of years and you've got to get a bit of acting behind you.'

'What part will I be auditioning for? Shylock? The Merchant?'

'No,' he said. 'A comedy part – Young Gobbo.'

'Well, that sounds more like me. I'll give it a go.' I did, and got the part. The director, Alexander Dore, explained the jokes and fashioned some sort of performance out of me. I based it heavily on Spike Milligan's 'Eccles' character and it got laughs. *The Merchant of Venice* was Richmond's 1960 Shakespearean production. Whatever play was the GCE subject for that year was the one they presented. This guaranteed matinees packed with reluctant students, and playing the comedy part was, sometimes, the only thing the kids enjoyed. Couldn't go wrong could I?

The following year the play was *Twelfth Night* and I had another classic role: the idiot knight, Sir Andrew Aguecheek. I thought I'd handled it quite well until, years later, I watched my friend Jonathan Cecil play the part and suddenly saw how it *should* be done.

I did three Shakespeare's at Richmond with Alex. I was so lucky to start in the legit theatre when directors were the governors. *Everyone* did what they said: their word was law.

Which is fine if you got a good 'un, and I had got a good 'un. Today directors are far too often 'nodding dogs', there just to massage the egos of the 'names' that bring in the punters.

I based my 'Young Gobbo' on 'Eccles' because I've always been a huge of Spike Milligan, both as a performer and as a writer. His novel *Puckoon* is the funniest book I've ever read and is always with me. Sadly, for me, *The Goon Show* doesn't stand up now. Comedy has changed – I won't say improved – and the recordings of the famous mould-breaking show sound forced and old-fashioned to me – and I loved them when they first appeared.

I was an extra in one of Spike's 'never-to-be-seen' TV pilots. It was called *The Performing Men Show* and I stood at the side of the set watching him change lines as he went along. The director eventually fled the studio and left it all to someone else.

Years later I put together a reading of Spike's poetry and prose, which made its way onto Radio 2 as *I Like Spike*. Broadcast live, in the middle of the show the director put a phone call through to the studio. It was Spike. He said how much he'd enjoyed *I Like Spike* and confessed he'd only listened to it because he thought it was about a well-known American comedy band Spike Jones and His City Slickers.

He invited me to dinner to say thanks for the show and we agreed on a date. 'I can't do it before,' he said. 'I'm in the looney bin till then.' Indeed he was phoning from that very place.

We met up in a restaurant where his great buddy Alan Clare was working. During the meal Spike produced his trumpet and he and Alan played together. He was accompanied by a tough American lady. They had a row during the evening and he left, but not before paying the bill. I was left with Al Capone in drag. I saw her back to her hotel and ran off before things got scary.

Shortly after my Shakespearian interlude, Morris got me an audition with Emile Littler, a famous pantomime producer who also owned the Palace Theatre on Shaftesbury Avenue. I did my stuff, and he offered me a short season doing a solo turn in *Archie Andrews' Christmas Party*. Archie Andrews was a ventriloquist's dummy operated by Peter Brough. They'd had great success on radio (I ask you, a vent on radio!) with a show called *Educating Archie*. Mr Littler offered me a choice – Archie Andrews or one of the Littler pantomimes. Yet again, the thought of working with a team won through and I settled for panto. One I'd never heard of, *Goody Two Shoes*. It was at the now long gone Empire Theatre, Leeds. I was to be one of the broker's men with the much better known than I was, Bill Pertwee.

We were due to rehearse in Leeds, and Bill said he'd drive the pair of us up there. He had a part in a sketch for a 'live' Sunday night TV show in London so after he'd done the job we set off for Leeds. It took all night to drive up there, and I was eventually dropped off at my digs around 6.30 a.m. I knocked on the door. A girl peeped out, said, 'Go away!' and slammed the door.

I wandered about for a couple of hours and eventually plucked up the courage to try again. This time the girl opened the door fully and said, 'Oh, *you* are the actor who's staying with us!'

'Yes,' I said.

'I am sorry,' she said. 'We've had *so* many suspicious characters forcing their way into houses recently – I thought you were one of them.'

As we went in, I looked in the hall mirror and saw an exhausted, unshaven figure with a mucky duffle coat, an ex-RAF kitbag and, of all things, a beret. She was right to be suspicious.

The girl was Marie Cowan. Her mum ran the digs and I stayed there every time I was in or around Leeds.

Later that same morning, Bill and I, two knackered unknowns, met the company. Sharing top of the bill were the great clown Charlie Cairoli, from the Blackpool Tower Circus, and Ken Platt, a Northern comic who had made his name on radio (his unforgettable catchphrase was 'I won't take me coat off, I'm not stopping').

Bill and I had cooked up a strange little double act, blending his impressions and my lightning cartoons. It wasn't bad. We shared a dressing room with Stuart Pearce who played the villain of the piece, the Yellow Dwarf. Even though he wasn't much older than us, Stuart was a throwback to the days of the repertory 'actor laddie' and made us laugh a lot. The rather shy wardrobe girl fancied him like mad and he always did his best to make her blush. One evening she came in to collect the washing and Stuart said, 'My dear, in the corner there, leaning against the wall, is my jockstrap. Take it away and run the Hoover over it would you?'

One morning I saw him in Boots the Chemists picking up things from the floor.

'What are you doing?' I asked.

'Collecting receipts for the taxman,' he said. 'We get an allowance for make-up, you know!' Another lesson learned.

One night he sent Bill and me an invitation.

*This evening, upon leaving the Temple
of Thespis, shall you repair to my
Chambers in Cobden Place for a
meeting with my bit of crumpet and a
small repast?*

We couldn't wait.

His girlfriend was a representative for Knorr foods so the 'small repast' was soup ... and to follow – more soup.

Playing an Old English sheepdog named Trousers in the panto was a little fella, Kenny Baker, who later achieved worldwide fame as R2D2 in *Star Wars*. Kenny's 'Trousers' was amazing: perfect in size, looks and behaviour. The kids adored him. Kenny studied dogs to get every movement right and once arrived for the show with a bandage on the end of his nose.

'I saw this beautiful Alsatian in the street,' he explained. 'I went up to talk to him and he bit my nose!' As Kenny was only just over three feet tall the dog didn't even have to jump up.

The dame in the show was a fascinating man, Henry Lytton Junior, the son of the great Gilbert and Sullivan comedian Henry Lytton Senior.

Every summer, Henry acted as ringmaster at the Blackpool Tower Circus alongside Charlie Cairoli, and every winter played in drag alongside him. He was another of the old school and he too taught me a useful dodge.

'When there's no matinee you can always go to the pictures for nothing,' he told me. 'It's an unwritten rule that if the manager knows you're from the theatre he'll pass you in. I'll show you.' So off we went.

'How do I know you're from the theatre?' asked the manager.

Henry pulled open his shirt collar and revealed make-up on the inside.

'In you go,' said the manager.

By this time, Ann was also a professional, and was in pantomime at the Hulme Hippodrome, Manchester. She came over to see our show, and I remember Bill and Stuart flirting outrageously with her.

'That is a very sexy bird,' Bill warned me. 'You'll have your work cut out holding onto that one.'

I did manage to keep them away.

At the end of the panto season I was told about a seaside concert party. The fart had found another exit route from the colander.

This one was a genuine, professional concert party. Professional, yet not so far removed from what I did with Tom and Doris Cooper. However, like the phrases 'half a crown', 'dog licence' and 'labour exchange', the words 'concert party' need a little explanation. A concert party was a team of performers who would provide a show featuring sketches, musical scenes, dancing, singing, specialities, comedians and comediennes. Developing from the minstrel and Pierrot shows, concert parties were *the* holiday entertainment in the British Isles – cheap and very cheerful.

When I joined, in 1960, the genre had moved on from the days of the Sand Rats of Tom Cooper's time. The usual line-up of performers was a top-of-the-bill comedian (not necessarily a big name – it was a specialized style), a comedienne, a second comedian/straight man and a male dancer/choreographer. There was also a baritone or tenor, a soprano, a soubrette (usually a pretty girl with personality who could pep up and front dance routines), four girl dancers and a couple of others doing something different: a magician, a multi-instrumentalist, a ventriloquist or a juggler.

So many beginners wanted to get in on a concert party because you were expected to do the lot. Everyone had to sing and dance and play in sketches as well as doing an act 'not longer than six minutes'! There were quite a few 'overnight stars' who went through this tough apprenticeship. Bruce Forsyth was one – that's why he's so adept at everything.

Yet again, I was lucky. Someone arranged an audition for me with Ronnie Brandon and Dickie Pounds for their concert party/summer revue *Out of the Blue*. I hadn't really got a solo act, so Eddie came along with me and we did our double act in their front room. No piano, nothing – a bit like the early auditions for *The X Factor*. Ronnie and Dickie kept an exercise book with their notes on every auditionee. Just a couple of years back I saw their entry about me: 'Not good looking, can't dance, but enthusiastic.' Nothing really changes.

The enthusiasm must have done the trick. Eddie didn't want to go away from home, so Ronnie and Dickie took me on as second comic for their 1960 season at Babbacombe in Devon.

Now, before you think, as I did when I first heard their names, that Ronnie and Dickie were a couple of chaps, I'd better explain. Ronnie was a little character man in rep and musicals who met and married a soubrette, Florence

Pounds. She didn't like being called Flo – who does? So she christened herself Dickie. They were unforgettable characters.

Dickie, about the same size as Ronnie, was an eccentric firecracker of a lady. It was she who auditioned the performers, devised the shows, organized running orders, did the lighting and directed us all. Ronnie was a dear gentle soul who worshipped Dickie – well, according to her! He fell in with all her ideas, suffered her tantrums, and agreed, mostly, with her choice of performers.

By golly, *Out of the Blue* was a baptism of fire. We did five different two-and-a-half-hour revues. The programme was changed every two days, which meant if you were on holiday in Babbacombe for a fortnight you could see our entire repertoire. And if you still wanted more we did four different Sunday shows. All sorts of Lord's Day Observance rules were in place at the time, so these Sunday shows were a parade of audience participation games – with prizes!

And what prizes! Mars bars, tins of baked beans, wine gums and sticks of rock. Eventually, someone put me on to a firm that supplied swag for fairgrounds, and the prizes became boxes of easily bent cutlery, alarm clocks that didn't go off, chalk models of dogs – and tins of baked beans.

These Sunday shows had always been a sort of tradition in Babbacombe, and it was by being spotted compèring these audience-participation shows (a trifle before my time I hasten to add) that Bruce Forsyth got his big break on the telly. The Sunday 'spectaculars' were all very well, but the weekday show was Dickie's thing. Through her eyes it was a Hollywood blockbuster with a cast of thousands and a huge orchestra, with choreography by Busby Berkeley (and Dickie Pounds!).

She loved dance and invented all sorts of strange ballets, which we were all in. She had her own version, in eight minutes, of *The Red Shoes*, where the principal dancer took her call on bloody stumps! Another, believe it or not, depicted the rape of a nun! Just the thing for a family night out on holiday.

But, the routine I've never forgotten was *The Punch Ballet*. In this, an old Punch and Judy man (Ronnie) was seen, half-cut, throwing his puppets into the corner of the room and refusing to let his wife (the soprano) make new costumes for them. The wife exits, sobbing, and the showman falls into a drunken sleep. At this, a giant Mr Punch (the boy dancer) leaps through the window, followed by the dancing girls as Judy, the Policeman, the Ghost and the Hangman. After a very bizarre dance routine, the showman is put on trial and sentenced to be hanged. A gibbet comes on from the wings, and the item finishes with the guilty one thrashing and twitching in his death throes, while Mr Punch and the company dance round him, laughing.

I had to follow this jolly little jape and, try as I might, my whimsicalities didn't mean a light. Well, I defy anyone to get a titter from an audience sitting with mouths open and eyes bulging in a state of shock.

Apart from her balletic aberrations Dickie was a great teacher and she would spend any amount of time with you if you wanted to get something right. Show business lore has it that she 'discovered' Norman Wisdom, David Nixon, Terry Scott, Hugh Lloyd, Clive Dunn, choreographer Dougie Squires and composer Cyril Ornadel. To which Dickie replied, 'No, I didn't. I was just lucky to have had them with me. They'd all have made it without me.' Her show was what her life was all about. Poor old Ronnie. Whenever *Out of the Blue* had a profitable season Dickie would take the profits and buy more lighting equipment!

We started rehearsals in a church hall near Regent's Park, and I found a soulmate as soon as we first heard the opening chorus. It began with us all entering through the cut-out of an aeroplane. We sang:

> *We could have flown to Majorca,*
> *Touched down in Athens or Bonn,*
> *Turkey or the south of France,*
> *Cairo or Rome perchance,*
> *Anywhere in the world you see,*
> *But BABBACOMBE is where we want to be!*

Like me, our baritone, Tom Howard, giggled his way through the last line. It wasn't the last time we shared a laugh.

Rehearsals in town over, the first two of our five programmes under our belts, we all got the train down to the West Country.

In the 1960s the theatre was still called by its Victorian name, the Babbacombe Concert Hall (now the more zingy Babbacombe Theatre), and today its summer show is one of just a handful that runs for months rather than weeks. Most importantly it has no big names, just good, young performers gaining experience. Long may it continue.

We arrived and were shown our dressing rooms – just two – one for all the lads on stage left and one for all the girls on stage right, down a flight of stairs.

To look out of our window was, for me, a sickening, sweat-inducing experience. We were perched at the very top of the cliff and way, way below we could see the sea with its toy boats and the matchbox-sized Carey Arms pub. In the corner of our dressing room, on the window-ledge, was a black box containing a reel of rope. A notice on its side said:

DAVEY ESCAPE APPARATUS.
In case of emergency,
tie rope around waist
and jump out of the window.

I looked at Tom and he looked at me. 'Well I'm not trying it,' he said.

'Nor me,' said I. So I tied a wastepaper bin onto the rope and threw it out the window. The black box clanked away and the bin and rope, *unattached to the box*, bounced down the cliff – never to be seen again!

Ronnie and Dickie had an evil poodle called Caramel Fudge. Spoilt rotten, Dickie adored Caramel, and Ronnie, ever doing his gentle best to please his missus, fed, shampooed and generally catered to all the little swine's needs. Caramel became famous for his unpleasantness throughout show business and there are still old *Out of the Blue*-ites and patrons of the show who shudder whenever his name is mentioned. He was, in the words of the prophet, a bastard. He attacked and bit anyone who crossed his path. Especially his owners.

Well not really bite – he'd give a nasty suck – because he was never given anything hard to eat and his choppers had disappeared many summers ago. When Ronnie sat in the front row of the stalls watching rehearsals, this snarling, toothless spawn of the devil would climb aboard his leg and vigorously give it one. Ronnie would call out instructions to us with the dog still attached to his leg.

Our comedian, Jimmy Edmundson, had bought a new suit for the season and went off to the loo to change into it – and amaze us. He returned in an electric blue mohair suit (mohair was *the* material for stage suits in those days). From that moment on none of us ever saw Jimmy out of that suit. Onstage, offstage, opening garden fêtes, boozing, fishing – the electric blue gave him away wherever he was.

One evening he wasn't at the hall for the show. Where could he be? From our dressing room window we saw, far away, out at sea, a tiny boat. In it was a fishing line and a tiny electric blue suit and, in the suit, Jim.

He eventually arrived back late for the show. He made his entrance halfway through the first half. Brushing the mackerel scales from the electric blue he explained to the audience, 'Sorry I'm late. I've been throwing sticks over the cliff for Caramel Fudge!'

This got a huge laugh from the customers, but Dickie didn't speak to Jim for the rest of the season.

Jimmy Edmundson was an original. Yet another offbeat talent who should have been allowed to do better. At one point in his act he would say, 'and now that great star of *Not As a Stranger*, Robert Mitchum'. He would then turn his back on the audience and, almost immediately, turn back again. There'd be an audible gasp because the resemblance to Mitchum was amazing. After a round of applause he'd comment, 'Well of course it's like him. That's why I do it!'

One night, I rather pompously told him how incredible the likeness was.

'Nah,' he said. 'If it's presented right they'll clap anything. Watch me tonight.'

I did and, after Mitchum, he said, 'And now, that great star of the silent screen, Francis J. Halford!' He turned away and back again with a grossly distorted face. It got a round of applause.

'What the hell are you clappin' for?' said Jim, laughing. 'There's no such person!' The applause embarrassingly faded away as he turned to the wings and said to me, 'See! What did I tell you? They'll clap any bloody thing!'

I had four summers with Ronnie and Dickie, from 1960 to 1963 and they were, without doubt, the most valuable summers of my professional life. Babbacombe was such a small place, the show relied on the locals to support it and recommend it to their visitors. We attended all sorts of odd local events to show our faces, including an annual church service in Torquay.

One year, the regular vicar was on holiday so a locum took the service. He got into the pulpit to deliver his sermon and introduced us to his 'little friend'. He reached down and produced a ventriloquist's dummy, hung its legs over the side of the pulpit and proceeded to deliver his sermon as a double act. Me, Tom Howard and Dickie couldn't believe it.

'Needs better material,' was Dickie's comment.

'Gog gless him,' was Tom's.

And mine was, 'If you put a few more bob in the plate he'll do it while drinking a glass of holy water!'

The dummy told me to 'gugger off!'

Whenever we were in the show together I shared a flat

with fellow giggler Tom Howard. Our favourite digs were a semi-basement couple of rooms we called 'The Molehole'. When we first arrived I turned on the water heater in the bathroom and the hot water tap: nothing happened. I wandered out to consult with Tom as to what was wrong, and was told it was no use just turning it on – it had to be lit first. I returned to the bathroom and lit a match. Boom! The gas exploded and I exited horizontally back into the living room without touching the ground.

Tom, the rotten swine, couldn't stop laughing but did, eventually, turn the gas off.

One season, for no reason at all, I thought we needed a pet, so I bought a hamster. What was it with me and hamsters? We called her Desiree and she entertained us and our after-show guests when we let her loose in The Molehole. She would run around, eat anything she could find and, best of all, climb up the curtains and hang from the pelmet. After one party we couldn't find her anywhere and, after hours of searching, we had to believe she'd escaped.

One evening, Tom and I sat in the digs and tried to trace a gentle scratching sound. It was coming from a device we very rarely used, the oven. Thank Gawd it was rarely used because Desiree had found her way between the oven's outer and inner wall and made a nest in the insulation. A tearful reunion – much like my reunion with Herbert many years earlier – followed and she stayed with us for the rest of the season.

I remember one very early pantomime season when Tom and I shared digs again – and very umpty they were too. The attic room in a university city student house. I cannot tell you the city or the landlady's name because her family are still there – though not touting digs any more – please God.

We arrived for panto rehearsals and were shown our lodgings. There was a bit of a dank smell in our garret, so Tom picked up the electric two-bar fire and held it above the bed sheet – it steamed. This and a roof that was just about a foot above where we slept – any sudden awakening meant you hit your head on the ceiling. As Tom said at the time, 'even the mice are round-shouldered'. But the landlady was a pleasant enough old stick who did do us a bit of supper every evening when we got back. Only one problem, she was a great fan of Mr Heinz – particularly of his baked beans. Every single night throughout rehearsals she gave us baked beans on toast.

Came the technical rehearsal, which in those days was on Christmas Eve, ready for the traditional opening on Boxing Day. This run-through went on for as long as the director wanted, and we didn't finish until near midnight.

As we made our way – exhausted – back to the digs all I could think of was baked beans.

'Bleedin' Christmas Eve,' I said to Tom as we trudged home. 'If she dishes up baked beans tonight, I swear I'll shove them in her ear'ole.'

We sat down at the table and, bless her, she was waiting for us. An unintelligible 'welcome' came from the kitchen and then we heard the shuffle of carpet slippers on the lino. In she came and slapped down in front of us – two plates of BAKED BEANS!

Now, I am slow to anger, but when I'm angry – look out! I could not believe it. About fifteen hours in the theatre and that's all we got. Slowly, the red mist engulfed me as I toyed with the familiar glutinous heap. But, hold on, my fork excavated something new: there, nestling in the tomato sauce, was a chipolata. I flipped.

"Oi, love!' I shouted. 'I think you've made a mistake. I've just found a sausage in my baked beans!'

'I know,' she replied. 'Merry Christmas!'

CHAPTER FIVE

'*Brilliant* young comedian requires new material'

I had my feet well under the table with *Out of the Blue* – and with Ann's mum, Alice, in Croydon. Things were beginning to look sort of all right. People convinced me I could earn a living 'showing off' and I took a chance.

Ann and I were married in May 1961 and we immediately moved in with the mother-in-law: the perfect start for a comedian. However, the difference was that, unlike Les Dawson, I had a lovely mum-in-law. Alice was the sort of person who would disappear whenever Ann and I had an up and downer, but be there to help us whenever she could. A perfect gem. I must have loved her because the first house we bought was next door to her.

In fact the first 'in-depth' interview I ever did was at that house in Tankerton Terrace, Croydon. The interviewer was a lady called Romany Baine and it was for *She* magazine. Romany arrived at the house with her young son and, as they came in, the lad tripped and cut his knee. As was her wont, Ann made a great fuss of the boy, until we saw – with horror – that he'd bled all over our brand new white carpet! Poor Romany was so embarrassed, I'm sure she gave me much more space in the magazine than she was contracted for. She eventually became a well-known television critic and has never given me a bad notice ... she remembers, and so do I!

Of course, come the summer season, I was anxious that Ann should join me in the show at Babbacombe, but there seemed little chance. Ronnie and Dickie weren't keen on having husbands and wives in their shows.

'They're always trouble, darling. We're such a small team, if they have a row the cast take sides and before you know where you are, no one's talking to anybody, and that comes across over the footlights.'

Ann, though, got a job with the big show in Torquay (Jewel and Warris and the Kaye Sisters at the Pavilion) so, Babbacombe being just a couple of miles up the coast, we were able to spend the summer together.

Their show didn't open until we were well under way in Babbacombe. The night before they opened they had their dress rehearsal and it went on forever – again, you had to stay until the show was right. So, long after our curtain had come down, they were still at it and I sat in the stalls at the Pavilion, waiting for Ann.

The finale of the show featured the whole company coming on in top hat and tails. The girls looked great and all was perfect until the last one came on: Ann. She was wearing a top hat that came down to her shoulders, she could have turned round and the hat would have stayed still.

'Stop!' yelled the director. 'Ann, where did you get the hat?'

'From the wardrobe,' said Ann, taking off the hat and blinking at the light.

'Has it a got a name in?'

'I think so,' she said, trying to read the label. 'It says T. COOPER.'

Yes, it had been used by the man with the biggest feet in the business and, now we knew, the biggest head as well – Tommy Cooper.

A great fan of *Out of the Blue* was a local probation officer, Tommy Scott (I always thought perhaps he was checking on past – or future – clients). One day he came to Ronnie and Dickie and asked if they would let us do an afternoon show in Dartmoor Prison. They agreed.

Our stage manager, Tony Clayton (who went on to run theatres, direct pantos and plays and marry Eric and Ernie's first television leading lady, Ann Hamilton), got busy, and managed to get a photograph of our girls onto the front page of the *Daily Mirror* under the headline, 'Bikini girls go to Dartmoor'. That didn't do the business any harm at all. Whether appearing at Dartmoor was good publicity or not was open to debate, but the whole company couldn't wait to see inside the legendary nick.

Once through the black, 'abandon-hope-all-ye-who-enter-here' gates, inside was a pleasant surprise: beautiful, well-tended flowerbeds, and a seemingly relaxed atmosphere.

In the hall we got ourselves together and I had a chat with the lighting man. As a National Serviceman he'd done the lighting for our RAF shows – Gawd knows what he'd done since then to send him to Dartmoor! There hadn't been a professional show in the place for years and it seemed that even if we were rubbish, the lads would have still loved us. Well, the girls anyway.

Around the perimeter of the hall were sort of witness boxes, and sitting in each one was a warder wielding a big stick. I endeared myself to the audience by referring to the one nearest the stage as Mr Punch and the next one as Judy. From then on I could do no wrong.

My agent, Morris, who was down to see *Out of the Blue*, came along, and he remembered our comedian that year, Freddie Earle, miming to a record of Jimmy Durante singing 'I'm the Guy Who Found the Lost Chord'. This went all right until he mimed to Durante's lines: 'Lock the doors! Nobody gets out of here!' At which the entire audience stood up whooping and cheering.

'It was,' said Morris, 'like Johnny Cash in San Quentin.'

At the end of the show we did what we always did in those days: stood to attention onstage and sang 'God Save the Queen'. The reaction was even better than the one to Freddie's miming. The lads stamped their feet, booed, jeered, whistled and used words I'd never heard before. I was scared they'd come up and tear us to pieces so, to the sound of Mr Punch on one side and Judy on the other banging their cudgels, the curtains were quickly closed.

'What the hell was all that about?' I shakily asked a warder.

'Ah, well,' he said. 'They don't like that tune. Most of them are here at Her Pleasure!'

Fair enough.

On my wall is a framed certificate, which was presented to Ronnie and Dickie by a group of prisoners. It's beautifully hand-lettered – and so it should be – it was done by a forger. It says:

Out of the Blue
you came to us at Dartmoor Prison and gave
us the happiest day of the year.
This souvenir of your visit is a sign of our grateful
thanks and sincere appreciation for so
kindly lifting up our hearts.
In the high spirits in which you left us we offer you
the

FREEDOM OF THE NICK

to ensure that you will come again.

At the bottom of the message was a real key.

We went again a couple of years later – and with an extra special guest. I suggested to Tommy Scott that he ask some of the big stars in the Torquay shows to come. Which he did.

A few days later he rang. 'None of them will come,' he said. 'Well, only one. Ken Dodd.'

I was as big a fan of Knotty Ash's Own then as I am now and jumped up and down with joy. 'Sod the others, Tom!' I said. 'Ken's all we need.'

If Ken had done then what he does now – go on for three or more hours – we needn't have bothered to go on at all. But he was almost human in those days and did what was required.

We did our two penn'orth and then the master came on. He started with his latest recording, the opening lines of which were: 'There is a key that will open all doors to me ...' and proceeded to bombard the lads with his unique machine gun-like patter. Of course, he paralysed them and he finished by saying: 'You've been a wonderful audience, wonderful. You've been so good that this evening, I'm taking you all on a cross- country run!'

Afterwards, when I asked Ken what made him want to entertain at Dartmoor, he said, 'There, but for the grace of God, go I!'

A phrase I reminded him – and the jury – of a few years later.

The next season's pantomime was again for Emile Littler, this time at the New Theatre, Oxford. It was *Dick Whittington* and starred a perfect pantomime performer, Richard Hearne, who everyone knew as Mr Pastry. Mr Pastry was a doddery old gentleman who was a surprisingly agile acrobat and slapstick performer. Second top was Ronald Shiner – a comedy film and stage actor who wasn't really right to play dame (but he did send me a funny Christmas card featuring the caption, 'From your old China Ronald Shiner').

Again, I was part of a double act – Captain and Mate. The Captain was a bloke I never saw or even heard of after that show, Bruce Gordon, who'd had a successful children's show on TV. I honestly can't remember what we did as a double act, but I do remember he had a huge knitting machine in the dressing room and I commissioned a white woollen dress for Ann. They were all the rage at that time. I took it home and she went off to the bedroom to try it on.

A howl of laughter came from the bedroom and out she came. The garment was the longest I've ever seen and she could just about be seen inside it – like a statue before it's been unveiled. Bruce was a nice bloke so I had to say it fitted like a glove – albeit a boxing one.

The first day of rehearsals Richard Hearne asked for volunteers to take part in his shoe shop sketch. Those were the days when everyone wanted to be in everything. I put my hand up, of course, and Richard picked me out.

'Hmm,' he said. 'Are you as funny as you look?' (Had he had a word with Gracie Fields?)

'I hope so,' I said, and I was in.

I played a yokel in a smock and big rubber boots, who had come in to purchase some new ones.

'Certainly, sir,' said Mr Pastry, and prepared to take off my footwear. Just then another customer came in and, with my foot under his arm, he served her, dragging me from showcase to showcase and up and down ladders. Then *another* customer arrived, and the business was repeated.

Eventually, they had all been served and he remembered I was under his arm. He sat me on a chair and it, and I, fell backwards (he taught me how to do that). Finally, he sat on the chair himself while I lay on the floor with my back to the audience. He managed to prise the boot off my foot to disclose a sock with a big hole in it. He carefully wound the sock back to show my bare foot. I loved this beautiful bit of business. He removed an imaginary 'something' from the underside of my foot, cast it aside and blew on the sole of the foot. He looked intently at the foot then at my face and informed me, 'You're going on a very long journey!'

That bit with Mr Pastry brought me my first review. It was in the university magazine *Isis* from Michael Billington.

At the end of the run Richard gave me a Parker fountain pen engraved, 'Thank you for a great performance – Mr Pastry'. I treasured it until some swine stole it from a dressing room. It was maroon with gold lettering along the side – if you see it let me know. From that day on I have always written with a proper ink pen. It makes anybody's writing look better.

Though he didn't know it, it was Ken Dodd who got me my first radio broadcast on the legendary *Workers' Playtime*. This 'live' variety show was broadcast at lunchtime on the BBC Light Programme from factory canteens all over the British Isles. The format was nearly always the same: a musical act opened the show, then a comedian, then a singer, with the star comic to finish. It was a pretty good showcase for beginners, which, in 1960, I was.

James Casey was Ken Dodd's radio producer. He was also the head of Variety at BBC Manchester, the writer and producer of *The Clitheroe Kid* and the son of the comedian Jimmy James (no one who had the joy of seeing Jimmy with his roll-up fag and his two 'feeds' Eli (Breton Woods) and the one in the long coat (played by all sorts of people, but most famously by Roy Castle) doing the 'Lion in the box' routine, will ever forget him).

Anyway, James Casey (also known as Jimmy) was visiting Ken at the Pavilion in Torquay to talk over their planned autumn series.

'I'd seen Ken's act a million times,' Jimmy later told me. 'So looked around for any other shows to take in. Ken told me there was a summer show at Babbacombe with a young comic he hadn't seen himself, but had heard good reports. I went to see – and saw –Roy Hudd.'

I knew nothing about this, but that coming autumn Jimmy booked me for a *Workers' Playtime*. You never forget your first time, and I can't forget mine – from the Ferodo

Brake Linings factory at Chester Le Street. Top of the bill was Jimmy Clitheroe (a pre-Jimmy Krankie and post 'Wee' Georgie Wood – a little fella).

I had no idea where Chester Le Street was, so I travelled there the night before the broadcast and stayed in a B & B. This cost me all the cash I had and the next morning I had to walk a long way to the factory in the rain. My precious stage suit was creased but dry, as were my precious band parts. When I arrived among the Ferodo brake linings, soaked to the skin, I was greeted by Jimmy Casey who explained that everyone in the show stayed in Manchester and was transported to the venue the morning of the gig: the BBC paid for hotel and transportation. Thankfully he did spring me the cost of the B & B or I'd never have got back home.

All the front I'd tried to put up – 'I'm a real "pro" with a nice suit and good music and I've done all this before' – went for a burton as I gave a dreadful impression of a sharp-as-a-tack patter comic. The spot I did went well – even the pianist laughed. I was on top of the world and, suddenly, I forgot all the previous embarrassment. Amazing just what getting a few laughs can do.

That *Workers' Playtime* was the first of many I did for Jimmy Casey. I was first spot comic with everyone from Albert Modley (who didn't use a script, just a page from an exercise book with six large lettered words on – the cues for his gags), Ken Platt, Cardew Robinson, Mrs Shufflewick and yet another hero – Ted Ray.

I did several broadcasts with Ted, who always did well. My spots were very much hit and miss. I was still learning the job. We did one at the factory that made Gannex macs (the coats that Harold Wilson put on the map). After the broadcast, we had lunch with the boss, Lord Kagan, who gave us all a mac, even one for Tiny Ross, the little fella in the Morton Fraser Harmonica Gang. I wore my Gannex for the next ten years.

Ted and I were catching the same train back home from Liverpool Lime Street. We had to wait an hour or so and, joy of joys, he invited me to have a cup of tea – in the Adelphi Hotel. It was the first time I'd ever been in a really posh hotel. The lounge where we were served afternoon tea looked like a Russian underground station.

I'd also never seen a local hero in his own manor before. As we entered the hotel all sorts of people ran towards us. Not just staff, but guests and management too. Ted was brilliant. He chatted to everybody – his Scouse accent coming and going depending on to whom he was talking. He did a few topical gags and reminisced with folk who'd known him when he was going by his real name, Charlie Olden. I so longed to be accepted as a real Jack the Lad as Ted was. I basked in his glory as the waitresses fussed around, giggling as he baited them with cheeky remarks. 'Oh boy! This is the life!' I thought. He is worshipped.

The broadcast that day hadn't been a good one for me and I confided to Ted, 'I do think I'll have to give it up. You're always on form, you get laughs out of nothing. You are the best. It's not worth me bothering.'

''Course it is, son,' he said. 'I can't work everywhere. There are lots of theatres where I'm not working. You get in there and learn the trade.' I still am.

My other memorable *Worker's Playtime* was one way down in Cornwall. On the bill was myself, Anita Harris, a harpist whose name I've never forgotten, Trifinna Partridge, and Rex Jamieson (known to all as Mrs Shufflewick), who I thought was a small genius. The show, from a naval station, did all right, and that night while Anita and Trifinna shared a sleeper back to London, I was sharing one with Rex.

'Hey up!' I thought. 'Watch yourself, son.'

We got into the cabin and Rex produced a couple of bottles of something.

'Shall we say goodnight to 'nita and the half-pissed?' Rex asked.

'Oh, yes please,' I said, hastily.

Anita and Trifinna let us in to their cabin straight away, knowing they had little to fear from Rex or the schoolboy-looking comic.

The outcome was a marvellous journey back, with Rex leading the laughter – and the drinking. We never went back to our sleeper and never slept a wink. The journey seemed to take about an hour and a half. We did get some very funny, and envious, looks when we left the cabin at Paddington.

It was *Workers' Playtime* that led me to meeting Eric Davidson. I'd done a few and some more were in the pipeline. Ronnie and Dickie had intimated that I might possibly be their principal comedian the following season. I started to feel like a proper pro and had the gall to put an ad in *The Stage* saying: '*Brilliant* young comedian requires new material, modern, off-beat, gags and sketches apply, etc.' I got quite a response.

There were letters trying to sell me gags and stories that I'd heard as a lad at the Croydon Empire; there were those who sent sketches that Ronnie and Dickie had turned down before the war; there were some in heavily underlined red and green ballpoint (they're the ones to watch); and there were some in pencil on pages torn out of exercise books ('They won't let us use anything sharp in here!'). Well, the advert only cost a couple of quid.

Then a rather smart, typewritten one arrived. It had a proper letterhead in red and black on grey paper. It said, in fashionable lower case:

eric davidson
comedy script writer
televison
radio
pantomime
revue
after dinner speeches

'This is more like it!' I thought. All those credits, and a very businesslike request to fill in and return the attached form, which was a questionnaire asking my age, height, weight, sex, accent, which comedian I most resembled, what sort of material I required, etc., etc. I thought this was even more like it and the address guaranteed it:

13a Draycott Place, Chelsea.

All I knew about Chelsea was it was the place where all the posh writers and nancy boys lived. I formed a picture in my mind of a tall whoopsie: a wavy-haired, cardiganed, corduroy-trousered, suede-shoed, pipe-smoking literary toff.

I filled in the form and a reply came back by return of post. It said he would be interested in writing for me and his charges were two guineas *a minute* for stage material – payable in advance!

I responded by return of post, saying that two guineas a minute was more than I'd ever paid before, and that I'd certainly never paid for material without even seeing it.

Of course, I'd never *ever* paid for a joke – seen or unseen. Mr Davidson wrote back and said why didn't I call round to his place and we could discuss money. Even naïve little me was a bit worried: his place – in Chelsea? Watch yourself, Huddy!

I made my way to Draycott Place and found a tall impressive terraced house. Number 13. But Mr Davidson lived at 13a. I looked down and there on the sub-basement wall was written, in chalk, '13a'. I climbed carefully over the mountain of coke (the fuel not the narcotic) that was piled up against the sub-basement door. I knocked and a lady with a baby in her arms answered.

'Mr Davidson?' I enquired. 'No, I'm *Mrs* Davidson,' she replied. 'Eric's in the back room. Along there.'

She took me through to where the 'posh Chelsea nancy boy' was pulling on a fag and drinking tea. I was disappointed he wasn't what I imagined, but was actually the caretaker of the building – hence the mountain of coke.

We chatted and reached a compromise: five guineas for three minutes.

The material arrived a day later and it made me laugh. I never used a word of it, but I liked Eric and he liked me. We liked each other even more when, after I confessed I'd never ever bought a joke, he owned up that he'd never ever sold one!

It was the beginning of a long and happy association –

except for when we argued. Eric wrote me several *Workers'*
Playtime scripts and, when it was confirmed I would be
principal comedian in Babbacombe for the 1962 season, I
introduced him to Ronnie and Dickie. Dickie, as I've already
said, was always looking for new things and she loved Eric's
ideas for sketches. For years, concert parties had relied on
domestic stuff, husband and wife, lovers hiding in the
wardrobe, all the men in the company in drag pieces. Eric
wanted to do different material. So did I, and so did Dickie.

That season he came up with all sorts of original ideas. I
did them all. We tried out a sketch set in a nudist camp,
another in a fortune teller's tent and one, my favourite, set in
Sherwood Forest – *Robin Hudd*. Some scored heavily and
others went down the Swanee. That was the joy of playing a
long season where no producers or talent scouts ever
appeared. It was a chance to make mistakes. Something you
can't do today on the telly. One flop and you're gone.

For two summers Eric gave up his holiday from the Hyde
Park Hotel (where he was the buyer of supplies) to be in
Babbacombe to direct the sketches and, when one flopped,
go back to the digs and write another.

He wrote lots of stuff for the later TV series, *The
Illustrated Weekly Hudd* and all my solo TV and cabaret
spots. He would spend hours sitting in front of me till I got
things right.

'If you don't put the hat on there, you won't get the roars!'
He was always right, nearly. We parted company as
performer and writer when I would insist on going off to do
plays and music hall. He liked writing gags and found a great
partner in Ted Rogers, who loved doing topical material.
Eric wrote, for TV, *The Mike Yarwood Show*, several series

for Cliff Richard and The Shadows and lots of shows for Des O'Connor.

He, unlike so many, wrote belly laughs, or 'roars' as he called them. We stayed friends until his untimely death at sixty-five.

I was so enjoying being with Ronnie and Dickie, and things got even better when, after auditioning her, they said Ann could join *Out of the Blue*. She did, and fitted in perfectly with Dinny Jones, June Fletcher, Carol Pearce, Vicki Lane, Dorian Claire, Harry Bennet, David Gardner, Tom and, of course, Arthur Tolcher.

On almost the last night of the 1963 season, as we were by the exit doors saying, 'Thanks for coming' to the punters, a rather fierce-looking red-faced bloke grabbed me.

'Who's the redhead?' he asked.

'My wife, if you must know,' I said quite sharply.

'A good dancer,' he said. 'I want her for my show.'

'Well,' I said, 'her agent's Morris Aza – sort it out with him.'

'I will,' he said. 'She's a cracker!'

'What a sauce!' thought I.

The next morning, as previously arranged, I met up with Frank Adey – the producer of *The Ocean Revue* in Clacton – he was the fierce looking red-faced bloke who fancied my missus! He greeted me with a big smile and, '*Who's* the redhead?'

He told me he'd come to see if I'd fancy doing his show the next summer, adding, 'You can bring the redhead'. And so it was that I did join *The Ocean Revue* for the 1964 season – but without the redhead: Ann was pregnant.

Being taken on, as principal comic, by Frank was a big

step up for me. He, like Dickie, was keen on Eric's sketches and, with Betty Martin (Frank's missus), I had the perfect comedienne to work with. As well as Betty we had six girl dancers, four boy dancers, a tenor and a soprano, a great speciality act and a twelve-piece orchestra. A big show, but it still retained the local appeal. All the good producers of summer shows made sure they – and their shows – were known to all the locals. They persuaded their comics, girls and boys, to open garden fêtes, judge baby shows, talk to the local Rotary clubs, entertain at old folks' homes, attend mayoral receptions and support local charities. After a couple of weeks, lots of the residents had seen the revue and the performers wandering about the town. With luck they had taken the casts to their hearts and became more than just customers.

In an odd way it wasn't too different from Butlins: you didn't have to be a world-beater performer, but you did have to have that warmth – on- and offstage – which, in spite of what you did for a living, showed you were really just an ordinary punter. A successful summer show top-of-the-bill couldn't be remote or stand-offish – the best ones always had a unique and natural style.

The Ocean Revue (presented in, believe it or not, the Ocean Theatre) was on the pier at Clacton – just. The pier was the place for entertainment and, apart from our show, there were lots of rides, a dolphin show and, at the far end, the Ramblas Concert Party, to my knowledge the last al fresco show left in England. Twice a day this little eight-man team would do their stuff from a tiny wooden structure to a deck-chaired audience. That same night they'd be at it again, only inside this time for their evening show in the Jolly Roger Theatre.

That the comic's wife was pregnant spread all round the town and the shout of, 'Any news?' followed me wherever I went. Eventually, on 1 July 1964, it happened, and I dashed back to Croydon to greet the son and heir. We were going call him Max, after my hero Max Miller, but then we thought further and, just in case he became an author or Prime Minister, we had him christened Maxwell Roy. But I've never heard anyone call him Maxwell. Only me, when, as a little boy, he got up my nose.

Ann looked blooming, but the little thing by her side looked just like Frank Adey when I'd first met him: red-faced and fierce! Don't all babies?

The next night, in the finale, the arrival of Hudd junior was announced to the audience. One of the usherettes called out, 'Thank Gawd for that – now we can all sleep easier in our beds!'

Ann and Max joined us in Clacton and he made his first theatre appearance at two weeks old. I carried him on and the cast and audience sang 'For He's a Jolly Good Fellow'.

A few weeks later, however, he wasn't such a jolly good fellow. Ann wanted to see the top of the bill at that week's Sunday concert. We had lots of big names for these one-nighters: Beryl Reid, Frankie Howerd, Arthur Worsley, Joe Mr 'Piano' Henderson, Terry Scott, Eric & Ernie. I had to compère the shows but I didn't mind. I could try out all sort of bits and pieces and knock off the odd gag from the stars. Ann came to the show and, after some persuasion, let me have Max in the dressing room.

'It'll be okay,' I said. 'I only pop on and off. He won't be left alone for more than two or three minutes.'

Against her better judgement, she agreed, took her seat

and the show began. In the dressing room, all went well, the angelic little eyes remained shut and I got on with the job. Then, as they always do, he woke up for no apparent reason and gave out a *terrifying* howl.

I finished the intro and ran down to the dressing room to see just a huge mouth, hear just a huge yell, and smell just a huge pong. His nappy needed changing. With one ear on what was happening on stage I tried. I got the old nappy off – cor dear! – and the new one lined up. The turn onstage finished, and back I went with my hands in my pockets ... they were slightly soiled.

Intro over, I returned to my diaper-less son. In my absence, he'd rolled *all* over the floor. The dressing room looked like H-block, but I battled on. It was now the interval and a smiling Ann came back to see that her baby boy was asleep and happy.

She screamed at what she saw: Max looked like Jolson – all over. Ann didn't go back for the second half, but efficiently did the nappy business and went back to the digs – while I was sent to the doghouse.

Frank Adey became a great friend and an invaluable adviser on all sorts of things – theatrical and otherwise. Much later, he advised my second wife, Debbie, 'Wherever he's working – go with him.' He was so right. Frank taught me how to lay out the running order of a pantomime, and not take myself too seriously. Like all those old summer show producers, with Frank the show was the thing. Nothing else really mattered.

One morning we were rehearsing in the theatre and Frank called for the girls to come onstage. They all did except one.

'Where's Valerie?' Frank enquired in his gentle tone.

'I'm sorry, Mr Adey,' replied the head girl. 'As we were coming out of the digs she slipped on the top step and broke her ankle.'

Frank threw his pencil on the floor and declared, 'Everything happens to me!'

By the next summer, 1965, I'd had a break too. A break on television, and Frank, even though he'd got me on a two-year contract, generously said, 'You don't have to come back next summer, son. You're doing all right on the box and you'll earn a lot more away from here.'

You may think it was even more generous of me to say, 'I will come back because I want to.' But I wasn't being that generous. I learned a lot that first year and I wanted to get more experience in front of an audience.

Frank was tickled pink because everyone watched the telly in those days and anyone who was on it, even a newsreader, could pull in audiences.

We did pack 'em in that year but, unwittingly, I almost single-handedly destroyed Clacton's famous style of summer show. It all came about because Frank did something he'd never done before: he splashed my name across the top of the advertising, five times bigger than anyone else's. Until then, the Ocean Theatre had always, quite rightly, relied on the name and reputation of the show, *The Ocean Revue*, to be the thing that brought the crowds in – *all* the cast's names were exactly the same size.

Years before me, Ted Rogers and Tony Hancock had both been principal comics with the show but, like I was in my first year, they were then unknowns.

Frank later admitted it was a mistake taking me back. By

the time the second year rolled round I was known through appearances on the telly and, OK, we did do terrific business, but I was no better than I'd been before. The eventual result was the punters expecting a 'name' every year, but there just weren't any around within Frank's budget.

At least I was able to turn up every succeeding summer and do a Sunday concert there. Because of those first two seasons I always did good business.

'Here's Huddy,' Frank would greet me. 'On another bank raid.'

It was through Frank and *The Ocean Revue* that I met Michael Harvey. Michael was part company manager, part assistant stage manager and part straight man in sketches. And he came to work for me. He played the villains in the pantos, answered all the letters, did my tax returns, poured drinks for welcome guests in the dressing room and helped the unwelcome ones out the door. He was a godsend to me in the days when I was doing everything.

He was great company, but I was so naïve that he worked with me for about five years before I realized he was gay, as so many of my best friends are. I finally found out he was 'Towards the Abbey' when, on walking home from a party in Torquay in the early hours, a car pulled up to give me a lift. It was driven by a nun, seated next to a man in a costume made entirely of bread, rolls, toast, bloomers and cottage loaves. In the back was sitting Amy Johnson – yes – Michael!

Being an old pro, Michael knew exactly how to organize whatever was needed. He answered the letters (I love answering letters, but when things were really hectic he would reply for me). He'd put in one-liners, topical gags and funny anecdotes. He was so good at putting together letters in my style that I'd read them and think, 'When did I write that?'

He kept the petty cash receipts and argued with my accountant. I had to sit in the accountant's office while he and Michael went through the expenses. I was, and still am, so bored by anything that vaguely touches on sums that I fell asleep in the middle of one meeting. I was woken by an unbelieving snort from the accountant as he read from Michael's claims sheet.

'Throat medicine forty-eight pounds,' he scoffed. '*Throat* medicine?'

'Yes,' answered the inscrutable one. 'From the Victoria Wine Company!' Even Michael had to concede that one.

Michael was horse-racing mad and we had many a great afternoon at meetings – especially those over the sticks. During that second season in Torquay, I was asked to open a garden fête at a Catholic school and Michael, being a staunch Catholic, made sure I did.

After the event, the Mother Superior wrote me a thank-you note and added as a postscript: 'I don't know if you're interested in racing at all, but one of our parents has close connections with Newton Abbot Racecourse and could certainly arrange free entrance for you.'

Michael replied by return of post, 'Yes, I am interested in racing – and so is my friend!' The tickets duly arrived and it was the start of some very happy and asset-stripping afternoons. One of the lessons Michael taught me was never to take a credit card to the course, cash only – and then only what you could afford to lose. Oh, and always buy a *return* ticket to the course: he had himself, in the past, having done his money, walked home from so many meetings.

Chesney Allen, of Flanagan and Allen fame, owned some successful horses over the years, and the first I knew of his interest in the sport was during a meeting at Newton Abbot. A few of us from the summer show were down there one day and spotted a horse named Edgar, owned by Ches, on the racecard. Of course, we all had a couple of bob on it – well we have to support our own. Edgar was a big red horse and, in the paddock, looked as if he could step over the jumps. He also had the smallest jockey we'd ever seen.

They were off! Edgar turned on his hind legs and, with the mini-jock desperately hanging on, completed the entire course the wrong way round. Years later I asked Chesney Allen if he'd ever had a horse named Edgar.

'Yes,' he said. 'The bugger did the Newton Abbot Racecourse back to front! Thank goodness no one I knew saw it.'

I nodded but said not a word.

Michael Harvey had started as a chorus boy and told me of appearing in *No, No, Nanette* as one of the Sunnicliffe Boys. A well-known musical comedy leading lady played Nanette and, at a certain point in the show, the Sunnicliffe Boys had to pick her up and perch her on their shoulders. This they happily did until one night when, as she landed on their shoulders, she let off the most devastating fart.

'Not a word was spoken,' said Michael. 'But in the interval her dresser brought the Sunnicliffe Boys a bottle of Guinness apiece.'

Michael had a song he always used as an audition piece. It was called 'You Don't Have to Tell Me – I Know'.

'It made directors laugh,' he told me. 'And got me more jobs than any acting could have done.'

Some time later, I found a song sheet of the number, which said on the front: 'Featured and broadcast by Betty Driver'. I duly sent the copy to the Rovers' favourite barmaid c/o *Coronation Street*, and her note of thanks advised me to watch the show on a certain date. I did and watched Betty Turpin drying glasses behind the bar of The Rovers Return while softly singing 'You Don't Have to Tell Me – I Know'.

Another magic moment.

At one stage in the 1950s the incredible Michael was the company manager/stage manager of a drag show. There were lots of these on tour then, the casts purporting to be ex-military personnel, hence shows like *Soldiers in Skirts* and *This Was the Army*. As you can guess, the performers were an odd bunch and Michael revelled in their eccentricities. He told me of characters like Isa Rex (called by her fellow performers The Mystery Girl). She was so named because of her strange way of making up, with her head practically *inside* her make-up box. She would shield her face with her arm so that no one could see 'the artistry'. It was later discovered she used an old trick. The make-up box had no bottom and she would sit down and put the bottomless box over someone else's make-up! A mystery girl no longer.

Another one was nicknamed Selina the Horse.

'He had', said Michael, 'a long thin face, exactly like a old mare.'

On the last night of one tour, the company received onstage all sorts of bouquets from their admirers. 'Some rotten sod sent Selina a bale of hay.'

Yet another of these boys was so hard up he couldn't afford a proper wig so he bought a couple of cheap dolls from Woolworths and stitched the hair together.

'The sight was horrific,' said Michael. 'And the poor soul was so thin that the first time he walked down the steps to "A Pretty Girl is Like a Melody", someone in the Gods shouted "Gawd! Git back ter Belsen!"'

One night he took me for a drink to a then notorious gay pub, The Salisbury in St Martins Lane. As we approached the bar, Michael, finger by finger, removed his leather gloves and handed them to the bloke behind the counter. 'Barman, dear,' he said. 'Put these in water for me!'

It was stories and behaviour like this that made working with Michael such a pleasure. We always seemed to be laughing – even when there was serious business to sort out.

Michael came from Romany stock and said he could 'see' all sorts of things. He never told me anything because, he said, 'I know you so well, I'll be influenced to tell you things I know you'd *want* to hear.'

He did 'see' something for me – us – just once though. One Saturday night, after the show, Ann and I were about to drive back to Oxford.

'Just a minute,' said Michael, as we were about to leave. 'Sit down for couple of minutes. I don't want you to leave yet.'

We did as we were told and left a bit later. On the road out of Clacton we saw two cars, upside down in a ditch. We stopped to help and a policeman on the scene said to us, 'Lucky you weren't driving along here five minutes ago – that's when it happened.'

I never sent up his belief in his visions ever again.

Michael was always ready to earn a few extra bob doing bits and pieces on the telly and, in an episode of the show I did for Yorkshire Television, he did a walk-on as Hitler. Before the show we sat in the canteen having lunch, with him in full Führer drag. Hardly had his soup spoon got to his mouth before the then governor of YTV, Donald Baverstock, arrived at our table.

'Hudd!' he said, waving at Michael. 'You've done this on purpose!'

'What?' I asked.

'Dressed Harvey up just to embarrass my guests!'

Just as I started to explain what the Hitler sketch was all about, Baverstock's sidekick entered the canteen, chatting to a dozen blokes in a language even *I* recognized. We got Michael out of the canteen just before the visitors from German Television had a chance to shout '*Seig Heil!*'

Michael's finest ad-lib was at the Victoria Palace. The occasion was a TV celebration, organized by Hughie Greene, of fifty years of the RAF. It featured a star-studded cast of ex-RAF lads and lasses including Jimmy Edwards, The Bachelors, Arthur Worsley and The Beverley Sisters, and was the first time I'd ever done an impression, in public, of Max Miller. One of the compères was Richard Burton, who did his announcement from a box. Apart from us backstage, no one knew he was being held upright by two RAF regiment policemen, both lying on the floor out of shot. He'd had a few.

This was during one of Burton's marriages to Elizabeth Taylor, and in the rehearsal Burton and Taylor had had an enormous row, and she swept out of the building. The last bit of the rehearsal was all of us lining up in the order we were to meet Prince Philip. I was standing next to Burton – who was standing a good deal less steadily without an RAF policeman hanging onto each leg.

Suddenly, Burton roared to the entire ensemble, 'Has anyone seen my wife?'

Michael Harvey, with hardly a pause, answered, 'I'm not sure. What does she look like?'

Now there *was* a pause, as we waited for Burton to land him one – but no. He gathered Michael into his arms, kissed him on the forehead and said, 'You're my man!'

The next day the press attributed that classic line to everyone – Jimmy Edwards, me, Arthur Worsley – but no one mentioned Michael. So that's what I'm doing now.

One of my first TV spots was in *The Billy Cotton Band Show*, and I shared a dressing room with the legendary Billy Cotton vocalist Alan Breeze and a young Welsh singer who was making his first TV appearance. He sang a song written by my fellow redcoat Les Reed – 'It's Not Unusual' – and the singer was, of course, Tom Jones. He paralysed 'em. After the recording our dressing room was besieged by agents, record producers, song publishers, TV directors – the lot. All, of course, surrounding Tom. I sat in the corner like the loser in a championship boxing match – and I honestly had done all right.

Into this collection of out-for-the-main-chance characters came Russ Conway, who was a regular on the show. He gave Tom a cheery wave, said, 'Great stuff, Tom!' and went to leave. Then he spotted the sad unappreciated comic and said, 'You did all right too.' I blushed becomingly and when he said, 'Come on, I'll get you a drink,' I stopped blushing and followed him out of the room. He could see how out of place I was and rescued me. We remained friends for many, many years. He was a thoughtful, kind and funny bloke.

The first week's music hall I did was with The Players' Theatre Company at Richmond Theatre (Surrey). As always with me it came about in a very odd way. The Players' Company, under the chairmanship of Mike Hall, had been booked for a week at Richmond by the boss there, Freddie Piffard. During discussions, Freddie insisted that a certain 'Roy Hudd' should be included in the show.

'Who's he?' asked Mike, quite rightly.

'He comes here every year and plays a comedy part in our annual Shakespeare play. He's funny and tells me he's really a comedian. They like him here, so put him in.'

So Mike had to – and did. I knew nothing about doing a music hall act, so I asked him what I should do.

'Get a music hall song to start and another to finish,' he advised. 'And do some jokes in the middle.'

'What sort of jokes? I asked.

'Well, what you usually do, but don't mention electricity, aeroplanes or Harold Macmillan.'

I remembered two of the songs that Gran sang to me, and into the routine they went. To open, 'Oh Nicholas Don't Be So Ridiculous' and to finish, 'Seaweed':

As soon as I touched me seaweed
I knew it was gonna to be dry/wet/hot, etc.

In between, a few classics like: 'She was a beautiful mermaid. What a figure! Thirty-eight, twenty-two and four and six a pound!'

Believe it or not it went all right.

About a week later came the phone call that changed my life completely. The phone call wasn't to me but to my agent, Morris, and the caller was the man who totally changed the face of comedy on television, Ned Sherrin. Ned was responsible for the mould-breaking show *That Was The Week That Was* (also known as *TW3*). He was, he told Morris, putting together a follow-up show on similar lines. He'd seen the music hall at Richmond and – heaven be praised – he wanted to see if I'd fit in as a member of the new team.

We did a handful of pilot shows from BBC Lime Grove. The thumbs-up was given, and yours truly was part of the team. And what a team it was. David Frost was the host, Cleo Laine, Annie Ross and Barbara Evans were the singers and the players of sketches included John Fortune, John Bird, Eleanor Bron, Michael Crawford and Willie Rushton. We had guests from Tommy Trinder to Gerald Kaufman, Hylda Baker to Mick Jagger. The show had the catchy name *Not So Much a Programme More a Way of Life*.

I was petrified, and really did feel completely out of place with this collection of university-educated, ex-*Footlights Revue* members, who read newspapers and knew real politicians. They were certainly a clever lot of smart Alecs.

The series was well under way before most of them would even speak to me: they weren't particularly nasty it was just that I wasn't on their wavelength. They were television performers supreme and got laughs out of satirical material I didn't even begin to understand. But then, Ned had booked me for down-to-earth, good standard jokes and songs. Far too 'obvious' material for them, it was stuff that I understood, *could* handle and get laughs with. They quite liked me doing it – probably because if I did it they didn't have to! And I started to appreciate their methods, and learned a great deal from them.

Ned didn't let me down as far as solo bits were concerned. Marty Feldman and Barry Took were constantly being courted by Ned to write 'something satirical'. They never would. Satire, they said, wasn't their scene. The only satirical thought they'd ever had was how much the Prime Minister, Sir Alec Douglas Home, looked like a ventriloquist's dummy.

'That'll do!' said Ned, and they came up with a belter. A take-off of the then famous radio show, *Educating Archie*. They called it *Educating Alec* and I played the Tory ventriloquist Edward du Cann. Ned had a terrific dummy of Sir Alec made, complete with tweedy plus-fours and a shotgun. All the jokes were based on the old idea of vents not being able to pronounce their Ms or Bs, and my favourite was where some stuff about France was under discussion.

'Two million Frenchmen can't be wrong,' said 'Edward du Cann'.

'Two million Frenchmen?' said 'Sir Alec'. 'That's a lot of Gauls!'

It was on this show that I first met someone who became yet another hero. Not a performer this time – a writer: Dick Vosburgh. Dick was an American who left home disenchanted with the Nixon presidency. He wasn't a bad judge. Dick was a brilliant lyricist, though at this time it was one-liners that were his speciality: 'I wouldn't say she was ugly but when she made up the lipstick backed into the tube!'

At this time John Osborne had written a new play, a farce, and so impressed was he by the brilliance of Ken Dodd, that he took the cast of his play along to Doddy's show at the Palladium to see how it was done. Knowing I didn't do a bad Doddy impression, Dick seized on this idea and wrote a sketch for me.

David Frost introduced the sketch by telling of Osborne taking his cast to see Ken.

'Does this mean', said David, 'we'll be seeing Ken Dodd in a John Osborne play?'

The set-up was the famous one from *Look Back in Anger*: the wife (Caroline Blakiston) ironing, and the hero's Welsh friend, Cliff (David Battley) watching. Into the room burst Jimmy Porter, aka Ken Dodd, aka me.

The sketch was a seven-page Dodd-type monologue with a few interpolations from the wife and friend. *Not So Much a Programme* . . . was a 'live' show, so once you started a sketch that was it. At the afternoon rehearsal I did all right – I battled through and, by visualizing each of the seven pages, I did the whole thing in the order it should have been done. In the words of the master, 'how tickled I was'.

Come the transmission though, things went slightly awry. I burst into the room OK, and got the first laugh. Now, drunk with power, I became even more frenziedly Doddified and followed the first gag with one from page three. I did seven minutes of this pick-and-mix solo (Caroline and David didn't say a word – they didn't get a single cue). I desperately dodged from page to page, but did manage to finish on a parody of 'Love is Like a Violin'.

After the show, some of the team said, 'Marvellous! How did you remember it?' To which Ned, who was passing, said 'He didn't!'

The musical director, Dave Lee, made my night when he said, 'For that bit I'm giving you one of the most useless things in show business – a vote of thanks from the band!' That was good enough for me.

It was on *Not So Much a Programme . . .* where I learned to never trust the autocue. The then American president, Lyndon Johnson, was telling his people that because of financial problems they should spend their holidays at home in the US. Dave Lee and Herbert Kretzmer had written a song about it, and I had to do it, but the words and music arrived so late there was no chance to learn it, so it was put onto the autocue – a very Heath Robinson affair at that time. I was nervous.

The song was a fast patter piece like 'The Darktown Strutters' Ball', and Ned had surrounded it with a production: drum majorettes marched around for a bit and then I was discovered, wearing a Stetson, camera round neck, and holding a big cigar.

The band was in a different room and, once started, they couldn't be stopped. I looked at the autocue and opened my mouth. It stayed open. No words came out. The words weren't there. I was looking at a blank screen. I smiled, moved my eyebrows up and down and waved the cigar. Still nothing. The music went on. The opening couple of lines appeared – too late! The band was sixteen bars into the song. I did a funny walk. I went past the camera to see if I could find the autocue operator. I couldn't. I went back to my start position and a few words from towards the end of the piece appeared.

This bizarre performance eventually squealed to a halt and I stood stock-still. The camera switched to a bemused and embarrassed David Frost, while I couldn't move. With some assistance, the floor manager dragged me, a rigid, wild-eyed, seized-up wreck, to a dressing room, where I immediately passed out. I was put in a taxi and sent home – still burbling.

Ann was no help. 'What were you doing mucking about in the song like that?' she said. 'You spoilt it!'

Too right I did. Once I had sobbingly explained what had happened she sent me to bed with a hot drink and much comfort.

I got no such comfort from the composer, Dave Lee. At the next rehearsal he walked out as I walked in, and it was three weeks before he even said 'Good morning' to me. He swore to whoever would listen that I had mucked up the number on purpose. Ned had to take him to one side and tell him what had happened.

From that dreadful moment on I either learned whatever I had to do or had the words written on whacking great sheets of cardboard.

Not So Much a Programme. . . had good writers and good performers but it didn't have the smack-between-the-eyes impact of *TW3*. Another bash at a similar format, *BBC3*, suffered the same fate. The satire boom was over.

I owe an awful lot to Ned Sherrin. By giving me the chance to do so many different things in front of the public he turned me into a 'name'.

For me, there was one terrific spin-off that came indirectly from *Not So Much a Programme* . . . Ned had commissioned a sketch for the show, based on the news that NCOs would no longer be allowed to sell insurance to their charges, and I played a sergeant major (a role I took into several other series) trying to flog policies to his regiment. The line-up of soldiers I had to address included John Bird, Irving Davies and Willie Rushton. At the rehearsal, Willie had realized that he couldn't be seen from the front so, as I approached him to deliver my first line, he closed his eyes. Written on his eyelids was, 'Piss off!' What a writer Willie was!

A pal of mine, film director Jimmy Allen, had been asked to come up with an idea for a TV advert for Lyons Quick Brew Tea. One evening, over a drink, he said he had an idea to use my sergeant major character in a Quick Brew commercial. He explained that the tea was in red and black packets (the colours of the sergeant major's uniform) and he thought the phrase, 'By the left – Quick Brew!' might work. We did a pilot and Lyons said OK.

The Quick Brew commercials went on for four years and, referring to the tea bags' selling point (lots of tiny holes in them 'to let the flavour flood out!') someone came up with the phrase, 'It's not me ma'am – it's me little perforations!'

In no time at all the phrase caught on and it was shouted at me by all and sundry. It was like having a hit song – and it paid very nicely too. So much so, that I was able to work at the Young Vic with Frank Dunlop. The money at the Young Vic was lousy, but the income from the commercials meant I could do smashing plays for next to nowt.

Throughout the entire Quick Brew campaign, there was really only one drama. Some right know-all wrote to the newspapers about the medals the sergeant major wore, naming the medals and asking whether Roy Hudd was entitled to wear them. I replied, saying all the medals were adaptations of the CDM – a gimmick from another commercial (Cadbury's Dairy Milk). We heard no more.

Over the years all sorts of young actors played the sergeant major's lads, the Quick Brewers, or QBs. When I see them on the telly now playing grandads I know I'm getting old.

The other series of commercials I did were for Danish Bacon. All I can remember about them was the make-up lady spending more time making up a slice of ham than she ever did making me up.

CHAPTER SIX

'Step onto that stage and you're done for!'

The satire boom may have been over but, for me, things took off – and how! Suddenly, I was the BBC's golden boy and they were falling over themselves to get me into other things. The first was a sitcom called, cleverly, *Hudd*.

I was, and still am, a great admirer of Jacques Tati. His sort of silent comedy really appeals to me and at that time it was something that, as far as I knew, had never been done on television before. I had a good storyline for the first episode. *Hudd* was taken home by his girlfriend to meet her mum and dad. He was a shy little creature and, anxious to make a good impression, got into all sorts of fixes. When he was shown to his bedroom – which dad had just finished decorating – he lifted his case onto the bed and made a long black mark on the wallpaper. He spent the rest of the night trying to get rid of the damage, and ended up re-papering the entire room. The girl's parents were kept awake all night and, at daybreak, burst into our hero's bedroom to discover nothing wrong.

The Beeb got two writers to work up my idea, George Evans and Derek Collier. The first half-hour went well, and people still mention that particular episode fifty years later.

My original idea was that the 'silent' comedy should come not from him being a mute, but by putting him in situations where one doesn't speak. Alas, the writers took it the wrong way and just made him someone who didn't answer when he was spoken to: they made him a simpleton rather than a normal young man placed in unfortunate situations.

The BBC seemed happy enough to do another series, but I wasn't. The 'silent' idea had come off the rails, so I asked if I could do a revue-type show, with sketches and the like. They said yes, and *The Illustrated Weekly Hudd* was born. They really went to town, giving me Sheila Steafel and Patrick Newell to play sketches with and one of their top producers, James Gilbert.

It didn't work, though. I wasn't ready or good enough to be able to headline a show as myself, and not clever enough to do sketches that required top-rate character work. Jimmy Gilbert spotted this straight away and gave up after one series, unloading me onto Michael Hurll. Michael had done almost everything in Light Entertainment, but comedy was not his strong point. It was the blind leading the blind. I needed someone who could successfully harness what little talent I had.

The BBC gave me enough chances. Two excellent performers to work with, Doug Fisher and Marcia Ashton. The writers were the best: Dick Vosburgh, Barry Cryer, Graham Chapman, Michael Palin, Terry Jones, Dave Freeman and, of course Eric Davidson. I was able to have my pal from concert party days, Arthur Tolcher, do all sorts of bits and pieces, alongside 'Nosher' Powell.

But despite all this, I wasn't really good enough. And, foolishly, I spent far too much time catching up with my lack of early development.

We did three series of *The Illustrated Weekly Hudd* from

1966 to 1968. Too much too soon for this lad: too much responsibility; too much sowing of wild oats.

Sleeping Beauty at the Sheffield Lyceum in 1966 was my second big panto as top of the bill. This one I shared with the Canadian musical comedy star, Edmund (Ted) Hockridge. He was extremely butch, with a glorious deep manly voice. Dick Vosburgh wrote a cod TV commercial that said, 'The new Edmund Hockridge aftershave – yes the one that comes in a hairy bottle!'

It was interesting being on the poster with Ted. We shared the top of the bill with exactly the same amount of space. It worked well for me. One of my first *Workers' Playtime* radio shows was with Ted Ray (for me the nearest patter comedian we had to the great Americans).

'That's clever, son,' Ted said to me one day. 'Using the name Roy Hudd.'

'It's my real name,' I told him. 'And why is it clever?'

'A short name like yours is great for the posters,' he said. 'If you're sharing equal space, your name has got to be bigger than a rival with a longer name. It's why I changed my name from Charlie Olden to Ted Ray.' He was right.

I knew I must have been becoming fairly well known during that season at the Lyceum because my life was threatened. One night I answered a call at the stage door phone to be assailed by a hoarse Lee Marvin-type voice with a Sheffield accent.

'Don't', said the weirdo, 'go onto the stage tonight. You will be shot!'

I started to laugh and the voice went up three decibels.

'Do not laugh Hudd! I mean every word I say. Too long you have been a curse on this Christian Nation. You will spread your evil no more! Do *NOT* step onto the stage tonight!'

While I was wracking my brain to see which of my chums could do an accent like that, the phone went down. A few minutes later the caller phoned back.

'Don't forget, you spawn of the devil! This is not a joke! Step onto that stage and you're done for!'

I giggled to myself and tried not to imagine Jack Nicholson saying 'Honey, I'm home', but I told the company manager what had happened. The police arrived within ten minutes. Apparently these sorts of phone calls had been made before and though nothing had happened, they would take no chances. For the next fortnight I had a police escort to and from the theatre.

The company, too, took every precaution. Whenever I was onstage with anyone they all stood at least six feet away from me. All except my two buddies, the classic double act Gordon and Bunny Jay. They addressed all their dialogue to me from behind pieces of scenery. For some bits they just poked their heads out of the dressing room. Never was so little seen of the pair of 'em. Ted Hockridge also kept his distance, and even the boys and girls did most of their routines in the wings.

Nothing happened. Probably the sight of a slosh-covered comic being escorted backstage, twice a day, by two straight-faced coppers frightened the embryo Jackal away.

Ann and I, the mother-in-law and Max had a house for the season. We had an au pair girl too, a nice Italian girl, Tania. Early one morning Tania crept into our bedroom and called to me softly: 'Meester 'udd, Meester 'udd! Excuse me but the bedroom is on fire.'

'Course it is,' I mumbled, burying my head in the pillows.
'Ees no joke!' she said. 'Please! Please! Come and look!'

Now Max, who was in her arms, started to join in, so, grudgingly, I investigated. The bedroom was on fire. Standing up in his cot, the bold Max had pulled a curtain down from the wall onto an electric heater. The fire was merrily making its way up all the surrounding drapes. I tried to remember all the extinguishing drills I'd read about in *Boy's Own*. Smother the flames – yes, that's it. I pulled the flaming curtains onto the floor and proceeded to jump on them.

As I jumped, my pyjama trousers headed floorwards. Straight out of bed I was and so, of course, I had no socks or slippers on and my feet and ankles *and* bottom (both cheeks), were all burnt to buggery. I'd just got over a fortnight of dodging the sniper and now I had two weeks of comedy walks without trying!

(I should have mentioned that during the initial discovery of the inferno I shouted out for water. 'Coming!' said Alice, the mother-in-law, 'Hot or cold?')

When all the panic was over Ann apologized to the embarrassed au pair.

'I'm so sorry, Tania,' she said, 'that Mr Hudd's trousers fell down.'

Tania blushed becomingly and whispered, 'In a case like zat one does not look!'

There was one great escape from the colander, which came through making a silent film. Frank Muir, who was the boss of BBC Comedy at that time, gave me a script written by John Law. John was the man who did so much for the success of Michael Bentine's classic TV series, *It's a Square World*. He died very young, so we can only imagine what he would have done if he'd hung around a bit longer. John's script was called *The Maladjusted Busker* and had no dialogue. It was simply the story of a London busker, a flute player (me), who, in the middle of Trafalgar Square, loses touch with his little band. The rest of the story is him trying to meet up with them again. It had some inventive, funny, sad, even romantic routines, and it was indeed like a Jacques Tati movie.

Frank Muir told me he liked the script and asked me what I thought of it. He confessed it had been turned down by every top comic at the BBC. Needless to say, I loved it and did it – directed by John Duncan, who had put together lots of bits and pieces on *Not So Much a Programme . . .*

I suddenly perked up. John Duncan was very different to the Light Entertainment directors I'd worked with. He was hugely inventive, he radiated enthusiasm and had the talent to be able to convey to me exactly what he wanted. And I always wanted to please him. We were both very proud of the finished result. (This bit is just for old time variety aficionados: halfway through the filming I discovered that the trumpet player in the busker's band was a man called Harry Hines, who'd been Dr Crock of the well-known comedy band Dr Crock and his Crackpots. So now you know.)

The film was intended to be the BBC's entry for the Golden Rose at the Montreux TV Festival, but the powers that be said it wasn't right for such a prestigious event and would only put it in on the fringe. They decided *Jeeves and Wooster* would be better, which the foreign judges found so confusing that they had to be issued with a glossary of terms used in the programme – 'Toodle pip, old fruit' = 'Goodbye, dear friend', etc. *Jeeves and Wooster* disappeared, glossary and all, but *The Maladjusted Busker* won the Press Prize from the European journalists.

A summer season at the Princess Theatre, Torquay, was a dream come true. Right next door to Babbacombe, where I'd made so many friends via *Out of the Blue*, I was second top to Frankie Vaughan. By this time, the family were so used to me being away in the West Country that when saying his prayers of an evening, Max would say, 'Our Father who art in Devon'.

I made another friend in that show, the comedienne Audrey Jeans. Audrey taught me more about how to behave and look than anyone before or since. She was a terrific performer and, in any other country but this one, she'd have been a star in musicals. I think perhaps she was of such value as a variety act she was kept away from the musical side of the business. She liked me and I used to call for her on the way to the theatre.

One evening, as we walked to work, she said, 'I'm walking on the other side of the road.'

'Why?' I asked.

''Cos you look such a bag of * * * * I don't want to be seen with you.'

That stopped me dead in my tracks – me? 'A bag of whatsit?' I was dressed in my usual duffle coat, black roll neck sweater, tubular trousers, red socks and Hush Puppies – so what was wrong? At the theatre, with the aid of a full-length mirror, she showed me. She was right – I was an almost perfect 'bag of * * * *'. Even more so standing next to her – the perfect showbiz star.

'I'll meet you here tomorrow morning,' she said, 'Bring your cheque book.'

The next day she marched me round all the good men's clothes shops and fixed me up from head to toe. It cost me the best part of two grand, but she was right. I felt a million dollars and people, when I came towards them, didn't cross themselves. The only people who came out of a stage door looking like I used to were the Sex Pistols.

I did pull a good 'un on her, though. I told her my wife was an alcoholic (nothing was further from the truth, I hasten to add) and to please *not* offer her a drink when they met. When the family came down to Torquay I took Ann along to Audrey's dressing room. She waved to Ann with one hand while throwing a large tea towel over her tray of booze with the other.

'She's very nice,' Ann said as we walked home. 'But she didn't even offer us a drink.' She did eventually.

Dear Audrey, who oozed class and lit up every room she walked into, was married twice and was on her second honeymoon when she was killed in a road accident. She was fifty.

I was up to the naughties again, but I did give Ann a nice surprise that season. She was dead anxious to drive herself – not easy when you haven't got a car. So I explained that I was late home because I'd managed to get her an old second-hand motor, and it was outside the digs. I'd been to the showroom and said I would buy a new mini on the condition that they could deliver it before I got home (in fifteen minutes). They did and Ann was knocked out.

That season was the first I'd earned any real money and I

ABOVE LEFT: Gran holding my Auntie Snowdrop; in front, the terrible trio (*left to right*) Evalina (my Mum), Ivy and Elsa.

ABOVE RIGHT: Any boy-child of that age wearing a dress is destined for the theatre. The young Hudd.

RIGHT: Evalina and me – modelling her latest knitted creation, summer 1940.

BELOW: The Maidford mafia, alias my cousins (*left to right*) Pat, Dennis, Alma, Valerie and Mavis.

ABOVE: This could have
been the last photo we
ever had taken. Me and
my brother Peter outside
the condemned cottage to
which we were evacuated,
just before the roof slid off
its rafters, Maidford circa
1944.

INSET: Gran and me in the back
garden at 5, Neville Road, Croydon.

ABOVE: I always
wanted to be a
ventriloquist, but
Peter just wouldn't
sit still!

BELOW: The happy
reunion on the sands at
Margate after my escape from
Birchington in 1947. (*Left to
right*) Gran, Auntie Snowie, me (at the back),
Peter and Uncle Len.

ABOVE: At RAF Waterbeach, pretending to play the banjo, circa 1957.

BELOW: My first panto, *Goody Two-Shoes* at the Empire Theatre, Leeds in 1959.

ABOVE: Butlins, Clacton, 1958. You see? I was *years* ahead of Ken Dodd.

BELOW: Early days of the Hudd and Kay double act. Eddie, me … and some hair.

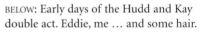

ABOVE: *Dick Whittington*, at the New Theatre, Oxford in 1960, with Mr Pastry (Richard Hearne), who taught me how to fall off a chair.

BELOW: (*Left to right*) Eric Davidson, me, Ronnie Brandon, David Gardiner and Tom Howard, at a 'fete worse than death' in Babbacombe.

ABOVE: *Out of the Blue*, Babbacombe, with Arthur 'not now, Arthur' Tolcher.

LEFT: Ann holds our baby boy, Max, while concert party maestros Dickie Pounds (*left*) and Ronnie Brandon (*right*) look on.

RIGHT: Max meets his hero. (*Terry Moore*)

BELOW: Ann and I brainwashing Max into following in our theatrical footsteps. (*Rex Features*)

ABOVE: A dozen puppies and their mother, Lily – who obviously doesn't trust the cameraman!

RIGHT: My friend Michael Harvey being molested once again! (*Isle of Thanet Gazette*)

LEFT: (*Left to right*) Billy Dainty, Morris Aza and yours truly. Morris was my agent for fifty years, until his retirement in 2009. (*Doug McKenzie*)

ABOVE: *Underneath the Arches*, 1981. (*Left to right, standing*) Joe Black, Tommy Godfrey, Billy Gray, Don Smoothey and Peter Glaze; Chris Timothy (as Ches) and me (as Bud) sitting at the front.

BELOW RIGHT: As Fagin in the 1977 production of *Oliver!*. Own nose!

BELOW: As Dogberry in *Much Ado About Nothing* at the Young Vic, with Barry Evans as Borachio, 1973.

ABOVE: The Royal Variety Performance, London Palladium, 1980, a thorn amongst five roses. (*Left to right*) Arthur English, Ben Warris, myself, Chesney Allen, Cyril Fletcher and Tommy Trinder.

RIGHT: About to doff my hat to another hero, Arthur Askey, the man who got me out of trouble, as Larry Beardsley (*centre*) looks on. (*Wimbledon News*)

RIGHT: Water Rats all. Me basking in the glow given off by two great stars, Sir Norman Wisdom and Danny la Rue.

certainly took advantage. Late nights at jazz clubs, drinking and laughing with the sax player, Red Price. At the end of the summer I got home and rang Morris straight away.

'I need some work,' I told him.

'But you've only just finished a long season at good money!'

'I've spent it!' I whined. The next day he arranged that all my wages went to him, he deducted his commission (not a bad judge) and part was put aside for tax. Thanks, Morris.

It was the summer of 1967 and I was about to do a show at the Winter Gardens, Margate, when someone sent me a cutting from the local paper. On the front page was a photograph of my Dad, Harry, with a woman I vaguely recognized as the lady I had met in Birchington years before. The headline read, 'The proudest parents in Thanet', and the piece explained how delighted my father and 'mother' were that I'd be next door to them for the summer.

I dismissed the story and carried on getting things organized for the season.

The show opened and went really well even though, at the end of the first performance, some bigwig on the local council, told the audience what a job they'd had getting *anybody* for the season. But, he confided, 'we scraped the bottom of the barrel and came up with Roy Hudd. And it's worked out quite well.'

Uncharacteristically, I didn't try to give him a mouthful there and then but – on the last night of what turned out to be a box office record-breaking season – with that councillor sitting on the front row, I came forward to say a few words and handed a barrel to the councillor. He was left with the barrel on his lap and my goodbye: 'Next year, have a scrape round that and see if you can come up with something as good!'

What he had said on that opening night had spread through the town like wildfire and his exit from the theatre was accompanied by mutterings, booing and lots of chuckles. A long time to wait for an ad-lib but, oh, so worth it.

Yes the show did do well and we'd only been open a couple of weeks before a very big deal happened. I was getting dressed for the first-half finale. This was – surprise, surprise – a music hall finale, and I would finish the scene in full drag, leading the company and the audience in a sing-a-long.

I was sitting in the dressing room in front of the mirror, dressed in a purple corset, high heels, fishnet tights, a huge red wig, enormous lashes and full slap. I was just attaching the first of two great sparkling earrings when a knock came at the door. It was my co-star Mark Wynter.

'And now,' announced Mark, in possibly the worst impression of Eammon Andrews ever perpetrated, 'someone you haven't seen for twenty years – your father!' With that, he threw open the door and there was someone I hadn't seen for twenty-*five* years – Harry Hudd.

Our memorable exchange was started by me.

'Hullo Dad!' I said, as I attached the second earring.

'Hullo – son?' came the reply from the bemused parent. Michael Harvey, burying his head in my corset, gigglingly handed me my Marie Lloyd-type jewelled staff, and on I went.

That, sadly, was the last bit of fun to come out of that reunion. I did so want to find out what he was really like. I'd been brainwashed by Gran and the aunties. They all told me what a dyed-in-the-wool villain he was, rotten to my mum, lazy – you name it and they called him for it.

I wouldn't dare admit it to the family, but I did have two good memories of him. I could remember getting into bed with him on a Sunday morning. He'd prop a chair under the eiderdown and turn it into a wigwam. Then he'd tell me great stories of cowboys and Indians. For years I kept the only present I remember him giving me, a marvellous book called *A Hundred and One Things a Boy Can Do*. It was full of things to make, experiments to try, magic tricks to amaze your friends with and ventriloquism for beginners. I managed to do about ten of the things most boys could do.

After the show we did have a chat, in a very stilted sort of way, but not once did he mention my brother. He didn't ask where he lived, what he was doing, or if he was alive or dead. I'm not a great family man, but I just couldn't forgive his complete lack of interest in dear Peter.

And that, as far as my relationship with the old man was concerned, was it. He did occasionally turn up at the box office – for a couple of complimentary tickets, and we did meet up again, me, Harry, Dorothy and a new half-brother but, alas, there was no spark from any of us. End of a chapter.

Now a story I've told many times but it is such an extraordinary one I can't leave it out. For years I had a recurring dream. Nothing sensational, it was just me walking around a house, looking through a window into an illuminated garden, and finishing up in the basement being looked at by several images of myself. It wasn't the least bit disturbing and I accepted it as just a slightly odd dream.

Ann and I were living in Streatham at the time, and an actor chum, Donald Walker, invited me to see a new flat he and his pal had moved into.

'Why?' I asked him.

'I think it will interest you,' he said.

Fair enough. So one Sunday morning we drove to Ackerman Road in Brixton, south London. As we turned into the road I knew exactly where we were going, even though I'd never been there before.

'This is the house!' I said, as I ran up the steps. Donald opened the door and I pushed past him. 'Let me describe the room through here,' I said.

I described it to Donald and, going into the room, proved I was right. As we went through the house, I continued to say just what the shape of each room was, where the fireplaces were sited, etc. I wanted to go down into the basement but it was full of rubbish so I couldn't.

'This is the house I've dreamed about all these years,' I explained. 'Why did you want me to see it?'

Donald told me that Dan Leno, a very famous Victorian music hall comedian, had lived there. Dan was a huge and much-loved star, particularly in pantomime at Drury Lane. I remember Gran used to say that whenever it rained really hard people would say, 'It's the angels crying with laughter at Dan.' He was a champion clog dancer and I put two and two together and suddenly worked out why, in the dream, I was surrounded by images of myself: dancers rehearse in front of mirrors and he could easily have worked out his routines in the cellar. It was getting stranger and stranger.

I told Donald about looking through a window into an

illuminated garden. We couldn't work that one out at all, until, many years later, I learned Dan used to have alfresco children's parties in his garden and that he was one of the first people to string lights powered by electricity out there. I was shaken, to say the least. I think it was simply because I'd never had any experience of that sort of thing before. Or since. I'm not one of those people who can 'feel' an atmosphere or a presence. There was no explanation.

It did, however, lead me into finding out as much as I could about Leno, and he was a fascinating comedian. Totally unlike any other of his period. When you read his patter you can see he was a forerunner of Spike Milligan, the Goons and Monty Python. He was also a founder member of the Grand Order of Water Rats in 1889. More about them later.

I told this story on radio and received a stack of letters from mediums and the like. They all said he was a benign influence and on my side. But several warned me not to go to where he was buried. Oh boy! I found out he was buried in Streatham, just round the corner from where we lived. As I've said, I'm not a believer in all that extrasensory perception stuff, but I've never been to his grave – better safe than sorry.

Dan died in a lunatic asylum. Long since demolished, it was sited on a plot that is now a children's playground called the Agnes Riley Gardens. I like to think that the man who made so many children laugh in pantomime still has a sort of link with juvenile fun today.

I also told the story of the dream to John Duncan, who'd directed lots of sketches in *Not So Much a Programme . . .* , and who later became the head of Light Entertainment at

Yorkshire Television. John was always terrific at seeing possibilities that no one else could see. He produced and directed a totally original solo TV show for me in the seventies. I am a great fan of monologues, particularly those of the Victorian columnist George R. Sims. I recited a few to John, including his most famous one, *In the Workhouse Christmas Day*. He had an idea that it might make a very different programme for Christmas. He called it *Poor Christmas* and we did it very simply – just me acting the material direct to camera. It got tucked away on BBC2 and George Melly, who was a TV critic at the time, said it was the one worthwhile programme on TV that Christmas.

Anyway, when I told him the Dan Leno story, John thought it would make a good creepy quickie for Christmas TV, and asked me to get together everything I had about Leno. Among all the photographs and songs and patter was a little book entitled *Dan Leno – Hys Booke*. It was a very funny 'pretend' autobiography. We both thought that, prefaced by the visit to Brixton story, it had the makings of something really special for television.

John approached the project in his own inimitable and highly inventive way, discussing it over a pint – or thirteen. That was the way he taught me the great wodge of dialogue, over a pint – or twenty-three. I don't remember learning it, but when I came round the following morning, I knew every word.

In effect it was me, as Leno, reading extracts from my 'autobiography'. John insisted I learned it all, no autocue, and after my experience with the song on *Not So Much a Programme . . .* I couldn't have agreed more.

There were a couple of film inserts, one of which was of

Dan going into the country to paint, his great hobby (when I told the late Sir Harry Secombe the story he gave me one of Leno's watercolours, which I'm looking at as I write). During this trip into the country Dan met up with a madman, and this was a bit we reconstructed. On our way to the location, John said we'd be picking up the actor who was to play the madman, and as we rounded a corner we saw a figure in a long overcoat and huge 'actor laddie' hat standing on the roadside, swaying slightly.

'That's him,' said John.

The epitome of eccentricity flopped onto the back seat, smiled briefly and declared, 'Morpheus – take me to your bosom!' Morpheus obliged … and that was when I first met Freddie Jones.

I love actors who really go for it, and Fred is one of them. He draws his characters with bold, totally truthful strokes. The actor he admires most is Charles Laughton and the actor *I* admire most is Freddie Jones.

Dan Leno – Hys Booke was, under the enthusiastic guidance of John Duncan, a fascinating piece of television. It was shown in 1968 as an episode in the *Omnibus* series and, by public demand, repeated three times.

After one of the showings I got a letter, via the BBC, from a man called T. (Tom) C. Elder. In it, he simply stated how fascinating it was to see something he'd written at the end of the nineteenth century, in a medium that wasn't even countenanced when he had put pen to paper. I went to meet him at his house in Surrey.

Just on a hundred years old, Tom was an extraordinary man who had only retired from his advertising business in Fleet Street a couple of years previously. He knew and enjoyed the company of luminaries from the artist Augustus John to General Booth of the Salvation Army. A writer all his life, he'd written comic novels under his own name and had 'ghosted' *Dan Leno – Hys Booke*. He never actually met Dan, but was a great fan and knew lots of his gags and patter, which he used as the basis of the book. For the rest, he took some facts and fantasies and 'Leno-esqued' them. You can't see a join between Dan's stuff and Tom's.

The last ghosting Tom did, so he said, was rewriting Edward Heath's speeches. I think if Leno had been delivering them the Tories would never have lost power! Tom died, at a hundred and four, in 1979.

One creepy thing led to another and in 1968 I was offered a part in a film. My first. It was a cheapo production, but did star Peter Cushing. Its title? *The Curse of the Blood Beast Terror!* It wasn't a comedy – well it wasn't *supposed* to be. . .

It was the story of a girl, played by Wanda Ventham, who, I can't remember how, was transmogrified into a giant death's head moth that ate people. The director was a legendary one, Vernon Sewell. He was just what I imagined a film director should look like – blue blazer, cravat and a riding crop which he kept slapping against his leg.

I was booked to play the mortuary attendant and I worked so hard learning every word and comma of the script. Well, it was a film and I'd seen all those credits: 'Screenplay by ...' so to me a film script was the Bible.

I turned up for filming at a tiny studio behind BBC Lime Grove at about half past six in the morning. I sat with the make-up girl and Peter Cushing. He was so smashing and asked me what I thought of the script. (Actually not much, but I wouldn't have dared say that.) I mumbled something non-committal.

'I think we can do better than that,' he said, and proceeded to ad-lib around the situation. Together we came up with some, to us, funny lines and we went onto the set. I was shaking like a leaf as Vernon prepared to start but Peter, God bless him, held up his hand and said, 'Roy's never done a film before, so I want him to meet the crew and I'll show him just what's what.'

He took me all round the set, which took all of forty-five seconds, pointing out where the lights would be and generally settling me down. We did our rewritten lines for the camera and got some laughs. I was feeling much better now. Our scenes were all set in my mortuary, which consisted of two marble slabs of deathlike proportions set close to the camera, with several more going off into the distance. Because the studio was so small they were made in perspective, as was the entrance to the place, which was about four foot high.

'You enter through the door,' Vernon advised me, 'And walk towards the camera. You'll have to come in with bent legs and straighten up as you get closer to the marble slabs at the front. Make the place look big.'

Was this how John Wayne and Robert Mitchum had to perform? Never mind – I was in a film.

The only two real 'bodies' on the set were the ones on the downstage slabs. They were two extras both covered with white sheets. Vernon, squinting through the camera, thought it would be more effective if an arm, covered in blood, hung out from beneath the cloth. At this suggestion one corpse pushed back his winding sheet.

'Blood eh?' he said. 'Well, above the elbow – more cabbage!' The assistant director did a quick financial calculation and we had blood – just *below* the elbow.

Eventually, all was settled and … ACTION! I made my entrance in the shape of a question mark and duly straightened up as I walked downstage. Before I could speak, the other corpse let out a huge snore.

Vernon threw his script on the floor and we went back to the entrance.

Peter's idea was that I should pull one of the sheets back, put down my plate of bread and cheese and eat it. Quite funny – but I had to go and push it that bit further. With my fork I reached between the corpse's legs and speared a pickled onion. It got a huge laugh.

'Cut!' shouted Vernon, throwing down the script again. I did manage to keep the pickled onion business in, but it was shot from a respectable angle and the laugh was killed.

I have to say, I haven't met a nicer actor than Peter Cushing. He was kind, generous and great to play opposite. A truly gentle gentleman.

Ann and Morris went to a preview and greeted the opening scene – natives canoeing down the river – with barely suppressed giggles. The river was obviously the Thames and the African canoeists were covered in goose pimples. When they recognized hardly concealed parts of Surrey they burst into guffaws and got slung out.

Quite right too. Us movie stars don't like to be laughed at.

The film often comes up on TV in the middle of long dark nights. I always know when it's been on. People shout at me in the street, 'Give us a pickled onion, Roy!'

Such was the memorable success of the mortuary

attendant that my next film role didn't happen until thirty years later. I played perhaps the only nice adult in a film called *Kind of Hush*. It was an adaptation of a very powerful novel by Richard A. Johnson. Based on the author's own experiences, it told a terrifying story of incest and child abuse. It wasn't a comedy.

I played a chef who befriends one of the abused lads and tries to help him to a better life. Difficult to believe but, at the time, there were so many TV series and films about the very same subject that it didn't get the attention that Brian Stirner's sensitive direction deserved. At the premiere I sat next to Les Reed, my old friend from the RAF and Nuffield days. Les, of course, wrote the title song, but the version used under the credits was a punk one. As it started we both slid under the seat …

In 1968, Ann and I saw in the New Year with a glass of champagne and high hopes. On paper, it looked as if I'd finally cracked it. What a year I had lined up: a thirteen-week BBC radio series of my own; my first series for Yorkshire TV; and a part in a brand new West End-bound comedy written by a playwright who was the flavour of the month.

Off we went. The radio show was produced by one of the BBC's top guys, Edward Taylor. We had a big band, with Norman Percival on the stick and just one other performer, Sheila Bernette. We got on and worked well together. But somehow it didn't quite gel and, after that first thirteen weeks, *The Roy Hudd Show* was never heard of again.

Not to worry – the 1968 BBC golden handshake show impressed Yorkshire TV and they took me, Freddie Jones and Joan Turner for a six-week series. They also took John Duncan from the BBC and he produced and directed the series, ominously titled *The Roy Hudd Show*.

John was always able to talk me into anything, and I believed, as he did, that the series would be given a late-night spot. It was packed with the most offbeat, strange stuff. Just the title of one of the sketches will give you a clue as to how unlike BBC comedies it was – 'A Soft Landing on God'. It would have been fine for a minority audience but ITV, in their wisdom – Gawd knows why – put it on at peak viewing time. It made the top-twenty ratings for its entire run, and people hated it. In those days *anything* on ITV was watched by the majority: it was entertainment wallpaper.

So, the second of my great hopes vanished without trace, too.

The third, though, was the 'best' of the lot. How could it go wrong? *The Giveaway* was written by Ann Jellicoe, whose previous play, *The Knack*, was a massive hit. It was produced by a top man, Oscar Lewinstein; starred Rita Tushingham and Dandy Nicholls; and was directed by a clever young man, the then unknown Richard Eyre (much later, *Sir* Richard Eyre, boss of the National Theatre).

We started in Edinburgh and all went well. The attraction of a film star (Rita), Mrs Garnett (Dandy) and me (well known on television – the Yorkshire series hadn't been on yet!), did pull the punters in. They laughed, but I felt it wasn't right. I told Morris I wasn't sure, but he said, 'With Oscar Lewinstein at the head they're *bound* to get it right before London.'

They didn't.

We got to the Garrick Theatre in Charing Cross Road

and did a dress rehearsal. Michael Harvey asked the theatre manager, who'd watched the run-through, if I could have a phone put in my dressing room.

'I should wait until *after* the opening night,' he advised. I should have known.

Came opening night and the queue for the gallery stretched down the side of the theatre that led to the stage door. Michael and I walked past the queue, with me doing my Butlin redcoat stuff chatting to one and all.

'I hope you enjoy it!' I ad-libbed brilliantly to one very large lady.

Her moustache bristled, 'We'll see!' she said, unsmilingly.

The curtain rose as our hopes sank. Not a titter for about half an hour. The palms were sweating and it was impossible to unstick the top lip from the teeth.

After wading through the barren waste for thirty minutes, the first laugh came. Rita, answering a phone call, pulled the phone wire out of the wall. They liked that.

Again, my rapier-like improvisation came to the rescue. To the frozen-to-the-spot Rita I suggested, 'Why don't you pop round to the Post Office and get them to send an engineer?'

'Yes. Thank you! Thank you!' she said, and was off like a startled ferret.

Dandy, who was playing my mum, shot me a look and said, 'Right. Now what are you going to do?'

I shrugged and panicked.

'What are you doing at the church concert this year?' said Dandy.

'Ah, yes!' I said – and went into my act.

It went quite well. Better than the play.

The curtain fell to the most blood-chilling sound ever heard in a theatre: booing.

Dandy and I got a smattering of applause for our bravery but they booed Rita, which was very, very unfair. She'd tried so hard to make a silk purse and was the best thing in the piece.

I reacted in my own sweet way: I 'replied' to the audience. The next day Morris got several phone calls from members of the press: 'Did Roy Hudd *really* tell the audience to * * * * off last night?'

'Certainly not!' said Morris in high dudgeon. 'As if he would!' But now it can be told – I did.

Directly after the first show, Morris and I waited in Leicester Square for the papers – and reviews – to appear. Around 2.30 a.m. the first one came. It was a stinker and they got worse with each new arrival, so much so that the newspaper bloke joined us in looking for the notices and he found the last one.

'Cor dear!' he chuckled. 'This is the worse one yet!' And it was.

Later that day, crafty front-of-house displays appeared – displays that only quoted *part* of the reviews like, 'TUSHINGHAM, NICHOLLS AND HUDD – FINE COMEDY PLAYERS ALL', forgetting to add, 'But what chance did they have with this sorry mess?'

We all parted company after six performances. I did a few bits later with Dandy but never saw Rita again – or Richard Eyre. I think *The Giveaway* experience was one he was happy to forget.

The unholy trinity of flops on radio and TV and in the theatre really did set me back. Suddenly I was poisoned ivy and no one would give me a job. Apart from a few things already booked, I was unemployed for nearly eight months: that had never happened to me before and hasn't, thank Gawd, happened since. The year headed towards its end with black clouds hoving into view.

Prospects for pantomime that year looked bleak and then Morris got a call from a famous agent, Billy Marsh. Would I be interested in doing a panto in Wimbledon. Would I!? I'd run out of money and Wimbledon was pretty near to Streatham where we were living. I could have walked to the theatre.

'Yes! Yes!' I cried, and duly turned up for rehearsals.

The Sleeping Beauty was not only a lifesaver, it also led to a bit of a rebirth for entertainment's reject. The star was Arthur Askey. Another legend. I found out later that Arthur had heard I was having a bad time and, when he was asked about Wimbledon, had said, 'Certainly, but I must have Roy Hudd with me. We work together very well in pantomime.'

I'd never even met him, let alone worked with him. What a marvellous thing to do.

I loved being onstage with him. He was a great ad-libber.

On Wednesday matinees at Wimbledon the production of an Equity card enabled out-of-work theatricals to see the afternoon show for nothing. With a legend like Arthur topping the bill, the place was always packed with admiring pros for these special matinees.

In the middle of the show, he, as King Arthur the Big Hearted, had to fall off his throne, at which I, as the Court Jester, had to ask, 'What are you doing down there?'

'Getting up!' was his snappy riposte, an answer every pantomimist had delivered since the time of Grimaldi.

I remember in the middle of one Wednesday matinee his reply to, 'What are you doing down there?' was 'I'm not giving all my best material away with all these pros in!' It was the best laugh of the entire season.

The morning after the first night at Wimbledon, Morris phoned to see how it went and asked if anyone had come backstage to see me.

'Just one person,' I told him. 'He turned up wearing leopard-skin jodhpurs and high boots and said he was a female impersonator. I thought he couldn't be much cop. He hadn't even got a panto. This beautiful-looking bloke said he was taking a show to the West End next year and would I like to be in it. I ask you!'

'What was his name?' said Morris.

'Oh, Danny something-or-other.'

'La Rue?'

'Yes, that was it!"

'Danny La Rue is going to be *the* biggest star we've produced for years,' said Morris, exasperated. 'And he is bringing a show to London next year! I'll ring you back.'

It was indeed Dan, and within a couple of weeks I'd signed for the show, *Danny at the Palace* (the Palace Theatre, Shaftesbury Avenue).

Danny had come to the show to see his old panto partner, Alan Haynes, who was our dame. Danny and Alan had played Ugly Sisters for years. Can you imagine Danny as an Ugly Sister? When he walked on nobody ever looked at Cinderella again!

I had to do a ten-minute solo spot and play opposite the great pretender in sketches. Again, I was with someone like 'Monsewer' Eddie Gray and Arthur Askey, someone who loved throwing in lines of his own to augment the scripted stuff.

The scripted stuff was perfectly tailored for Dan by, in the main, Dick Vosburgh and Barry Cryer. I'll never forget the first night when in one sketch I introduced Dan to the audience as the UK representative in the Miss World competition. I had to interview this gorgeous creature – and gorgeous he was. I fancied him myself. He came on in a bikini that hadn't got a single bulge in the wrong place. The gasp from the audience told you exactly what spot 1,400 pairs of eyes were focusing on.

'I know what you're thinking,' said Danny. 'I've been doing it so long I just whistle and it goes away on its own!'

That was what he was all about. He was one of the audience. He was just a mate who got dressed up as a woman to make you laugh. It was this contrast between the most stunning-looking wearer of the most sensational drag and the deep-voiced sender-up of himself that made him a star. Plus his charm and that indefinable charisma, of course.

Before we opened, I confessed to him I was worried about how I would do with his audiences. I explained I'd never played to a gay audience before.

'I don't play to a gay audience,' he said. 'My audiences are mums and dads. Families.' And they were: just folk wanting a good night out, especially a night of honest vulgarity.

Dan insisted I had my name in lights alongside his outside the theatre and he never had an important visitor to his dressing room without asking me along to meet them. Everyone came to see the rage of London – from Liberace to Billy Jean King to Rudolf Nureyev to Noël Coward. I spent nearly two years at the Palace before leaving the comicking and sketch-playing to a great pal, Joe Church.

Danny is no longer with us. He died just this year, 2009, and I was asked to say a few words at his funeral. The service was a very heavy Catholic affair (Latin and handbags on fire), and three priests stood behind the high altar. Another priest, Father Peter Stoddart, was scheduled to deliver the sermon but he hadn't arrived, so Father Christopher Vipers stepped down from behind the altar.

'He's caught up in traffic,' said Father Christopher, 'so I suppose I'd better have a go.'

At this point Father Peter ran down the aisle removing his crash helmet and backpack. With immaculate timing Father Christopher cast his eyes upwards and announced to us all: 'You see? There is a God.'

I swear I heard Danny's unmistakable chuckle above everybody else's.

So much has been said and written about the amazing Dan, but I would like to get my two penn'orth in. He was the one person I've known who genuinely loved being a star, and he was one – whatever you imagine a star to be. Somehow it doesn't have a lot to do with actual performance. He was a fairly ordinary comedian, not a great singer or dancer, but he carried himself like a star. When he walked onstage he was in total command. Of course he had an ego that made Michael Winner seem shy, but it sat easily with him. This terrific self-confidence didn't ever seem offensive as it does with non-stars.

Dear Dan had a sad, sad end: throat cancer. But he did pay off his debts, debts that were incurred on his behalf by a pair of swindlers. He was lucky to be taken care of by a loyal friend, Annie Galbraith, but he should have been lording it in a stately home somewhere, seated on a throne and dispensing anecdotes, advice and champagne to his adoring mates.

Danny La Rue, bless his name, had put me back in the public eye and, more importantly, boosted my confidence after the shocks of 1969.

One of the greatest moments in my showbiz life happened in panto season. It was *Dick Whittington*, at the Bristol Hippodrome in 1971. We had a smashing cast. My pal Wyn Calvin MBE, also known as the butchest dame in the history of cross-dressing was there; principal boy was Peter Noone of Herman's Hermits; Alderman Fitzwarren was played by the ebullient and golden-voiced Ivor Emmanuel.

There was a collection of tiny flats attached to the Clifton Hotel where lots of the pros stayed, which was perfect if you were, like me, in the city for a few weeks. I tried to get home most weekends and, on returning to Bristol, I'd go into the hotel to order a cab to take me to the Hippodrome for the matinee.

One Monday morning I did just that. On the reception desk was a fancy cake with the inscription, 'Lovely to have you back in Bristol'.

'Oh really, darling,' I said to the receptionist. 'You shouldn't have bothered – I've only been away one day!'

'It's not for you,' she sniffed. 'It's for him,' indicating a man standing in the bar.

I did the very best double take I've ever done. 'Him' was Bristol's very own Cary Grant. Honestly. I immediately became a gibbering, cringing, worshipping fan. I went over to him.

'You don't know me, Mr Grant,' I stuttered. 'But I must

say thank you for so many er, laughs, so many er brilliant performances, well really for er. Oh yes. Thank you very much.'

'I *do* know you,' he said. 'You're Roy Hudd and you're in the pantomime here. I'm coming to see it tonight. I always go to the panto when I come home. It's good to meet you. Will you have a snort with me?'

'Certainly,' I said, desperately trying to think of what sort of drink 'stars' drank. 'Whiskey,' I said. 'On the rocks.' I'd never drunk whiskey before and had little idea what 'on the rocks' meant but I had my 'snort' with Cary.

My cab arrived and he bid me farewell with a cheery, 'See you tonight, Roy.'

At the theatre I told no one. I thought there must be some mileage in that meeting.

After the matinee, Peter Noone grabbed me. 'You'll never guess who's coming in tonight,' he said.

'Who?' I enquired, disinterestly.

'Only Cary Grant, that's all!' he said.

'Oh, really?' I responded, doing up my shirt and tie. 'I know him.'

'Bugger off!' said Peter. 'Well he is coming in and I've laid on a drink for us all after the show in my dressing room – if you want to come.'

'I'll try,' I said wearily.

Soon, everyone was telling me about the forthcoming visitor. To them all I confided 'I know him', information greeted by all with derision and raspberries.

Come that night, a few minutes after curtain down, I heard the Grant party arrive backstage and go into Peter's dressing room. I listened to the cast running downstairs and dashing to meet Mr Grant. I waited until the very last excited dancer was in Peter's room, and then strolled along myself. I walked in to see the most handsome man in the world surrounded by the cream of the chorus. He looked up.

'Hi, Roy!' he said.

'Hi, Cary!' I responded.

Just the *greatest* moment of my life in show business.

CHAPTER SEVEN

'I can hear the whisper of
wheelchair on Wilton'

The mid-seventies saw the second of the three times I've been poleaxed by a pretty face. I was away in summer season and at a 'welcome to the resort' party for all that year's performers, when I experienced an 'across a crowded room' moment. I couldn't take my eyes off her – and didn't for six years. A pal of mine introduced us and that season was one of total joy and abject shame: total joy we were together and abject shame because I knew it meant curtains for Ann and me. I have to admit, I'd mucked about for ages, but this was the real thing.

By this time Ann, Max and I had moved to a rather posh house in Oxfordshire. It was Ann who found it, in a little village called Nettlebed. She'd been driving around that area and stopped her car to look at a house opposite the church. A man came out and asked her what she was up to. She said she was looking for a house to buy.

'This one's for sale,' he said. 'Come in and have a look.'

She did, and we bought it. I remember proudly showing Morris around the new place. His verdict? 'I like it – every brick a tea bag!'

The season finished, but the affair didn't. I spent every

moment I could with this lady, getting back to Nettlebed late at night – if at all. We went everywhere together while Ann stayed at home. For the most part of six years I seemed to be in a dream. When I look back now I wonder what I was up to. But at the time we made plans and looked at places to move in to together. Eventually, I decided I just couldn't take that final step and we parted. Ann and I battled on.

I fled to Paignton for a summer season with *The Black and White Minstrel Show*. The first spot comic that year was Michael Barrymore and we spent a lot of time together with Cheryl, his late missus. Michael was very down at the time and about to pack it all in. I told him not to. I wasn't struck with what he did on stage, but I could see the public were and he did have a unique something.

Cheryl worked like a lunatic to get him to the very top – and she did. His eventual fall from grace was a tragedy. What is it with original comics? If there is anyone, or anything, that doles out talent with one hand they, or it, just as surely seem to take it away with the other. So many of the great ones seem to have had a cross to bear: booze, sexuality issues, drugs, depression. I'm glad I'm not a great one.

The Paignton season was a memorable one for a terrific charity event for the Entertainment Artistes' Benevolent Fund (EABF). One of the Minstrel lads came up with the idea of a Showbiz Olympics. All the local shows produced teams and, under the stewardship of a great Water Rat, Joe Church, we set about it. Another Water Rat had advertised the event in a spectacular way. Bobby Roberts of Robert Brothers' Circus paraded his elephants along the seafront with all the info on special saddlecloths. The crowds that turned up to watch the parade of the teams from Torquay,

Paignton, Teignmouth, Babbacombe and Brixham made the Lord Mayor's Show look like a street-corner gathering.

They followed the parade to the sports ground. There, a lone runner arrived in charred vest and shorts and blackened face. It was Glyn Dawson from the *Minstrel Show*. His Olympic flame just about made it in time for the release of the dove – well pigeon, actually – and the games began. The events were all angled to the local performers and included a 'Quick Brew Tea-Making Obstacle Course', the 'Larry Grayson Mince for Men' and the 'Tug of War – Hattie Jacques Versus the Rest'.

For me, it was what show business is all about: giving the crowd a great afternoon and being able to give a few thousand quid to the EABF's residential home for old pros, Brinsworth House in Twickenham.

The EABF is one of two showbiz organizations I've been involved in. Originally The Variety Artistes' Benevolent Fund, the charity cares for entertainers all over the UK who have fallen on hard times, become ill or simply get older. The one event that helps keep all the balls in the air – the running of Brinsworth House, the pensioners the Fund supports and all the expenses involved in living (and dying) is The Royal Variety Performance. It is a charity that everyone in our business should support.

The names of people the Fund had helped over the years reads like a *Who's Who?* of variety and circus. I'd been invited to serve on its committee and, eventually, at the behest of Bernard Delfont, I was made chairman in 1980 and held that post for eleven years. I thoroughly enjoyed doing what I could, and became so involved with fundraising that Morris used to get the right needle when I turned work down so that I could deal with the Fund's business.

It was towards the end of that eleven years that I saw just how nasty some, though very few, of the people involved could be. One afternoon I had a phone call from an unpleasant bully connected to the Fund. With hardly a 'Hello', he launched into a vicious attack. With a voice getting ever more excitable he proceeded to tell me to 'Get off your arse and do something for the Fund'.

'You're useless,' he exclaimed. 'Get out of the organization!'

I listened to this rant, thinking of the dozens of shows I'd organized and been in all over the country; the Open Days myself and my oppos had got together; visiting Hylda Baker in a mental hospital along with the charity's general secretary Reg Swinson; and vowing that we would have a proper nursing wing at Brinsworth (which, after lots of drumbeating and ear'ole bending, we got).

The voice got higher and higher and eventually shrieked, 'You only got involved with the Fund to get a gong!' I put the phone down without mentioning that five years before I'd been offered an honour and turned it down. I was hurt and disillusioned but most certainly didn't want to carry on, knowing that I would have to associate with this devious creature.

Reg Swinson was about to retire, and I waited until he'd had his party and then wrote to every member of the committee and our supporters explaining that, due to a clash of personalities, I couldn't continue as chairman. A very sad farewell for me but, for those who wanted it, success.

One good thing that came out of my years with the EABF was my friendship with Mike Ford. Mike is a most generous supporter of all sorts of charities – especially theatrical ones and particularly the EABF, of which he is now honorary treasurer. I knew I liked him for something! He and his partner Sarah are great chums of ours and we've spent many hilarious hours in their company.

One time when I was staying with Mike and Sarah I was delighted to discover that that evening, joining us for dinner, would be Bert and Maggie Weedon. Bert, of course, is the man who taught the world to play the guitar via his mega-selling book, *Play in a Day*. Lots of people have never forgiven him! Bert and Maggie had no idea I'd be there so I carefully dressed as a cross between Alan Titchmarsh, Shadrack Dingle and Worzel Gummidge.

I always carry a false moustache with me – just in case. With moustache on, hat pulled down and a wheelbarrow full of weeds, I hid behind the garage to wait for the Weedons' arrival. The car pulled in, which was my cue to push the barrow out.

''Ello! Can I 'elp you?' I enquired in my best Mummerset accent.

'Good afternoon,' ventured Bert (what an ad-libber!) 'We're here to have dinner with Mike and Sarah.'

'Oh, ah, – 'ang on,' I said, then called very loudly to the hiding Mike and Sarah, 'Mister Ford! Mister Ford! There's a ginger-haired old poof and his tart to see you. Yes, you're right Mister Ford – it is Bert and Maggie Weedon!'

Bert, diplomatic as ever, prepared to make allowances for the village idiot, smiled and looked slightly bemused, until I removed the moustache and enquired if he wanted to buy it.

Then came an expletive followed by an imperative. One of my more subtle characterizations.

The other show business organization that I've been delighted to be involved with is the Grand Order of Water Rats – a pompous sounding name for a jolly, funny and unique organization. I had noticed a pin in the lapels of several of my comedy heroes – Bud Flanagan, Ted Ray, Norman Wisdom, to name a few. It was an emblem of a small gold rat. Actually a water vole – also known as a water rat. They were Water Rats, members of an exclusive band of performers who get together once a fortnight to enjoy each other's company and raise a few bob for charity.

How it all began is well worth telling – so I will. In 1856, a couple of music hall comics were working in Newcastle. The owner of the theatre, Richard Thornton, a well-known impresario in the North-East, was also the owner of a little trotting pony, Magpie. Thornton convinced the comics that the pony would do well racing in London, so they bought shares in the trotter. At the end of their week's work they had to get Magpie back to London. Knowing nothing about horses, apart from the odds they carried when they backed them, they bought an extra first-class train ticket and the pony travelled back to the Smoke in the carriage with them.

Once in town, they organized stabling and a venue for regular racing: a straight mile between two pubs in south London. Magpie never lost a race. He was an ex-circus pony and his owners used that well-known method of circus training – bribery. At the start, his nosebag would be put over his head. After a couple of mouthfuls it was taken off and rushed to the winning post a mile away. Once he got

there, it was put back on again. A few goes at this and it
became a routine he knew well. A comment at the time was:
'Well, you'd shift if you knew you were going to get your oats
at the end of it!'

The races were held on Sunday mornings and the pub
became a very popular meeting place for everyone
connected with the music hall business.

Magpie did well for all his supporters and after one
successful Sunday morning meeting he was being walked
back to his stables in Kennington, near the Oval cricket
ground. It was pouring with rain and his thick coat was
dripping wet. A cab driver, who recognized the pony's
minder, a famous comedian called Joe Elvin, called out,
'What have you got there, Joe?'

'A champion trotting pony!' Joe proudly replied.

'A trotting pony?' said the cabbie. 'It looks more like a
bleedin' water rat!'

Magpie's name was changed to The Water Rat, and his
supporters held meetings and social events under the
banner, 'Friends of The Water Rat'. They were making a lot
of money from backing the little demon, felt guilty about it
and so decided to give some of the profits to charity. It was
the start of a long – and unfinished – business of raising
funds for worthy causes.

Eventually everyone realized the pony could not be
bested and he retired, like Joe Calzaghe, unbeaten. The
Friends, though, stayed together, changed their name to The
Grand Order of Water Rats, and today, a hundred and
twenty years later, are still functioning.

Just a few years back, while sorting out a mountain of
Rats memorabilia, there came to light four separate hooves

on pedestals labelled, 'A genuine hoof of The Water Rat'. Not long after, a fifth 'genuine hoof of The Water Rat' was found! No wonder he ran faster than any of the others.

The more I got to know the Water Rats and the more I learned about their history, the more I wanted to be one. They were, almost a hundred per cent, lads I got on well with. To be one was, to me, another step closer to becoming a real 'pro'.

The word 'pro' is an odd one. When I was a lad a 'pro' was a prostitute – still is to some folk – but in show business it is short for the word professional. So anyone who does what they do for money is a 'pro'? No. Certainly it does usually mean someone who earns a living in show business. But it also means someone who has a special, offbeat, sense of humour; someone who can genuinely laugh at themselves; someone who is in love with the job and is ready to help their compatriots out of trouble. It's what everyone in the biz should aim to be – a real 'pro', accepted by your brother performers.

I hung around the Rats I knew in the hope they'd think I was OK and might become one. I was quite well known and just waiting for the invitation to join. No one said a word. It took me months before I found out you had to ask. I did and, almost immediately, was invited by the ex-bandleader, disc jockey and agent, George Elrick to do a cabaret in Jersey. I did it and, on the flight back, George gave me a handsome cheque with the comment: 'If you could see your way clear to handing that cheque to the Rats Charities Fund it may help.'

It did and on the evening of 18 November 1973 that year's King Rat, George Elrick, installed me as a member.

I'm not a Freemason, but I believe the Water Rats' set up is a bit like the Masons. There are all sorts of passwords, all sorts of odd rituals, but ours seem to be gentle send-ups of the Masonic ones, devised to bring a bit more fun to the gatherings.

When I was waiting for a decision as to whether I would be accepted into the Order I was advised to go backstage and meet a Water Rat who would be good to have on my side. He'd been King Rat of the Order three times. (The King Rat is the member who is elected by his brother Rats to be the front man and head of the organization for a year.) I was suspicious about it as this man was renowned for the terrible gags he pulled on the unwary. His name was Bud Flanagan. But I was desperate to actually talk to the great man and so I turned up at the theatre and was invited into his dressing room during the interval.

He could not have been nicer – which made me even more suspicious – but no. He asked me about what I was up to, what I wanted to do, and finally, as the Tannoy announced: 'Act Two, beginners!' he said, 'Been good to meet you. Would you like a souvenir?'

Of course I would, so he took his famous battered straw boater from the table top and gave it to me. I stammered my thanks and asked what he would wear for the second half.

'I'll be all right,' he said and, opening a case, he picked out another boater from about two-dozen identical hats, punched the top out and bent up the rim. 'All the best,' he said, and disappeared stageward.

I wore that hat every night throughout the run in *Underneath the Arches*, a musical based on the lives of Bud, Ches and The Crazy Gang, of which more later.

I was totally bowled over to be elected King Rat for the Order's centenary year in 1989, and even more flattered to hold the post for a second time in millennium year. You have to find your own after-dinner speakers for the great Annual Ball and I invited Glenys Kinnock to speak on behalf of the ladies. I'd done a couple of panel games with Glenys and so enjoyed her company: she likes a laugh.

'Can I bring my husband?' Glenys asked me.

'Of course,' I said. 'As long as he doesn't speak!'

Their arrival at the Ball was the only time I've been ashamed of the Rats – several anti-Neil members booed and we're supposed to be non-political. I apologized to him and he assured me he'd had far worse receptions.

My ace in the hole that year was Ken Dodd to reply to my toast to the guests. He said he'd be there, which was a real scoop as it wasn't long after his tax trial where it was disclosed he kept lots of cash in shoe boxes, so people couldn't wait to hear what he'd say.

Came the night of the Ball and Debbie and I sat at the top table with two thousand guests – well one thousand, nine hundred and ninety-eight. There was no sign of Ken and his lady, Ann. He used to be notorious for arriving for a gig just in time to walk on, so I was sweating cobs while still doing my Butlin's smiling for the customers.

The meal had come and gone and I was just about to start my two penn'orth when he came bustling in.

'Just made it, young man,' he said, and he and Ann took their seats. He immediately produced a big pile of postcards held together by an elastic band. I glanced at them and each card had just one or two words on. Like Albert Modley, all those years ago on *Workers' Playtime*, this was his script.

I did my bit and Glenys did hers, and now our greatest living comedian got to his feet. As he did, hundreds of five-pound notes fluttered down from the balcony above him. Water Rat Peter Regan had organized two suitcases full of prop fivers for just that moment! It was a hell of a good gag and the laugh grew and grew as Ken picked up every single one before he spoke.

I've had so much fun and so many adventures with the Rats. As I hope you've gathered from this book, I'm not a namedropper (I don't know enough names to drop), but I will drop a couple here. One year, our King Rat was one of my best friends, Wyn Calvin MBE. Wyn had the great privilege of welcoming Bob Hope to the Order. I've never stopped thanking Wyn for sending me to the Savoy Hotel to pick up Bob and bring him to be made a Rat.

At the reception desk at the Savoy I said I'd come for the great Bob. Before, every time I'd been to the Savoy it was to work and I was always snootily sent to the cabaret venue. Not this time.

'Of *course*, Mr Hudd,' said the man on the desk. 'Go straight up to his room.'

I did and there, at the breakfast table, was Mrs Hope and, at the other end, that so-familiar nose poking over the top of a notepad.

'Come in, Roy,' said Bob (did he know I was a friend of Cary Grant?). 'I'm just dotting down a few lines to say thanks for making me a Water Rat.'

He then tried out the stuff on me, asking what I thought. He could have read me the side of the cereal packet and I'd have said, 'Perfect!'

It was around the time when a rash of books had been

A royal page! ABOVE: The Royal Variety Performance 1980, at which the Chairman of the Entertainment Artistes' Benevolent Fund meets a certain Patron. (*Professional Photographic Services*)

RIGHT: Sharing a joke and a jar with Princess Diana.

BELOW: The Queen Mum not looking the least bit disappointed that she *didn't* win the TV when she came to see *Underneath the Arches* in 1982.

ABOVE: *Babes in the Wood*, Theatre Royal, Plymouth, 1991. Jack Tripp holds my trousers open while Geoffrey Hughes perpetrates a subtle piece of comedy.

LEFT: *Mother Goose*, Theatre Royal, Plymouth, 1995. Me looking suitably surprised at being allowed to be on the same panto stage as the great Jack Tripp. (*Adam Eastland*)

ABOVE: My very favourite time in any panto, bringing the kids up on stage.

BELOW: Recording *The News Huddlines* with Chris Emmett and June Whitfield. Hard to tell which one of us is going to 'corpse' first!

ABOVE: Debbie's favourite
picture of herself – and mine.

ABOVE: No, I wasn't giving her away – I was
marrying her! 25 September 1988.

BELOW: The Water Rats Ball, 1989, with our guests Glenys and Neil Kinnock.

RIGHT: Debbie and I with our best friends, Morris and Sheila Aza.

FAR RIGHT: At the Water Rats Ball, Doddie looking delighted after picking up a suitcase full of fivers.

BELOW: With that 'well-known explosion in a mattress factory' and radio producer extraordinaire Jonathan James-Moore and the entire cast of *The News Huddlines*.

ABOVE: As evil Harold Atterbow with his organ in Dennis Potter's *Lipstick on Your Collar*, 1993. (*Whistling Gypsy Productions*)

LEFT: As John Parry in Billy Ivory's *Common as Muck*, 1994.

BELOW: The Pet Shop Boys? No, Albert Finney and his press agent in Dennis Potter's *Karaoke*, 1996.

RIGHT: Proudly showing off the gong to the cameraman before Debbie took it to the pawn shop.

BELOW: HRH The Queen pins on the OBE in 2004.

BELOW: The *original* Calendar Girls with their pin-up boy.
(*Terry Logan*)

ABOVE: I was awarded an Honorary Doctorate of Civil Law from the University of East Anglia in 2007, another proud moment. (*Left to right*) Elizabeth and Laurie Bellew, The Doctor, Debbie, Mike Ford and Sarah Clarke.

RIGHT: As Njegus in *The Merry Widow*, English National Opera, 2008. (*Clive Barda*)

LEFT: The gathering of the clan in our Suffolk garden. I'm standing with daughter-in-law Janet; Debbie is sitting with grand-daughter Emma and my son Max. Emma is holding the lovely Bella.

published in which the children of stars wrote horrible things about their parents, and Bob wanted to get something in about them. 'All these terrible things the kids are saying,' he said. 'Now I know why some animals eat their young.'

Mrs Hope nodded and I laughed. So did the two hundred guests at the special lunch. But he'd told it to me first.

It was my idea to put on a show, 'For one night only – every hundred years!' at the London Palladium to celebrate our centenary in 1989. Almost all the living Water Rats did something that night, and those who weren't living were impersonated by those who were.

The other event I was so glad to have masterminded was in millennium year – a tribute lunch to three special Water Rats. I called the lunch – 'Two Knights with the Samba King'. They were Sir Henry Cooper, Sir Norman Wisdom and the bandleader Edmundo Ros OBE. It was a packed-out do, full of naughtiness, wit, laughter and even a couple of tears – of admiration.

And that's all the namedropping – for now.

But back to the late 1970s. Around this time I was really perfecting my 'fart in a colander' image. Morris's advice to get some in with the 'straight' acting was bearing fruit. I was so happy working at the Young Vic with Frank Dunlop and his assistant, another lady who made me laugh a lot – Denise Coffey.

Further up the road, the Old Vic had had a big success both there and in the West End with Tom Stoppard's *Rosencrantz and Guildenstern Are Dead* and, on the play's first revival in 1973, Frank gave me the chance to play Rosencrantz opposite a smashing actor, Andrew Robertson.

Playing the tiny part of Hamlet in this play was the late Ian Charleson who was later so terrific as Eric Liddle in *Chariots of Fire*. God was I lucky to be alongside this sort of talent. I thought I was a proper actor now – playing in the theatre instead of working a week.

Frank, great Shakespearean scholar and all that, was the man who made me believe I could do the job; and made me realize that going for laughs was OK. He was a great believer in having a team of players, a company, and so am I. My happiest times in show business are those I've spent as part of a company. Amateur Boys' Club shows, Butlins redcoating, seaside concert parties, pantomime, musicals, plays – anything where you get to know your fellows and, together, you strive to get it right. I have had success in what's now called 'stand-up' but I've never really relished being out there by myself. If I don't get the laughs I've got no one else to blame!

Also in 1973, I played Dogberry in *Much Ado About Nothing*, again at the Young Vic. Ian Charleson and Jeremy Irons were in this one, and Denise Coffey played Beatrice. I will never forget her 'visually interpreting' Hero's description of her:

> **'Look where Beatrice, like a lapwing, runs**
> **Close by the ground, to hear our conference.'**

Her 'close by the ground' running alone was worth the price of admission.

Call me a male chauvinistic porker if you like but at that time there were very few women onstage who made me laugh. Most of the funny ladies I'd seen were the turns at the

Croydon Empire and I found them aggressive, butch and not *very* funny. Until Victoria Wood came along I didn't think stand-up was for girls. Victoria proved they can be laid back, sexy *and* very funny.

Denise Coffey, much to the sadness of everyone who knows, admires and loves her, has taken herself away to the West Country where she paints, fishes and enjoys herself enormously away from the show business rat race. She is a rotter.

In late 1976 I was playing Birdboot in Tom Stoppard's *The Real Inspector Hound* at the Young Vic.

During rehearsals a lot of time was spent trying to elicit the meaning of a certain line. I thought it was a joke, but all sorts of dark theories were advanced, until Frank Dunlop got Tom Stoppard himself to come to rehearsals. As the controversial line was uttered we all asked him what it meant.

It's meant to get a laugh,' he said. 'It's a joke.'

It was the only time a genius and I have shared an opinion.

One evening, before the show, an odd couple appeared in the canteen to see me. One bore a remarkable resemblance to Rasputin and the other looked like a fourteen-year-old head prefect. They were a team I got to know very well: Robin Midgley (who ran the Haymarket Theatre, Leicester) and Cameron Mackintosh (before his knighthood – just out of short trousers).

The show they were about to mount was the classic, and for my money the very best British musical ever, *Oliver!* And they wanted me to play Fagin! I'd never done a musical and I practically gave them both a big French kiss. I just couldn't believe it. The Butlins redcoat, variety turn, concert party comedian being offered *the* plum role in a failsafe winner.

'Yes,' I said, in an attempt at understatement.

The picture of Alec Guinness as Fagin in the classic David Lean film was always in my mind, and so a lady from the National Theatre spent an hour and a half transforming me into the old villain. The wig, from a famous TV and film wigmakers, was perfect but after a couple of wearings it started to fall to pieces. The treatment it received during the cut and thrust of live theatre performance was too much for a creation that was meant for film and TV. The problem was solved by ordering a heavy-duty piece from a pal of mine, Bert Broe. His Dad (also called Bert) was a very famous wigmaker, and Bert Junior owned a magical shop called The Theatre Zoo. Here you could not only get every possible stick of greasepaint known to mankind, but pantomime cows, donkeys, cats, dogs – even giraffes. I wore the wig Bert Junior made for me for nearly two years. It went back to him for a retread about four times. I think it saved Cameron enough money to mount *Cats*!

So much for the hair, but the make-up lady's masterpiece was the nose. She built up the magnificent hooter with a substance called morticians' wax. Too much information. After a couple of goes myself I thought I'd sussed it and so, for the dress rehearsal, I laid on the wax like a good 'un.

My first entrance was a smasher. I was discovered, toasting fork in hand, with my back to the audience, cooking a sausage. The Artful Dodger coughed and I whipped round to discover him and our hero.

'Fagin!' said Dodger, 'I want you to meet my new friend, Oliver Twist!'

At this, Oliver bowed low to me and I bowed low to him. We met in mid-bow. When he stepped back he had my nose on his forehead.

'You've found a good 'un Dodger. He's pickin' noses already!' said I, one of my better ad-libs.

The morticians' wax was banished to the bottom of the make-up box and, as my missus advised, 'Your own nose is perfect for the job.'

We toured the show all over the British Isles and, as always happens when you are doing a piece eight times a week, all sorts of odd lines and business creep into the performance: some good and some lousy. With my concert party background I was always trying bits out. I did find one winning piece of action.

Fagin is awake late at night, all his boys having gone to sleep. He gets his jewel box from its hiding place and proceeds to check the contents. After counting guineas and trying on bits of jewellery he produces a long string of pearls. He silently counts them, gets to the end of the string and realizes one pearl is missing. So he counts them all again, sees the missing one on the floor, picks it up and is happy. It always got a good reaction.

We were at the New Theatre, Oxford and were told Lionel Bart was in the audience. Like everyone else, I was tickled pink about this but I was scared. How would I shape up against Ron Moody and all the other Fagins? Was I doing it right? Too kosher or not Jewish enough? Was I bending the songs too much? Cameron told me he'd be bringing the great man round afterwards and I was sure he'd put me right and have a go if he didn't like it.

All went well till it came to the business with the string of pearls. As I pulled it out of the jewellery box the string broke and, to a hushed audience, about seventy individual pearls bounced around the stage. Even now my stomach gives a lurch whenever I think about it.

I waited until the last renegade pearl had stopped bouncing – giving myself time to think of how to cover the disaster. My mind went blank. I only knew Fagin would never leave valuable pearls lying around, so I started to pick them up and put them in a bowl. I picked up every single one. It took forever, but I was still thinking. By now some of the audience were pointing out ones I hadn't noticed. Eventually I sat down with a bowlful. I was dripping with sweat – but still thinking.

'Oh well,' I finally thought. 'In for a penny . . .' I counted the pearls, realized there was one missing and worriedly took a swig of coffee. Something was in the coffee. You've guessed. I removed from my mouth a pearl (which I'd surreptitiously hidden) and put it with the others. The round of applause I got *didn't* make it all worthwhile, however. It seemed to me I'd held up the proceedings for at least an hour and a half and I feared that Mr Bart would only come backstage to give me the heave-ho.

I sat in the dressing room with fingers crossed thinking, 'Perhaps he didn't notice!'

Eventually there was a knock on the door and in came the smiling legend. 'Hey, Dad!' he said, 'I loved the *schtick* with the pearls!'

I blushed modestly, my heart commenced beating again and I sadly informed him it would never ever be seen on any stage ever again!

Lionel Bart was in big trouble at that time. He'd blown the

fortune he earned from *Oliver!* on parties, booze, drugs – you name it. He'd sold the rights to the show – and the rights to shows he hadn't even written yet.

Cameron gave Lionel a weekly salary, which he didn't have to do, to supposedly oversee the production, especially Fagin's gang. Lionel and I travelled to a few of the venues together and I got to know and like him very much. He explained how the tunes in *Oliver!* all stemmed from the one song 'Where is Love?', even the upbeat numbers. We'd sing music hall songs on the journeys and he would ad-lib brilliant new lyrics. He was inventive, enthusiastic and a joy to be with. He just needed a kick up the bum – I thought.

A few years later I saw a chance for me to help when he told me about two unproduced shows he'd written. One was a musical adaptation of Fellini's film, *La Strada*. This was a fascinating little movie starring Anthony Quinn as a travelling one-man circus. Lionel sang me a great song from his version, 'To Be a Performer'. The other was *The Hunchback of Notre Dame*. Lionel had some stunning demo tapes, with full orchestra, and a set designed by Sean Kenny, the chap who designed *Oliver!*

I'd just finished doing *Underneath the Arches* at Chichester and, thinking that a brand new Lionel Bart musical would be a real scoop for the theatre, persuaded the boss there, Patrick Garland, to have a listen to the shows while Lionel sang and described them.

I laid on a car to take the pair of us down to Chichester and called for Lionel at his house in Acton. The door was opened by a white-haired lady who looked and sounded like Barbara Mullen (Janet the housekeeper in *Dr Finlay's Casebook* – her, or a friend of Lionel's in drag). She explained that Lionel wouldn't be coming with me – he wasn't well. Having arranged everything, I was furious. I pushed past her into the Bart boudoir. He was sitting up in bed with a ladies' leather flying helmet on.

'I'm not well, Dad,' he moaned.

'You won't be if you don't get out of that pit right now!' I couldn't believe what I was saying, but it did the trick. He was in the back of the car with scripts, demo tapes, the lot, while 'Barbara Mullen' was still protesting his ill health.

We met up with Patrick Garland and Lionel sold the shows as only he could. Patrick, I think, was impressed with what the author had to offer. I wanted so much to work with Lionel, even though I had been warned by a mutual friend that any collaboration with him would be murder. How far the proposed productions got I don't know, but the outcome was the discovery that Lionel had sold the rights to all sorts of people all over the world – anyone who would give him a few bob for drink or the dreaded drugs. Even now, people are turning up with bits of paper, fag packets and bus tickets on which Lionel's signature guarantees them a piece of the action. Who actually did own the shows no one ever found out, but I doubt whether we'll ever see *The Hunchback* or *La Strada* on a stage. God, he was a clever bloke – if only someone could have harnessed that talent.

The story of our production of *Oliver!* getting to the West End is worth telling. The whole shebang was to run for a few weeks in Leicester and then be taken on the road. Cameron fixed a good tour although, unbelievably, we played just a week in each theatre. We never opened on a Monday. It took two days to put the set on stage. It was the original Sean Kenny set, complete with revolve and London Bridge flying in. Just five days in each town, and at every venue we were packed out, such is the magic of that show. People would say, 'Oh you're bringing the punters in all right.' But no, it wasn't me: the show itself is the draw. Like *Phantom of the Opera* or *The Mousetrap*.

The big treat for us was going to be the last two weeks of the tour: a whole fortnight in the same place, Cardiff. A fortnight was like a season to us.

We were in Wolverhampton when the boss told us we wouldn't be going to Cardiff. He'd been offered four weeks over Christmas at the Albery Theatre in the West End. He reckoned we'd do great business with a show that hadn't been in London for twenty tears. I had my doubts. Foolish boy. We opened to great notices for the four-week run and, five years later, the show closed. Now you know why Cameron's got a knighthood and I've got an overdraft.

I was nominated for a SWET (Society of West End Theatres, now known as the Olivier) Award. But that was the same year that Michael Crawford was working his magic in *Barnum*, so I lost out.

I stayed with the show for two years and looked forward to going into work every day. It was then, and still is, a huge thrill to be part of the West End theatre scene. The only pain in the neck was the constant changeover of lads in Fagin's gang. The law allowed the boys just eight weeks in the show per year. This meant virtually non-stop rehearsals – if you cared about the job, and I did.

I rapidly discovered that a gang of lads working together are like one big blob. If one decides to play a blinder they all do and if one decides to 'mark' it, so do all the others. I cared so much about this show that if the gang didn't try I had to have a go at them. One afternoon they were really lazy and couldn't care less. At the interval I rushed up the stairs to their dressing room, toasting fork in hand. I was just about to go in and sort them out when I heard one of them leading off.

'Bloody Roy 'udd! The old bastard'll be up those stairs in a minute shoutin' and hollerin', you see!'

'Hang on!' said another lad. 'We were rubbish out there this afternoon. He's got every right to have a go. You know he's up here just as quick when we do a good 'un.'

A mumbled, 'Yeah – that's right,' went round the room, and I turned on my heel and went downstairs thinking that at least one of them knew what I was all about. His name was Nick Berry, of *Heartbeat* fame. Another lad from that gang did all right too: Perry Fenwick from *EastEnders*.

When I came out of the show (I couldn't take the constant geeing up and telling off the boys any more), we had a bit of a farewell party in my dressing room. The high spot of the do was someone wheeling in a record player and putting on an unlabelled LP. I was thrilled to hear the recording. With the agreement of the band, the soundman had recorded all my numbers in the show – and in actual performance. What a thing to be able to keep.

Then there was the extra stuff! The LP was turned over and, loud and clear, came a chat between myself and the girl who was playing Nancy's friend Bet. This particular actress was about twice as old as she looked, and a very sophisticated, cigar-smoking little person. Unbeknownst to us, the soundman had caught us chatting just before the second-half curtain went up one night. It was very atmospheric, you could hear the sound of props being set, people humming the next song and the orchestra tuning up.

'What a week I've had!' I said. 'I had a corn removed on Monday, a tooth replaced on Wednesday and a hair transplant on Friday!' Just then the music started for Act Two ... and you can just hear me shouting after her as she ran up the stairs, 'And I'm having a cock transplant next week!'

And you can just hear her reply, 'Oh! Can I have the old one?'

All sorts of wicked things had been recorded in a really evil way. The sound guys had left my radio mike on all the time, so everything I'd said over a week and a half was on tape. Everyone was in the room for my farewell party – the cast, the crew, the band, Cameron and Robin Midgley. I didn't dare think what would be coming up next.

Taking over from me, as Fagin, was Roy Dotrice and we'd met and chatted about the part. On the recording I was telling a 'friend' who had popped into the dressing room in order to get me to make terrible comments, all about Roy and me meeting.

I began: 'I told him it's a marvellous part in a marvellous show. The only problem is the boys. You honestly never know if they're going to work or just schlep about.'

'Well, Robin Midgley had assured me the lads are perfectly trained and always give great performances,' Roy replied.

'Well then,' said I, 'If Robin Midgley thinks that, then Robin Midgley is a * * * *.' Robin actually laughed.

The two main culprits who would come into my dressing room and ask me things they knew I'd be rude about were Nancy (Gillian Burns) and Mr Sowerberry the undertaker

(Graham Hamilton). Graham is much more respectable these days. Or is he? – he's the president of our trade union, Equity!

I still have the explosive LP. On the cover is a drawing of a spider about to pounce and it's entitled 'Blackmail Productions Present – The Real Roy Hudd!' After everyone had been insulted and left the room and my legs had stopped shaking, I nabbed the sound guy and he assured me he had taken the rest of the tapes and burned them. I hope he was telling the truth or I could be rivalling Jonathan Ross and Russell Brand.

As one of my favourite lyricists, Sammy Cahn, once said when asked how he wrote a song, 'It all starts with the phone call', and that is exactly how twenty-six years of *The News Huddlines* began. It was from a BBC radio producer Simon Brett (now a very successful novelist).

'Are you doing anything next Thursday lunchtime?' he asked.

Ever suspicious that it might be someone wanting something for nothing, I hummed and harred for a bit. 'Not really sure,' I hedged. 'I'll check with my agent. What exactly is it about?'

'I've got an idea for a show.'

'Oh yes? [haven't they all']?

'A sort of topical revue, with you as the Kenneth Horne figure, doing a monologue to start off and then introducing the sketches.'

'Can I read it?' I was interested.

'No. I haven't got anything yet. It's got to be really topical and I do know a few mates who'd like to have a go.'

Hudd thinking, 'A few mates who'd like to have a go?'

'And it's this Thursday?' I asked.

'Yes. We can do a pilot.'

Hudd thinking again, 'A pilot, this Thursday, with no material?'

'Oh yes?' I said.

'I'll be honest,' he told me. 'All I've got so far is a title.'

Hudd, heart sinking, 'Oh yes? What is it?'

'*The News Huddlines.*'

Hudd, perking up, 'Oh – I like that,' thinking quickly that if, by any odd chance the pilot's a success, no one else can head it. 'What time and where?'

'Ten o'clock. The Paris Studio, Lower Regent Street.'

And that was it. Simon got together a three-handed team of performers: a comic playing himself, me; an actor who specialized in voices and excellent impressions, Chris Emmett; and a highly experienced actress and comedienne, Janet Brown. We had a musical director, Nick Rowley, who gave up a career as a doctor to play the piano. He could play every instrument. On one show we had a Scottish sketch and he bought a set of toy bagpipes just to do a Scottish play on.

I was doing panto in Cardiff and on the day of the England versus Wales rugby game the hotel I was staying in was taken over by fans from both sides. As I was leaving for a matinee a man stopped me.

'You're the one who's keeping my son from doing a proper job!' he said.

'Your son?' I asked, thinking he didn't look anything like Prince Phillip.

'Yes,' he said. 'He's Nick Rowley.' Nick's dad was the

doctor to the England Rugby team and he did eventually get his son back to medicine. Nick's now one of the world's leading naturopathic doctors. Whether he makes people happier dispensing herbal remedies than he did with his music is open to debate.

Simon Brett himself never actually produced a single show. He put us in the care of a fresh-faced boy producer (with a wicked old bastard's sense of humour), John Lloyd. Not a bad choice. He was a great judge of material and would constantly throw back sketches to the writers if he thought they weren't up to his standards. Long after he left us he produced *Not the Nine O'Clock News, Blackadder* and *Spitting Image.* Like I always say – once they leave me it's downhill all the way.

John came up with a couple of phrases I've never forgotten. As *Huddlines* was recorded at lunchtime (edited in the afternoon and broadcast that same evening) we often had a fairly elderly audience in the Paris Studio.

'Are the audience coming in?' I asked him just before one recording.

'Yes,' replied John. 'I can hear the whisper of wheelchair on Wilton.'

The other line became folklore at the Beeb:

'What has eighty-two legs and no teeth?'

'The front row of *The News Huddlines* audience.'

I had a birthday during an early series and the party was on a Thames riverboat. The invitation insisted that guests should come dressed in 1936 clothes. John came as Hitler. A quick glance around his fellow guests showed him there were quite a few Jews there. In a flash he removed the swastika emblems, replacing them with unreadable ones made from the gold paper in a fag packet. He then quickly announced to one and all that he was a stationmaster.

We did the pilot and within four weeks me, Chris and Janet had been booked for a ten-week series. Not that the show was so marvellous that the Beeb couldn't *not* give us a series, but rather that these were the golden days of radio and TV, the days when the powers that be didn't play recordings to rooms full of 'cross-sections of the public', or leave decisions to committees or wet-behind the ears university graduates elevated to positions of thumbs up or thumbs down.

In those golden days you could take an idea to the Head of Live Entertainment who would, if he liked the idea, send you to the producer who he thought might be interested in the embryo programme. Then it would be in the hands of the person who could bring it all to life. A pilot could be arranged in days. Today I know of so many good writers who are kept waiting for months for a decision and they are never told why if their ideas are given the elbow.

Some of the early shows were recorded at the Shepherds Bush Empire, and the usual place for a quick after-show nosh was a restaurant called Oddis on Shepherds Bush Green. My one memory of the place was a fruit machine in the bar downstairs and one night Morris and I went down there to spend his commission and spotted Tony Hancock playing the machine. We watched as he put in tanner after tanner: not a sausage. Finally, he walked away and over to the bar. Then, from a shadowy corner came – who else? – Sid James. We watched as he put three sixpences into the machine, the third of which brought an enormous cascade of silver coins. Everyone in the bar watched as Sidney gave his familiar laugh and scooped up the jackpot. Morris and I just watched Hancock's face in the mirror behind the counter. He never turned around, and his expression slowly changed from surprise, to trying to blot out the crash of cash, to the realization that Sid had won again, and the final, exasperated closed-eyes defeat could have been written by Galton and Simpson. Morris and I had had a private performance of understated, unspoken, unequalled, unique Hancock.

Huddlines was, to the best of my knowledge, one of the few shows that used unsolicited material. Today, most comedy shows are written by the performers themselves – a two- or three-handed team. Our show enabled so many people to get a foot in the comedy door. Talking of the comedy door, the one we used as a sound effect throughout the whole twenty-five year series was the famous one used by all of Tommy Handley's characters in the legendary *Itma*. It always gave me a kick to know that Mrs Mopp, Colonel Chinstrap and the rest had passed through that very door. *Huddlines'* most famous knocker on the door was Mr Friggins, an invention of Charlie Adams. Friggins, with the perfect voice from Chris, paid regular visits to his doctor (me) and always to get medical advice about problems in the vicinity of his genitalia. The classic diagnosis was in a Christmas edition when Friggins, who'd been carol singing, complained of a prickly sensation down below. The doctor examined our hero and declared, 'No, no, no, Mr Friggins, the phrase is "deck the *halls* with boughs of holly"!' The laugh went on for nearly a minute.

Anyone could send us jokes and sketches. They were all read and, if they were judged to be good enough, they made it onto the show. I was always being tackled by followers of the show as to the number of writers credited at the end of the programme. 'It's longer than the list of fatalities in the First World War,' one listener wrote. Yes, I know we probably could have got a couple more items in if we'd dropped those credits – well, perhaps a very short sketch, given the way our announcer, Richard Clegg, used to rattle them off.

Richard did the announcing for us for fourteen years, and only once did he have to do a retake. He maintained this fantastic professionalism despite continually being molested, kissed and goosed by yours truly.

I felt it was important that every jokesmith should get a name check. It did bear fruit. First-time scribes were so knocked out to hear their names on the air that they'd be inspired to send in more jokes. All the more to choose from . . . Hee! Hee! Hee!

What a collection of writers we had to put terrific words in our mouths. At the very start, in 1975, two of our main lads were Peter Spence (who later came up with *To the Manor Born*) and David Renwick (who went on to have great success with sketches for *The Two Ronnies*, Ronnie Corbett's monologues and his own huge hit shows: *One Foot in the Grave*, *Jonathan Creek* and *Love Soup*).

We had two lyricists who wrote most of the songs, Jeremy Brown and Richard Quick. What a joy it was to sort out the music with our giant musical director, Pete Moss, and his regular lads, Dougie Henning on bass and Will Hill on drums. We had lots of different pianists, including Paul Maquire who sometimes played for me in cabaret.

Among our writers, we were so lucky to have, as beginners, Andy Hamilton (*Drop the Dead Donkey, Who*

Dares Wins, etc.) and John Revell – the excellent stand-up comic and contributor to every panel game or discussion that requires wit, opinion and truth. Douglas Adams managed to get a couple of quickies into the show, but we weren't really his scene. He later made a slight impact with *The Hitchhiker's Guide to the Galaxy.* I'm delighted he did write *Hitchhiker's* as he used me in an early radio episode playing Max Quordlepleen – the compère at the Restaurant at the End of the Universe. *Hitchhiker's* became a worldwide hit and I still get the odd royalty cheque. Thanks Douglas.

One week, our usual producer being off sick, the show was put together by John Dyas. After years of pretending he was a masculine, dark-suited BBC man, John suddenly came out. At last, the BBC came round to the idea that being gay wasn't tantamount to treason, and John revelled in the release. Overnight, leather jackets and jeans were the order of the day for 'Dolly' Dyas, and the carefully modulated dark brown voice became more sibilant than an afternoon in the reptile house.

He was witty *before* the transformation, but now he was Larry Grayson, Julian Clary and Graham Norton rolled into one over-excited package. One of our top writers, Terry Ravenscroft (a reet broad Northern lad), submitted a sketch about cock-ups in schools. Dyas read it.

'Where did you read this story?' he enquired.

'In the *Times Literary Supplement,*' answered the scribe.

'Really?' said the new Kenneth Williams. 'Who read it to you?'

Chris Emmett and I went to John's funeral. The place was packed and, just before the service started, an arm reached between us for a hymn book.

'Excuse my long arm,' came a cultured, malevolent voice. We both recognized the man who made horror top box office. We turned to nod to Vincent Price.

'Gawd!' I said to Chris. 'Look who he's sitting next to!' It was Frank Williams, the vicar in *Dad's Army*. 'The Antichrist and the vicar!'

Vincent Price was a great buddy of John Dyas, as was Vincent's wife, Coral Brown – she whose ad-libs made Paul Merton sound dull. It was John who told me of Miss Brown coming out of Brompton Oratory after a session of Catholicism. A male dancer friend called out from the other side of the road, 'Hello dahlin'! How's your sex life?'

'F**k off!' replied the lady. 'I'm in a State of Grace!'

The end of *Huddlines* after twenty-six years on Radio 2, during which time it became the longest-running comedy show with an audience in the history of broadcasting, didn't really come as a shock. I had taken on the part in *Coronation Street* and Granada couldn't guarantee a regular weekly day off.

The Beeb reassured us, and the listeners, that the radio show would return once I finished my stint in the *Street*. During my eighteen months in Manchester the response to listeners' enquiries changed to 'we have no plans for a further series', and then nothing.

My warning that we were on our way out came with the unloading of the one-time producer of *Huddlines* and then Head of Light Entertainment, Jonathan James-Moore, one of the most enthusiastic and inventive blokes to hold the post. He was replaced by a puppet boss whose name I can't remember. He took me to lunch, over which he told me what they really wanted was for me to be more like Jonathan Ross!

For perhaps the only time in my life, I was speechless. Then I was furious. A show that for all those years had worked one hundred per cent because it was like nothing else on radio. The combination of music hall style comedy, on-the-button topical stuff, great vocal cartoons and songs that were perceptive, funny and moving, was unique.

'Be more like Jonathan Ross!' I left the restaurant without a word.

CHAPTER EIGHT

'Where the Gusy Gungle Gees
Are Gusy Guzzing'

Late 1980, *Robin Hood and the Babes in the Wood*, Theatre Royal, Nottingham. It was just another pantomime season in another city ... but this one turned out to be a bit special.

I arrived at rehearsals in a not-too-happy mood. The director was Bill Roberton, who wasn't a fan, and didn't seem very interested in me or the show. The good and bad robbers were The Krankies, Ian and Jeanette, who've been friends of mine ever since; Barry Howard (the ballroom dancer in *Hi-de-Hi!*) was the dame; brother Water Rat Barry Kent (the original Lancelot in the musical *Camelot*) was Robin; and Rita Morris was Maid Marian. I was Simple Simon.

I looked around the rehearsal room and at the dancers. No girl dancers look their best in rehearsal. They wear all sorts of funny outfits: leotards, Max Wall tights and boots, weird trousers, T-shirts with the name of their last show printed on, no make-up and hair brushed off the face with Alice bands or pulled back into pony tails. Within half an hour of work the sweat is beginning to show.

This team were exactly true to form. Except for one. She was as sweaty as the rest, but she had a nice smile, which stayed on her face while all around were scowling with concentration. I thought, 'Hello, I'm in trouble again.' And I was.

I saw little of her during the rest of the rehearsals. Usually the dancers put their routines together in one place while the principals rehearse dialogue and their comical capers elsewhere.

When the show opened, though, I saw her twice a day. I was moonstruck. I tried to chat her up at every opportunity. I didn't seem to be doing too well until I made her laugh in the schoolroom scene. As I entered, I threw her a packet of sweets and with a lustful leer whispered, 'And there's plenty more where that came from!' That did the trick – and I've been trying to make her laugh ever since.

She came out with me for supper and we enjoyed each other's company, even though I was, and still am, twenty-two years older. She made me laugh when she told me her name wasn't the one in the programme, Deborah Colinroy, but Deborah Flitcroft. I swore she'd made it up – but no. I persuaded her to use Flitcroft from that season on because it is an unforgettable name and it makes people smile.

The season was a happy one, despite a difference of opinion on nearly everything between myself and our director. One of my very best spots for panto is my cake-making scene. I can claim, without any fear of contradiction, it is the messiest slapstick routine in the business. Ask anyone who's ever been part of it. Sadly, so many stage directors don't like it. They don't like the thought that the 'slosh' *might*, possibly, spill onto their stage. It doesn't if the crew set everything correctly.

My only defence is that it's four minutes of the *biggest*

laughs I've ever heard. Real slapstick is irresistible. The cleverest spoken gag in the world cannot compete with two gallons of gunge down the trousers or a custard pie slapped up the dame's jacksey.

Our director was adamant he didn't want the scene. I was equally convinced we should do it.

'All right,' he said, reluctantly. 'But this is the only place it'll fit in.'

The crafty swine had placed it where I had to practically follow myself back onstage for the next scene. But I would not be denied and gave it a go. I would come off at the end of the slapstick scene with custard everywhere: head, face, chest, and especially round the nether regions and oozing out the bottom of the trousers. I looked like a multi-coloured snowman. But I had to get cleaned off, change clothes and back on again within thirty-two bars of a song from Maid Marian.

I stood in the wings, whipped off all the kitchen clothes and, naked as nature intended, scraped off the gunge. I was into clean gear and back on in a flash! I never missed. I wouldn't dream of losing those marvellous laughs.

One evening Rita (Maid Marian) glanced into the wings where I was cleaning off my private parts. She spluttered through the rest of her song. It was 'Love is Where You Find It'. The theatre manager got a letter from a little lad who wrote, 'When the lady was singing I saw Simple Simon's bum.' I sent him a signed photo.

Jeanette and Ian – The Krankies – were terrific fun and marvellous with an audience. They were great social creatures and could party till the early hours and still be on top form for a 10.00 a.m. show. I worked very hard trying to keep up with Debbie. So much so that Ian and Jeanette's last night present to me was a record, 'The Oldest Swinger in Town'.

Things were decidedly dodgy between Ann and I, but we managed a rather uncomfortable holiday together in Scotland.

Back home, I couldn't stop thinking about Debbie, even though 1981 was one of the most traumatic yet theatrically exciting years I've ever had.

It began with the return of my show *Just a Verse and Chorus*.

It all started actually a couple of years before, when Robin Midgely, the guv'nor of the Haymarket Theatre in Leicester, not only helped me put together my first one-man show and starred me in farce, but was the first to encourage me to write shows.

One of the shows I put together for Leicester was a music hall called *Victorian Christmas*, a show based on how the Victorians invented the Christmas we know. Another was *While London Sleeps* – a Victorian musical drama based on the writings of George R. Sims (the man who wrote 'Christmas Day in the Workhouse' (the straight *clean* version!)) and another was *Beautiful Dreamer* – the story of the American songwriter Stephen Foster.

Wracking my brains for a 'different' musical, I was searching through my collection of songs and came across many written and composed by R.P. Weston and Bert Lee, who were the Andrew Lloyd Webber and Tim Rice of the early twentieth century – only much, much more prolific. Weston and Lee had published more than seven hundred songs, and many classic music hall songs were theirs – from

'Joshua' to 'Knees Up Mother Brown'.

The First World War couldn't have really happened without Weston and Lee. They wrote practically every song used in the film *Oh! What a Lovely War*, including the most touching and evocative war song of them all, 'Good-bye-ee'. I had about five hundred of their songs but could find out little about the two men themselves.

I wrote to the then *London Evening News* to see if anyone could help me. Among the dozens of letters I received, all quoting songs by Weston and Lee, from 'When Father Painted the Parlour' to 'Roll Away Clouds', just one told me anything about them. It was from Bob Weston's two daughters, who lived in the same house where Bob and Bert had met every day to pen their miniature masterpieces. I hurried round to see them.

It was like a *Play for Today*. The two maiden ladies, both in their eighties, lived with their younger brother, John, in Staines. They showed me the room where the great team had met to do the business. It was Miss Havisham's house rekindled. Their father had died in 1936, yet there was a piece of manuscript still on the piano. The attic, which I never had the chance to look over, was packed with everything he and Bert, whom they referred to at all times as 'Mr Lee', had written. I kept hinting that I would love to see the attic but they wouldn't have it. I think if I had been allowed to go up I'd have been there still.

They were a couple of dear old ladies, but not of this world. I asked what they had done for a living.

'Nothing,' they both said. They had lived pretty well for fifty-odd years on dad's royalties. They said that as soon as things were getting tight someone would revive and record a Weston and Lee song: Tommy Steele 'What a Mouth'; Val Doonican 'Paddy McGinty's Goat'; Roy Hudd 'With the End of My Old Cigar'. The stage show and movie versions of *Oh! What a Lovely War* produced a bonanza for the two sisters and their brother. As I was leaving one sister confided she had worked once: she had rolled bandages in the First World War.

I continued my quest.

'I think they wrote stuff for Stanley Holloway,' Morris said.

Did they? Just a bit: 'With Her Head Tucked Underneath Her Arm', 'My Word, You Do Look Queer', 'Brahn Boots', to name a few. I phoned Stanley to ask if I could come over to talk to him about the team. He agreed and I arrived at his house near Brighton.

'Hullo, Roy,' said Stanley, opening the door. 'What have you come for?'

'Oh dear,' I thought. 'He's lost it. I'll get nothing here.' I explained it was to talk about Weston and Lee and Stanley's eyes lit up.

'Of course,' he said. 'Bob and Bert. Come in, come in.' He had known them both very well indeed, and for the next couple of hours he told me facts and anecdotes about the incredible pair.

I put all the bits and pieces together and took the script to Robin Midgley and his musical director, Ian Smith. They cut out lots of the biographical stuff and showed me ways to present the story using songs and sketches.

The show played a Christmas season in the Haymarket's Studio Theatre. Robin encouraged me to put the show together and directed that first attempt. Pan forward to

1984, and the Greenwich Theatre got in touch to say they'd like to do the show, but only if I'd be in it. I immediately plumped to play Bob Weston (a Cockney) and approached a hero of mine, Billy Dainty, to see if he'd play Bert Lee (a Northerner).

Typical of Billy, he watched a video I'd had taken of the Leicester production, but wasn't sure. The next few weeks were taken up with friends of his viewing the show and giving their opinions. If one liked it he'd say 'I'll do it.' If they didn't, 'Sorry, son, not for me.'

Someone, I think it was Morris Aza (who was Billy's agent too), advised him there was something in the show and he should give it a go. Billy said he would.

The money at Greenwich was not the best – seventy quid a week each – and Billy, like a lot of great comedians, had long pockets and very short arms. He rarely took on anything he couldn't make money from. Billy lived in Guildford – a fair step from Greenwich – and I told Morris, 'He won't make any money out of this – the fares alone are more than seventy quid.' Morris swore he would.

He did, in a way that only he could have pulled off: he bought, and paid for, a long-term season ticket from Guildford station to Greenwich. At the end of the contracted four-week run at the theatre, he went back to the booking office and said, 'I bought this season ticket in good faith and now, would you believe, I've got the sack.' Sympathetic British Rail refunded the entire cost of the ticket!

Billy was a real hero of mine: what a talent. A terrific eccentric dancer, a good singer and my favourite sort of comic, the sort that makes you smile as soon as he walks on. He had a personality that lit up the theatre and, offstage, any room he walked into. He was knocking on a bit for the lunatic dancing he'd always done, and he was pleased that his role as Bert Lee meant only the minimum of hoofing. I explained that the part didn't call for funny walks and eccentric movements. I also wanted everyone to see him for the excellent actor he was.

We rehearsed for three weeks and he was a revelation. He squeezed every ounce of humour out of the material and, towards the end of the story, played the drama beautifully. Throughout that three weeks, he had me in tears of laughter and sadness.

Came the dress rehearsal and a few stray members of staff and stagehands sat out front and watched it. On came Bill and did all sorts of things he'd never done before in rehearsal: funny walks, outrageous cod dry-ups, out of character ad-libs – a masterclass in how *not* to do it.

'Well, that didn't go too badly,' he said, back in the dressing room. I went berserk.

'Badly? *Badly!*' I shouted. 'The whole three weeks wasted! Everything we got together you forgot. You did your variety act! All the stuff you've always done only here, for seventy quid a week. I didn't believe you were Bert Lee – you were Billy Dainty at the Met Edgware Road!'

Billy Dainty in variety was a small genius, but I had seen something very special from him and I was heartbroken to see him throw it away. Looking back, I realize that he was scared to do things his public had never witnessed before and, like any comic would, he reverted back to what he knew best.

I don't think he'd ever seen me so angry before. As I've said before, I am slow to anger, but seeing someone selling themselves short is enough to get me at it.

'Well, I'm sorry you weren't happy,' he said, slowly taking off his make up. 'The best thing I can do is come out of the show. I'll stay until the understudy's ready and then I'll leave.'

'Yes. Good idea,' I said, and we went our separate ways home.

The next night was press night and we didn't speak to each other till we got onstage. When we did – oh boy – he played the show exactly as he had done in rehearsal, and instead of just laughs he got everything that was intended. At the curtain, I wept. The next day the first review I read was headlined, 'Billy Dainty is a star at last'. I'd won – and his leaving the show was never mentioned again. We packed 'em out for the whole four weeks.

Under the guidance of a lovely bloke, Bob West (who'd been Cameron Mackintosh's production manager), we took *Just a Verse and Chorus* on the road. My son Max, who by now was seventeen, was assistant stage manager and, in his own offbeat and inventive way, added all sorts to the show. It was good for us to be together. We made each other laugh and he was a bloomin' good organizer.

We had a terrific cast: Caro Gurney, Sally Smith, Graham Hoadley, Tony Jackson and Peter Durkin. How could we go wrong? There's a well-worn and well-respected cliché in our business: never put your own money into a show. Even a hoary old clown like me can get caught. I was so confident that *Verse and Chorus* would click that I put my life savings into it.

We did well at every date: Bromley, Norwich, Bournemouth, Wolverhampton, Richmond and Chichester. Just two let us down badly: Sunderland and Belfast. Belfast was the worst as it was the furthest to take the scenery. We had to pay for the driver's digs for the whole week too. Once there, the show was wrongly billed as a music hall show and Union Jacks were used to decorate the theatre! Despite Billy and me being interviewed on the local telly by Eamonn Holmes, before he turned into a toby jug, nobody came.

In Sunderland we announced a press call for the morning of the opening day. One man came. He didn't tell us what newspaper he was from – I've a feeling he was there to empty the bins and get a small glass of warm white wine. To cheer us all up the stage management team and wardrobe came dressed as reporters, with the name of their papers tucked into the bands of their trilby hats. There were several from *Gay News*.

God, it was a depressing sight walking to the theatre. There didn't seem to be any lights outside the place and what looked like just a candle blazing away in the foyer. Again, nobody came.

By the time we got to our last date, Chichester, I'd done my money. Just before the show one night Billy came in.

'It's cost you, this tour, hasn't it?' he asked.

'You could say that – yes,' I told him. Then he did something I imagined a man of his financial prudence would never do: he took out his chequebook! Admittedly, it was printed in Latin, but he got out a pen as well (quill, of course).

'You gave me a chance to do something really good,' he said. 'How much do you need?'

I was so touched. I buried my head in my briefcase and managed to mumble, 'Thanks, Billy, but I took a chance and I've only myself to blame.' And before anything more could be said, I heard a great sigh of relief and the chequebook and pen disappeared as quickly as they had appeared. My pal Billy would argue over who would pay for a cup of tea, but when it came to a big problem he was there. Like a fool I didn't pursue the matter. Who cares? I'd had the great joy of being half of a double act with a genuine one-off. An inventive, lovable, highly underrated, brilliant clown.

We did a routine in the show, a ventriloquist and his dummy, singing a Weston and Lee song, 'Where the Busy Bumble Bees Are Busy Buzzing' (which of course became: 'Where the Gusy Gungle Gees Are Gusy Guzzing'.) The routine ran for three minutes when we started. By the end of the tour it ran for eighteen minutes, simply because we so enjoyed each other's company and thought along the same comedy lines.

There was one ray of hope regarding the lost savings: a West End management wanted to take the show into town, but not until after Christmas, as both Billy and myself were committed to pantomime. So I went to Plymouth and Billy to Nottingham, where he was taken ill and sent home: he had the dreaded cancer, and within a year he was dead. It was suggested I take our show in with somebody else, but I couldn't contemplate it without Mr Dainty.

All through his illness his house was never empty of friends. Eric Davidson was often there, as was the writer Vince Powell. I went one very cold afternoon. He was in the front room with a miserable fire just about staying alight. There was a stack of logs on the hearth but he wouldn't waste them. Finally I offered him ten pence for a log – he took it and we all warmed up.

The pantomime producer Peter Elliott, was there. Peter

had just got Billy to sign a contract for next Christmas's show, 'just down the road' in Guildford. We all knew Billy wouldn't be with us by the following December, but Peter insisted he sign. Good for Peter. Old pros always know what will please other old pros.

Without his lady, Moya, knowing, Billy had a mate plant flower bulbs all round the garden. Come the following spring, hundreds of them flowered. He was no longer there but what a way to be remembered.

In the early eighties John Brooker, an expert on old films, particularly B Westerns, came up with an idea for Anglia Television, *Movie Memories*. It was a magazine programme. The subject? The clue's in the title: a collection of film clips based on viewers' memories. I say 'based on' because the cost of showing just thirty seconds of top movies would have paid for two years' worth of *Anglia Tonight*. I was taken on board as the host, while John fiddled around in his own collection and somehow managed to produce a good little programme on a shoestring.

The memories were the first half of the show but the second half was my favourite: interviews with British stars of not so long ago. I had the great joy of meeting and talking with so many legendary names: Diana Dors, Ann Todd, Robert Beatty, Muriel Pavlov, Geoffrey Keen, Richard Greene, Anthony Steel, Roland Culver, Harry Fowler and Jack Warner. The most memorable interview was with the *Carry On* star, Charles Hawtrey. Even now, over twenty-five years later, I'm shaking as I write this.

Charles was lavishly entertained by Anglia TV (there's a first!) – a trifle too lavishly, in fact. He arrived on the set doing a fine impression of a newt. Try as I did, I couldn't get any sense out of him and he never stopped stroking my knee. On the transmission I think he said, 'Hello,' and then it cut to me telling all his stories. After showing a few clips there was just time for him to say, 'Goodbye' before he fell off his chair. I did warn them what he could be like (I'd seen Charles and his 'friend' Joan Turner, another secret lemonade drinker, ejected from the Arts Theatre Club bar – no one ever had had that honour before!) But the powers that be still kept saying, 'Do have another Mr Hawtrey.' It was so sad because, sober, he was a lovely, funny bloke.

We did about four series of *Movie Memories*. I enjoyed the cosy, old-fashioned way in which Anglia Television was run. When it comes to showbiz autobiographies, my favourite is definitely David Niven's *The Moon's a Balloon* – it has to be the best and the funniest autobiography ever. He too worked at Anglia TV, in an episode of *Tales of the Unexpected* and he christened the company *19th* Century Fox.

I was doing all right, and it was around this time that I got an invite to appear on the *Michael Parkinson* TV chat show. I love doing chat shows – you don't have to learn any lines – and this one was extra special as I'd be on the couch with Chesney Allen, the straight half of the Flanagan and Allen double act and, vocal wise, the bass underscore to Bud's gentle, melodic cantor. I'd worked for Ches in panto in Belfast and couldn't wait to see him again. Ches and Bud had retired years earlier, and Bud had died in 1968, but the public always held them in great esteem, there was a true and enduring fondness for their act.

A couple of days before the recording for *Parkinson*, Ches

rang me and said they wanted him to do a couple of Flanagan and Allen songs on the show.

'I can't do duets on my own,' he said. 'How about it?'

Well, what do you think?

The afternoon of the show we ran through a couple of classics with the pianist and Ches told me the secret of Flanagan and Allen's unique sound. 'Bud was always the gnats of a beat behind the orchestra,' he told me.

No one else could ever do what Bud Flanagan did with a song, but I did enough for Ches to approve and the show went well.

A couple of weeks later, Patrick Garland, who was the boss at the Chichester Festival Theatre, rang to ask if I'd be interested in playing Bud in *Underneath the Arches*, a new musical about the legendary pair and the Crazy Gang, that had been commissioned by Chichester.

You betcha!' said I. 'Send me the script.'

It arrived and it wasn't right. OK, all the facts were there, all the haunting songs, but not enough team play, not enough anarchy and not enough laughs. It had been put together by Brian Glanville – a well-known football correspondent whose father, bizarrely enough, had been the Crazy Gang's dentist. Brian agreed it wasn't right as a show and, I think, welcomed my input. Naturally, I asked who would be playing my partner, Ches. I was told Christopher Timothy. My immediate reaction was, 'You mean the vet?'

Chris had become a huge favourite playing James Herriot in *All Creatures Great and Small* on BBC television. It was indeed him, and he worked on the part until he became just marvellous as Bud's partner and straight man supreme.

Patrick was all set to hold auditions for actors to play the

Crazy Gang and this for a start was, I felt, wrong. I pushed for real old comics to play the old comics. Patrick asked me how many old comics I knew. I answered, 'Skips full!' and he booked, to my huge delight and relief, Don Smoothey, Joe Black, Tommy Godfrey, Billy Grey and Peter Glaze (who fed heaven knows how many comics on TV's *Crackerjack*). They were all highly experienced guys who had served their apprenticeships doing crazy-type comedy – and my brother Water Rats, Don and Joe, had both been top-of the-bill variety comedians. Boy, did they know how to work an audience.

We started rehearsals with Roger Redfarn directing. I was going back to digs every night and writing the next day's sketches. The Crazy Gang were in like Flynn with all sorts of suggestions and ad-libs. But, on opening night, I was cream crackered and, literally an hour before curtain up, Chris Timothy and I had a discussion about how we should play the parts.

The show opened and really did go well. The posh Chichester Festival Theatre had never seen anything like it: comics running through the theatre, pinching people's drinks at the bar, covering the punters with dust sheets and projecting, to the back row of the stalls, classic ancient gags and sketches. Patrick Garland acknowledged that the show brought people in who had never been near the theatre before.

Chesney Allen, who lived just down the road from Chichester, had been trying for ages to persuade Patrick to mount a show about him and Bud and, now it was on, Ches was as excited as the rest of us. His involvement with the show was of paramount importance. He always came up with just the right gag that was needed, and was responsible for a truly magical theatre moment.

Towards the end of the first half came the great meeting of Flanagan and Allen as a double act. I, as Bud, was told to wait and 'meet' Chris, as Ches. I stood on the stage and, shading my eyes, looked towards the back of the auditorium.

'Chesney Allen?' I called out.

'That's right,' came the answer from a figure walking through the audience to join me. It was the *real* Chesney Allen, and an appearance by Elvis wouldn't have been better received.

To so many of the audience Ches represented everything that epitomized the British wartime spirit: togetherness and hope. When, together, we sang the famous songs, there wasn't a dry eye in the house – and two of them were mine.

The late Tommy Godfrey, who you often see popping up on television in films and series from the sixties and seventies, was, for me, funnier than any material we could give him. He spoke funny with a Cockney accent that made anybody in *EastEnders* sound like Noël Coward. He looked funny and he walked funny. He said of his legs: 'I tossed a sparrow for these – and lost!' In drag, he looked like something out of *The Picture of Dorian Gray*. He had just one tooth left in the middle of his smile: 'That's for central eating!' he ad-libbed one night.

Just before we started in Chichester, Tommy had a call for a TV commercial.

'I went into this room,' he told me, 'and they all started laughin'. I knew the director and I asked him what the bleedin' hell they were all laughin' at. He told me the commercial I had to audition for was the Colgate ring of confidence!'

I was doing a Sunday morning records and chat show for Radio 2 at this time, *'udd's 'our an' 'arf*, and I told the Colgate story, adding, 'You all know Tommy – the man who gives Arthur Mullard elocution lessons!'

When I got back to Chichester for the Monday show Tommy was there to meet me. He gave me a big grin and showed me his mouth was completely void of choppers.

'What happened?' I asked.

'You, you sod,' answered Tommy, 'I was listenin' to you on the wireless and you told the Colgate story. Then you added the bit about Arfur Mullard and I laughed out loud. As I did the last "hampstead" shot out across the room and I've never seen it since!'

I can guarantee, he was just as funny toothless.

The show really was a sensation and, as always happens when you're filling the theatre, all sorts of managements came haring down from London to see if they could get on board. They all said it was fine for the provinces but wouldn't mean a thing in the West End. Chris and I were sharing a dressing room and after the last performance we agreed it had been an experience and what a shame it was that we didn't get a crack at London. Just then, a knock came on the dressing room door and it was Lord Bernard Delfont.

'Boys,' he said, with tears – honestly – coursing down his cheeks. 'I've just seen my life out there. Which of my theatres would you like?'

In the middle of all these dramas I was ringing Debbie nearly every day but, eventually, when I rang her home, she was never there. She was, of course, but she made her mum answer the phone. Debbie was giving me the bum's rush. She told me that she didn't know how to have an affair with a married man. I suspected the age gap between us might have played a part, but she never mentioned it.

I spent the rest of that year trying to keep all the balls in the air work-wise while still trying to get her back. Her mum was all for it but Debbie wouldn't have it.

We were both booked for pantomime at the Pavilion Theatre Bournemouth (with Clive Dunn and the only two female Ugly Sisters who have made me laugh, Peggy Mount and Dottie Wayne). While we both said it might be better for us not to be in the same show, I secretly hoped she would be there. And she was.

After a tentative reunion we found we were still on the same wavelength and, heaven be praised, we were together again.

On 26 February 1982, *Underneath the Arches* opened at Lord Delfont's Prince of Wales Theatre. It was an opening night no one who was there will ever forget. Morris was in the audience and recalls the show finishing with the whole company in evening dress with silver-knobbed canes singing Ralph Reader's 'Strollin'. On the last note, they struck a pose and the stage blacked out.

'There was', said Morris, 'absolute silence, and I thought, "I don't believe it! The show's died." Then the lights came back to full up and a huge roar filled the place as the entire audience stood up cheering, shouting and crying.'

I'd borrowed an idea we did in *Out of the Blue* and got all the cast to go into the audience to say goodnight. As I went down the steps, the broadcaster and sax player Benny Green, whom I'd never met, grabbed hold of me and wouldn't let go. He just said, 'Marvellous! Marvellous!' as tears streamed down his face – and I knew we had a blockbuster hit.

Advance bookings for the show hadn't been too tasty but again an appearance on the *Parkinson* show played a part in its success. John Fisher, Michael's producer, had seen *Arches* in Chichester and gave the whole hour of the show to us. We did the songs, the sketches, the dance routines, the anecdotes – the lot.

By lunchtime on the day after transmission, the theatre was practically sold out for six months. In those days, you knew a West End show was a hit when a well-known busker played the bagpipes to your queues. We got to know every note of his repertoire.

Several royals came to see the show, but we were most thrilled when the Queen Mum came. The Victoria Palace – where the original Crazy Gang held sway – was always referred to by King George VI as, 'my local'. He and his missus loved the Crazy Gang, and we were on tenterhooks as to how the Queen Mother would react to us. We needn't have worried: she laughed at all the gags (she probably knew them by heart) and joined in with the songs. A favourite moment was Chris announcing to the audience that underneath one of the seats was a red spot. Whoever was in that seat would win a spectacular TV set. Of course there was a red spot under every seat in the house, but the first person to spot one was the Queen Mum who raised her hand and called, 'Over here! I've got it!'

A couple of weeks later she shook hands with Ches at a parade of First World War veterans. Her comment: 'Mr Allen, we must stop meeting like this –people will talk!'

I suppose it was because of the Queen Mum's love of The

Crazy Gang and of *Underneath the Arches* that a few years later, in 1985, the BBC asked me to deliver eighty red roses to Clarence House for her birthday. I was greeted at the tradesman's entrance by her aide, Sir Martin Gilliatt, a lovely crusty old throwback to another age who I'd met before at Royal Variety Performances.

'How terribly, terribly kind,' he said as I handed over the flowers.

'They're not for you, Martin,' I said. 'They're for the lady of the house.'

'Of course,' was his deadpan reply. 'Do have a sherry.'

As we sat there jugging up, the lady of the house appeared and, in time-honoured fashion, asked what I was doing. I bit my tongue as I was about to tell her *The News Huddlines* had just won a Television and Radio Industries Club Award, but I wasn't sure she appreciated the good hiding we used to give the Royals every week – or June playing her as Irene Handl. So I told her I was about to start rehearsals for the tour of *Just a Verse and Chorus* and that I was working with a favourite of hers, Billy Dainty.

'Ah,' she said. 'A very funny man.' Not everyone gets a notice like that and Bill was tickled pink when I told him.

Back in *Underneath the Arches*, Ches would go on and do that unforgettable finish to the first half whenever he was in London. We never knew when he'd appear, but he told me, 'People will keep coming in the hope I might turn up.' Saucy devil.

He left his make-up box in my dressing room, which I don't think he'd used since he retired in 1946. He would always carefully make up and was the last person I ever saw put those red dots of make-up in the corners of his eyes.

One night a message came up for him. An elderly lady was at the stage door to see Mr Allen. She was an ex-Sherman Fisher girl dancer who'd worked with Bud and Ches years previously. Ches stopped putting the red dots in and said, 'Would you sort her out Roy? The wife's in tonight and I don't want any trouble.' I did chat to her and she was a bit of a darling.

My dresser, a good old comic, Jack Francois, was filling in before panto. He left the show just before Christmas and my son Max, who had just left school, took over. There were thirty costume changes and Max handled the whole thing like a veteran. He was then, as he has demonstrated many times since, very fond of unrehearsed comicalities. One tiny scene showed me, as the boy Bud, practising the song of an early music hall star. As I sang, one of the chorus boys, as the star, came through a door behind me and said, 'Well done, son – you're getting it.' This particular evening the chorus boy was off and the door was opened by Max, who gave me a half-crown and said, 'Well done, *son* – you're getting it!'

As the original Crazy Gang had always done, our 'Gang' would mingle with the audience in the stalls, the circle and the bars before curtain up and in the interval. They were inspired and ad-libbed all sorts of business that the crowd lapped up. My favourite was three of them covering the first nine rows of the stalls with a decorator's sheet before starting to paint the theatre. Tommy Godfrey was in the bar (surprise, surprise) doing his worst, when a punter clapped him on the back.

'Here he is – good old Arthur, Arthur Mullard!'

'No,' growled Tom. 'Not Arfur Mullard – Tommy Godfrey.'

'Get out of it,' answered the know-all. 'I know you, Arthur. I'd know you anywhere Arthur Mullard!'

This exchange went on for some time, until the show started. Tom told me all about it in his own colourful way.

'If 'e carries on in the interval I'll 'ave 'im,' he swore.

In the interval, needless to say, the know-all *did* carry on. Don Smoothey came back to the dressing room.

'That geezer started calling Tommy 'Arthur' again so Tom chinned him!' Chaos reigned in the bar, but thankfully almost everybody was on Tom's side.

As I said, the members of our Crazy Gang were all dyed-in-the-wool old pros and during the performance they had a couple of longish breaks. Well, long enough for them to slip out of the stage door for a quick one. The very thoughtful landlord at the pub they used had arranged for a Tannoy to be connected to the show relay and fixed in his hostelry. They never missed a cue – or a pint.

Sadly, during the run Peter Glaze died and the company laid on a coach to take us all to the funeral. We arrived and this strange collection made their way across the cemetery to the church. The procession was headed by a couple of six-foot-tall showgirls; following them came the always immaculately dressed Don Smoothey; a jean-clad wild-haired crew member; then Tommy (he of the one tooth and sparrow legs); a collection of motley backstage lads; Chris; and various shapes and sizes of dancers, wardrobe girls and boys, and Joe Black smoking a cigar that was almost as big as him. Max and I followed them. This odd parade passed two old girls who were tending a grave. They both looked up from their flower arranging to savour the strange spectacle.

'They must be from a circus,' said one. She wasn't far

wrong. After the service I told Peter's widow, April Young, about it.

'Peter would have loved that,' she chuckled.

After a year of sheer pleasure, Chris and I left the show in February 1983. The Gang stayed on and I was convinced, as one of the writers, that the show was good enough to no longer need Chris and me.

It was just the best feeling ever to be part of a show that cheered everyone. To be involved from conception to production – and in its success. In 1983, *Underneath the Arches* brought me the Society of West End Theatre Award for 'Best Actor in a Musical'. It should have been for me *and* Chris: very few, except those who know, appreciate the straight man.

The Royal Variety Performance of 1982 was a dream come true for our Crazy Gang. Chris and I did a Flanagan and Allen medley and all of us did a sketch – in drag – as old girls selling flowers around Eros. We'd finished our rehearsal, and as we sat in the dressing room the door opened and in came the surprise star for that show, Ethel Merman. She was getting ready and wore a real 'showbiz' dressing gown (worn wool with cuffs that had been rolled up twenty-five years before and never rolled down), bedroom slippers and hair in curlers.

'Sorry boys!' she said, in that voice that could shatter a beer glass, 'Wrong room.'

'No it's not, dahlin',' said Tommy Godfrey, grabbing the lady. 'I've bin waitin' for you for years!'

'You'll do for me!' said the great diva. 'I'm stayin' here.'

And she did – for nearly an hour – telling us stories of Vaudeville, Broadway and Irving Berlin. It's a horrible life, show business.

The Royal Show, no matter how well established you are or how much you are – or aren't – a fan of royalty, is still an ordeal. I've done three of them, and at one I shared a dressing room with about a dozen well-known names. There was a loo in the corner of the room and, for two hours before and throughout the actual performance, it was never unoccupied. As Michael Ball emerged after his fourth visit, he memorably commented, 'Is adrenaline brown?'

I was in the show the year JR (Larry Hagman) made his unforgettable appearance. *Dallas* was the top TV show and Larry came on to that terrific theme tune wearing a big Stetson. He took off the hat and, as he waved it to the audience, hundreds of dollar bills fell out. What an entrance. But, as so often happens, from then it was all downhill. He started to sing a parody – and it was a funny one. Then, would you believe, he lost the words. He started again, with the same result. I was standing in the wings watching this with Larry's mum, the great musical comedy star, Mary Martin. Suddenly Mary grabbed me.

'Jesus! He's blown it!' she said, and with that she dashed on to the stage and together, as mother and son, they stopped the show.

The performance was recorded and Larry was told his spot could be tidied up in the editing and no one would know what had happened.

'No!' he said. 'The old girl got me out of trouble – let everyone see it.' And they did. He is what we call in the biz, a toff!

The Royal Variety Performance is staged in aid of the EABF, and the charity always held a lunch for the performers the day after the show. At one such lunch, Debbie had a bread roll on her plate that bore a remarkable resemblance to fossilized genitalia. I pointed this out, just in passing, to Peter Elliott, who was then a fellow committee member on the EABF, and added what an amazing likeness it was to that of a mutual friend. We both found it impossible to explain to Lady Delfont why we were giggling into our side plates all through the meal.

And that, I thought, was that, till we got home and Debbie produced from her handbag the *very* offensive object. We put it in the freezer for an inspirational day. That Christmas, it formed part of our season's greetings to Peter, who returned it as part of his New Year good wishes. Back and forth went the, by now, enviably hard thing. It helped us, and Mr Elliott, convey our congratulations on birthdays, Bank Holidays and anniversaries. Its final trip was inside a chocolate Easter egg. I believe a lady friend of Peter's opened the egg and, on finding what was inside, dropped it, whereupon it disintegrated into a thousand pieces. The end of an eggciting eggscursion! Well it will soon be panto time.

I was still, in my totally ludicrous way, trying to keep the family together. I paid the bills, went home as often as my obsession would allow and, in front of Max, tried to behave as normally as possible. It didn't work. If I'd given Ann a hard time before, this was an impossible situation for her: Debbie living with me in Clapham while I was still Ann's husband.

Then, in late 1983, Ann had a baby – it wasn't mine. Eventually, to the relief of both of us and everyone we knew, we were divorced.

We'd actually been there a few years before, when I was with Danny La Rue at the Palace. One night Ann was driving me to the theatre and I stopped to get a evening paper. On the front page was the headline: 'Roy Hudd sued for divorce'. I knew nothing about it.

'What's this all about?' I politely enquired.

'Oh, yes,' said Ann. 'I meant to tell you about that.'

Of course, I was as guilty as hell and we did actually get to court, but at the last minute we said we'd give it another go.

The proof of my guilt was confirmed by a private detective Ann had hired. After the petition had been withdrawn, he waved at me across the court and gestured, 'Let's have a pint over the road.' We met in the boozer and I recognized him: he was the palmist from Butlins Clacton!

Ann and I tottered along together for a few years, but I was still misbehaving and the inevitable happened. We split for good.

We'd got married on 13 May 1963, and divorced on the same date twenty years later. Ann had been a good 'un. Together we'd suffered all the slings and arrows that go with trying to make it in show business. Ann had worked while I tried to. Whether she'd have wanted to continue as a performer I've never found out, but she was a good dancer with a great personality. She gave one hundred per cent on stage. In one show the girls said she was overdoing it. The director said, 'No she's right – you're all *under*doing it!"

I gave Ann a terrible time and I still don't know why. No one could have had a better or more loyal wife. I can only think we were too young to be married. I know I was twenty-seven, but I was a very late developer and, the old cliché I'm afraid, being away from home so much meant I needed company.

I honestly did worry about her running the ship with just Max and her mum. I needn't have: I only discovered recently that Morris kept more than an eye on her. I would have agreed to anything she asked – I felt so guilty – but we settled for Ann keeping the house in Nettlebed and me having the one in Clapham.

A new beginning for both of us.

CHAPTER NINE

'I only just met her in the car park!'

I was chuffed when, in 1983, Cameron Mackintosh asked if I'd like to go to Toronto with *Oliver!* Would I! A favourite part in a favourite show, and a chance to catch up with my cousin, Dennis, who lives there.

We flew by Air Canada and the cabin crew weren't the smiling robots they usually are. When they found out we were with *Oliver!* they jumped up and down and disappeared into their behind-the-curtain private place. The chief steward welcomed us aboard and his entire staff joined with him and sang 'Consider Yourself' and a selection from the show over the Tannoy (several of the lads fought each other as to which of them would sing 'As Long As He Needs Me'!). Air Canada used to have a TV commercial that said, 'We're so good you won't want to get off!', and after the generosity of the cabin crew – with ballads and booze – we agreed with that wholeheartedly and had to be unwillingly 'helped' off.

Toronto was a big disappointment. The crew at the Royal Alexandra Theatre were totally Union-bound and seemed completely disinterested in their jobs apart from what money they could earn. The audiences were as good as ever, but again it was the backstage staff who were the spoilers. A local children's hospital had asked us to go along and do some stuff from the show for the kids. We put together a potted version of *Oliver!* and rehearsed it. Just before we were due to go to the hospital the wardrobe department refused to let the costumes out of the theatre unless they went with them and were paid. I, and everyone else, got the red mist and refused to do the show: a company from England raring to do a show for Canadian children being stopped by Canadian grown-ups who wanted to be paid? Madness!

Toronto itself was spotlessly clean, to the point of sterility. I complained to Morris that it was so immaculate I was sure no human beings had ever set foot in the place. I missed, I told him, signs of humanity. A few days later a parcel arrived. It was full of fag ends, balls of fluff, old envelopes, chocolate wrappers, polystyrene boxes and some unrecognizable nasty stuff. A note was enclosed: 'Scatter this around the apartment and you'll soon forget your homesickness!'

The one great joy of this escapade was working with Jimmy Edwards. Jim played Mr Bumble the Beadle, and was the only person I ever heard get a laugh from that classic Dickensian line: 'If the law believes that then the law is an ass!'

I came to like him very much. A sweet geezer, he was totally the opposite of his macho huntin', shootin', fishin', fiery-tempered, crumpet-chasing roué image. Yes, he did like hunting but I never saw him lose his temper (well only with people who were trying to pull strokes or were rude) and he never chased crumpet. In fact he was gay. When this news broke – the story sold to a Sunday paper by a boyfriend out for a few bob – it was a huge surprise to everyone. Especially me. I had an apartment below his while in Toronto and we spent a lot of time together. Me, the sharp, streetwise Jack the Lad that I am, never noticed a thing.

Such was the affection in which Jim was held, that when it was made public, everyone – fellow performers and punters – showed their support for him more than ever. That's something that, thankfully, has changed since the days that when folk were 'outed' it meant they'd be ostracized.

Jim had a terrific War record and indeed was awarded the Distinguished Flying Cross (DFC). He taught many Canadians to fly and our time in Toronto prompted a constant round of day-off lunch and supper dates from his ex-pupils. Knowing how totally useless I was at self-catering he always took me along.

Mr Bumble's inamorata was the Widow Corney, played by Meg Johnson (who has been, and still is, a regular in every soap from *Coronation Street* to *Emmerdale*). The constant catchphrase during our time in Canada was the ghastly, 'Have a nice day!' This *did* get up Jim's nose, and mine, and his reaction to this greeting was always a growled 'S*d off!'

Meg, who he was very fond of, is a staunch Catholic and on our way to a lunch on our day off Jim said, 'We have to drop Meg off at the church.' We did, and as she made her way up the path he called after her, 'Have a nice pray!'

On return to the UK we toured all over the country and, on almost our last week, we played Norwich. As his last night present to the entire company, Jim took us all for lunch at a place called Bumbles, which was brilliant thinking as the building had actually been the Parish Workhouse. We all sat down on benches at wooden tables to much laughter – especially when we saw at the top of the menu: gruel.

The laughter died when bowls of greasy, vile-smelling yuck were put before us. Evil Jim had consulted with the chef, who found the original recipe for Workhouse Soup – and that's what we got. We all had a spoonful and it was awful ('I put salt in it to give it some flavour,' said the chef – it didn't). When Jim had stopped chuckling, he treated us all to a slap-up proper job.

During the UK tour, I started a little running gag just for me and Linal Haft, who was playing Bill Sykes – at least I *thought* it was just for us! After Bill Sykes had made his first entrance at the opening of the second half, and sung his great song 'My Name', he would exit from the pub in a foul mood and I, as Fagin, would hurry after him. One particular night, assuming my microphone was off, I followed him off and called after him 'Don't rush off, Bill! I've found this little gay club just round the corner!'

Linal enjoyed it and so did I – until Cameron came round at the end of the show and enquired, 'Where is this little *gay* club then? All the audience want to know!' My microphone *wasn't* off and my ad-lib gave the relationship between Fagin and Bill a very new slant.

Linal himself was definitely responsible for changing the character of Bill Sykes at one matinee. As he was clubbing Nancy to death, a child's voice piped up from a box, 'Daddy!' It was his baby son watching the show for the first time. Maybe Bill Sykes wasn't such a baddie after all.

For just a few minutes on that last tour I had a very good

co-writer. We were in Leeds and it was Linal's birthday. Our Artful Dodger, Russell Nash, was about to have his bar mitzvah so we had a party for both of them onstage. During entrances I had written a parody song to the tune of 'Hava Nagila' for the two 'slightly' Jewish lads:

'Linal – Russell and Linal . . .'

I'd extended Fagin's curls and donned quite an insulting nose. I was all set to do the song as a rabbi. But, try as I might, I couldn't get a good tag to the song. Just before I was due to go on, who should turn up to the party but Victoria Wood, whom Debbie and I knew from panto in Plymouth. Poor girl, she didn't have a chance. I rushed her into a dressing room and stood over her while she finished the parody. It got big laughs, especially the tag. I never told a soul who wrote it. I should have hung on to that one.

The director of that UK tour was the famous Peter Coe (who had directed the original stage version). He wasn't a very nice man. At the start I was so pleased that someone with his reputation was going to be our governor. On the first day of rehearsals he gave us all a copy of the novel and declared he was going to go back to the roots of the story and work from there. Being a Dickens fan, I was delighted. However he didn't come every day and we were soon left to create our own production.

I don't remember him ever coming to see the show once we were on the road. It was only when Cameron was trying to take the show into London for Christmas that he suddenly took an interest again. He appeared towards the end of the tour and, quite unjustifiably, sacked the two youngest principals of the company for no other reason than to show he could.

To Jim and I, a grudging, 'I suppose I'd better buy you a drink,' was the nearest he got to an in-depth analysis of what he'd just seen us do onstage. He did take us for a drink and sat with us, silently playing with the coaster.

Jim, for all his bluster and roaring, was a sensitive soul who always needed his confidence boosting as do I, along with ninety-nine per cent of my fellow thespians. We all need someone to tell us we're doing it right or, if we aren't, put us right. Nothing came from Mr Coe.

'You know, I'm just like an old horse,' Jim declared after a few minutes of embarrassed silence. 'I happily do what I'm asked, but I do like a knob of sugar now and again, just to encourage me.'

Peter Coe silently took a knob out of the sugar bowl, shoved it in Jim's mouth and patted his head.

Like I said, he wasn't a very nice man.

The tour finished with Cameron saying, 'Keep yourself free this Christmas. I'm taking the show into town again.' But, try as he might, no one wanted to know. As Christmas got nearer I thought of all my friends having to go without presents and the family without Christmas pudden.

Cameron, seeing how my clothes and possessions were all disappearing down the pawnshop, assured me that a Merry Christmas would be mine, adding (can you believe this) that if the show didn't get into London he would pay me my pantomime money (I immediately phoned Morris to get him to put some extra noughts on the panto money!).

I thought it was too good to be true, however, when Mr

Mackintosh added, 'That's what I'll do – *if* I can't get you a pantomime.'

My dreams of wallowing in well-paid idleness went out the window when he got me one.

I was the late entry into the cast of *Dick Whittington* at The Theatre on the Green in Richmond, Surrey. And – without knowing it – Cameron had got me into a show that would influence so many of my later years in the business.

Being so close to London, the panto at Richmond was always packed with good names, as it meant that those who lived locally could easily get back home for Christmas. Because of this perk the money wasn't great, but the talent in the show was amazing. The year I was elbowed in was no exception. Among a stellar cast we had John Hanson, Hugh Lloyd, Richard Murdoch, Honor Blackman, Jack Tripp and June Whitfield.

The show was musically directed by Will Fyffe Junior and directed by the man who put the Theatre Royal Plymouth on the map, Roger Redfarn. And it was this show that led me into two of my longest and most enjoyable friendships – on- and offstage – with June Whitfield CBE and Jack Tripp MBE.

From the first couple of days' rehearsals I knew Jack Tripp was someone very special. The show he had been most associated with was a very famous and hugely popular summer revue called *The Fol De Rols*, but *The Fols* weren't really my cup of tea – I had only seen them on television and they came across to me as being old-fashioned, twee and rather camp.

In rehearsals I always try to stand back when I'm watching someone I've not worked with before, to see if I can find out just what they're about. What things do they do to get laughs? Would their style clash with mine? Were they open to suggestions? Do they share my sense of humour? Do they know where to get a drink after hours?

When Jack took the floor, playing Sarah the Cook, it didn't take two shakes of an eyelash to see he was unlike any other dame I'd seen before. I've always enjoyed butch, obvious blokes-in-a-frock-type dames like Billy Dainty, Terry Scott or Les Dawson – but Jack wasn't one of these. He was a quite brilliant character actor. One who, when he walked onto the stage, made the audience immediately smile and relax back into their seats, knowing instinctively that they were in safe hands. They knew somehow, before he had even opened his mouth, that a 'lady' like him would never embarrass them or confuse the kids with smutty gags and innuendo-laden one-liners. He looked like everyone's favourite auntie (the one who, after a couple of Guinnesses, would kick her legs up and dance like a Dervish, sing a cheeky song, flirt with all the men, confide in all the women and behave like one of her nieces and nephews).

Jack could, if required, bring a tear to your eye, too. He looked bright, clean and colourful, only *just* over the top. Not for him the giant tomato, traffic lights or sausage-on-legs-type dress with a fried egg and bacon hat. Not for him the ghastly, female impersonator-type make-up and grating camp voice. He was a lovable, almost real, middle-aged bundle of cheeky fun.

I interviewed some tots for a radio feature about panto and one six-year-old lad, when asked about the dame (Jack), said, 'I wish I had a mum like that!'

I love to act with people who give you the truth. If they

can make you believe the situation, and that they, as characters, are real, the work is an absolute joy. When you look into certain performers' eyes you get all this. I immediately think of Sue Nicholls, Albert Finney, Stephen Lord, Neil Dudgeon, Billy Dainty and Jack.

Actors and actresses often say how they'd like to play comedy. Is it so different? The best note I ever got on playing farce was from the master farce writer, Ray Cooney. I was in his, for my money, very best comedy, *Run For Your Wife*, and I was worried whether I could cope with Ray's almost fanatical precision for words and moves. I think he counted six laughs per page and you had to get them all. How?

'No funny walks or face pulling – play it like drama,' he told me. He was right. His writing was so clever – the pauses before the tag, the double takes, the quick exits and returns – were all there in the words.

For all his effortless dancing, his infectious smile and his charisma, Jack Tripp did indeed 'play it like drama'.

Back to looking into people's eyes. So many performers, onstage, will say their lines to you but they're looking at just above your eyebrows. It drives me crazy and throws me. Sometimes with Jack I'd believe I really was his son. His truthfulness was infectious and though pantomime is so often plagued with crude, coarse, careless comicking ('It's only pantomime – take the money and run!'), it wasn't with the master. He knew *exactly* when to push, when to lay back and when to just look. His tiniest gesture and intonation got right to the back of the hall.

Class. That's the word.

Lest I should make him sound prissy and pedantic let me

say he was pedantic. He would take endless trouble over the timing of a gag or a bit of clowning, and would insist I did too. That's why I had such joy playing opposite him. One season we were stuck for a comic scene that used just the two of us and he remembered a piece that the great high camp cabaret and dame comedian Douglas Byng had taught him. It featured a huge mirror. In a blackout, the audience heard the smashing of glass. When the lights came up the comic, holding two broken bits of glass, was discovered stepping through the frame that had contained the mirror. He explained that this was the Dame's favourite antique mirror and that she will go spare when she finds out what he's done. Then a quick look offstage and:

'Here she is! Don't say a word!' A quick exit – through the mirror frame and we were away.

The Dame enters, thinking she'd try on some new hats she'd bought in a sale. As she walked to the mirror the comic, dressed identically to her – dress, wig, shoes, the lot – became her reflection.

We worked on it together and it did become one of the high spots of the panto. In fact it was so popular we elbowed it into every one we did. The routine is a very old one (it's done beautifully by the Marx Brothers in a film) but we made it our own. Our version is preserved for posterity at the Theatre Museum.

A young researcher, from a TV company Jack was going to do an interview for, waxed lyrical about the mirror scene.

'I understand it goes back to the 1920s?' he said.

'I should think 1920 BC!' corrected Jack. It was certainly done in ancient Greece.

Jack was lousy at learning lines, mainly because what he

said naturally was so much better than the words people tried to put into his mouth.

Like every comic from Grimaldi onwards, I always tried to put topical references into the panto. Once, when we had a villain with a rather peculiar neighing laugh, I suggested that Jack referred to him as Shergar, after the racehorse that went missing. Jack could never remember the name and Debbie, as principal girl, had to stand next to him in the scene so she could whisper 'Shergar' to remind him. But by the time he'd worked out what Debbie had said, the scene was over. One night, some six years after the horse's disappearance, Jack shouted out, to the audience's total bemusement, 'SHERGAR! – Got it!'

Jack's partner was an excellent performer, Alan Christie. Not only was he superb in sketches and scenes, he was a good actor and an effective, if rather strangulated, tenor.

Late in life Alan converted to Catholicism. Jack, the least religious of men, paid little attention to Alan's beliefs.

'Converts are worse than the real thing!' he'd say.

On the whole, Alan shared the same sense of humour as Jack, but not where his religion was concerned. The day Alan was received into the Church was, naturally, a very special one for him. He returned to their flat to have the door opened to him by a nun – Jack! For sure, Alan would have hooted at this … if he hadn't brought the priest back with him.

Jack said it was the quickest quick change he'd ever made and, 'Alan didn't speak to me for three months.'

Thankfully, their long friendship won through, and the years before Alan's death were happy ones. When he did die we all thought Jack would retire, not be bothered with all the nuts and bolts of panto preparation that Alan had always taken care of. But he carried on, I think, better than ever.

Debbie and I often popped down to Brighton for lunch, and a lot of laughs, with my hero. Again he surprised us by laying on very classy lunches. Alan used to do all the cooking and we wondered just how Jack would cope without him. The first time we visited, post-Alan, I offered to take Jack out to eat, but he said no and laid on a smashing meal.

'Courtesy', he said, 'of my caterers, Mr Marks and Mr Spencer.'

He did like greeting you in eccentric ways. Our last visit was typical. He pressed the buzzer to let us into his block of flats and, on stepping out of the lift, there he was, lying half in and half out of his front door, wearing the worst red dame's wig ever, a roll-up in his mouth, an empty gin bottle in one hand and a jam jar full of meths in the other. A caption round his neck said, 'Available for work and a little light dusting'.

He was, believe it or not, a very shy bloke, not a great partygoer or a show-off, but he did come out with some lovely ad-libs, onstage and off.

My favourite was the time he did panto with Ivan Owen. Ivan was the voice behind, and operator of, Basil Brush. After a Sunday at home, away from the show, the company always met for a cup of tea before Monday's curtain up. Chatting about their various weekend activities, Ivan told them that he had got home to find his house had been burgled.

'And,' said Basil's boss, 'the most amazing thing – they didn't take a single thing!'

'Oh!' said Jack. 'How humiliating!' Boom! Boom!

Not long before he died in 2003, Jack was awarded the MBE. Now most performers who get these gongs are cited as it being for (that blurred-at-the-edges phrase) 'charitable work'. Jack's was awarded for 'services to pantomime'. He is the only person ever to get an honour for that.

For me, it was an honour to know and work with and hear an audience acknowledge Jack's special genius. The actor Jonathan Cecil wrote an article about Jack and, for me, it conjures up his work perfectly:

> **Eternally young, his sense of magic untarnished, the irrepressibly droll Jack Tripp embodies the true comic spirit of Christmas past, present and future.**

I'm sorry if I have rambled on about Jack but he was a great influence on my thinking about pantomime and, if I achieved any sort of reputation as a player in the genre, it was by rehearsing, watching, working with and listening to someone who, if he hadn't stayed loyal to so many people, producers, agents and performers, would have been a star.

The second great meeting that took place at that memorable panto in Richmond was with June Whitfield and, I hasten to add, her husband, Tim.

June is an inspired, accurate, inventive creator of characters. Later, I spent fourteen years standing at a BBC Radio 2 microphone with her, and her expertise never failed to amaze and surprise me.

As I'm sure you know every panto has some rhyming couplets as the epilogue of the show. You know the sort of thing:

OUR PANTOMIME IS OVER
OUR TROUBLES OVERCOME
WE GIVE YOU ALL A CHRISTMAS WISH
AND ABANAZAR A KICK UP THE ......!

June suggested that we try and do a topical gag, in rhyme, as part of the traditional farewell. I thought I was pretty good at this sort of thing but she was better. It's so smashing to work with a legend like June and discover she's still as clever and, more importantly, as keen as the youngest chorine.

After the panto curtain went down, June and I would share a drink in my dressing room while we waited for lifts home. One evening she asked what I was up to once the panto finished. I said I was into another series of *The News Huddlines*, but there was a problem. I told her we were looking for a girl to join Chris Emmett and me.

'We've tried every girl in radio,' I said. 'But none of them are quite right.'

'Oh,' said she who never misses a trick. 'I've done a bit of radio ...'

'Ah, yes,' I said, remembering her classic Eth Glum in *Take it From Here*. 'But this show is very different to the stuff you've done before.' (You're right: I was getting more than a bit beyond myself.) 'You see, it isn't just funny voices,' I burbled pompously on. 'It's all satire. We get the boot in and have a go at everybody we think deserves it. Not your cup of tea at all.'

'Oh,' she said. 'What a shame.'

'It's horses for courses see, love?' said I, becoming even more patronizing. 'Now, if you could do an impression of

Mrs Thatcher you may stand a chance.'

And that was that? Not quite. The next afternoon, in the matinee, June, as Fairy Bowbells, had to introduce and referee the big fight between the Cat and the Rat. She stepped into the centre of the ring and spoke in a voice that could cut through steel. She just got out the first two words and everyone clocked it. This lady *was* for turning. Without a handbag or a welded hairstyle, she had turned from the immortal into the Iron Lady!

'Now then,' she said to the combatants. 'I'm not *asking* you – I'm *telling* you – go to your corners and come out fighting!' They did, very quickly. The audience gave her a round of applause.

'June! You've got the job!' I shouted across the stage. It was the start of fourteen years together on radio and the beginning of a friendship that, happily, still flourishes today.

She is, without doubt, the finest comedy actress we have. On radio she was an inspiration. Her voices were always perfect. To stand next to her at a microphone was uncanny. She is tiny, Barbara Windsor size, and when she let loose a burst of Barbara's *Carry On* chortle, you'd swear she was her. But when June did Janet Street-Porter she even *sounded* taller. There were two accents June hated doing – Welsh and Geordie. I tried so hard to put her on the spot. I'd preface quite ordinary sketches with things like: 'Now, here's a lady I want to talk to. You, madam, are Mrs Blodwyn Davies from Cardiff.'

Her face was a picture as she struggled with a vague Taffyshire accent. Drunk with power, I later tried: 'Good morning. I believe you were born and brought up in Newcastle?'

'We moved years ago,' she replied quickly. You couldn't catch her twice.

I tried and tried to 'corpse' her, all to no avail, until one day I discovered a sound that always cracked her up: a raspberry (well, that's the polite word for the disgusting noises I'm *really* good at). I say they always cracked her up, such is her self- control that the only indication I got that I'd made her laugh was a slight pause in her dialogue and a smack round the head.

A radio show is so easy to edit which is why I love it. Years ago, all you needed was a razor blade to cut the tape with – and now it's even easier. I knew that, on radio, I could improvise to my heart's content if I felt the audience were in the mood. Chris Emmett was on my wavelength and together we could be uncontrollable. Well, uncontrollable by everyone except June. She, who knew exactly when we were getting boring, would jump in with a line like, 'Yes, well, more to the point . . . '

It is so good to be in her company. Wherever you go with her people stop and smile.

There were two rather strange and wonderful exits from the colander in the mid-eighties. The first came my way via David Furnham, an eccentric yet full-of-ideas film-maker. Well, I say film-maker. David lectured in film-making in Brighton, but I think the series we did together was almost his first excursion into actually doing it. David had been commissioned by Channel Four to film the *The Peep Show* by Walter Wilkinson, and he got in touch. I knew the book because when I dabbled in puppetry as a boy it was the only one the library had on the subject. It had enchanted me then, and now it weaved its magic all over again.

In the mid 1920s, Walter Wilkinson gave up his job as a bank clerk to walk across Devon and Somerset. He made himself a set of glove puppets and a theatre (a booth on wheels, it's in the Theatre Museum). Bored with the usual Punch and Judy Show, Wilkinson invented his own characters and storylines. He stopped wherever he thought he might drum up a crowd, and lived on what he could earn from a collection at the end of the show. I was delighted to agree to play Walter.

How David got the commission I'll never know. He must have been a damn good talker because the script was non-existent, just a few notes. But I knew we were in for a real adventure when we did the very first shot in Wells, Somerset.

'Now,' said David, 'You're pulling the booth on wheels. You enter camera right and exit camera left. OK? Let's go!'

'I got "enter camera right" and "exit camera left",' I said. 'But what about the bit in the middle?'

'Oh,' said David. 'You'll think of something. Action!'

A baptism of fire, but that was the way he worked. Eventually we got a system. Myself and the actors who would be filming the next day would retire to my room after dinner and read through the parts of the book we'd be filming. We ad-libbed around what was required, and the next day we did it.

On his journey, Walter Wilkinson met all sorts of offbeat characters – more than fifty – and they were all in our film. David had no experience of booking actors, so Debbie went through my address book and persuaded all sorts to take part. The first bit of casting was just the job. To play Walter's chum, William, we had Jonathan Cecil, an old pal from my *Not So Much a Programme* . . . days. Since those couple of weeks on location Jonathan and I have become good friends. We both laugh at the same things, love the same performers and share the same loathing for those that sell us short and generally dumb down what we think acting is all about. A chat on the phone, a drink, or dinner with him and his missus, Anna, is one of my most eagerly anticipated pleasures.

This eat, read, rehearse and shoot system worked but, oddly enough, I found that the younger actors were the least able to cope with the improvisations. The elder thespians loved this way of playing. Victor Maddern was terrific and George Coulouris was a revelation. He was well over eighty when we filmed, and I apologized that there was no actual script.

'Thank God for that,' said George. 'No words to learn.' He played an itinerant tinker and we sat by the roadside and chatted. His opening line blew me away.

'Ah,' said the slightly-to-the-left Coulouris, 'so you are the Puppet Master. Lenin was very fond of puppets you know. Oh yes …' and then proceeded to give me a rundown on how the art of puppetry had played such an important part in the establishment of the Soviet Union.

Throughout most of the filming we stayed in a strange little hotel. The landlord obviously hated the hotel business – and us. On our first night there, after the main course, he came out of the kitchen red-faced and sweating, with a big knife in his hand. He glared at us all and angrily demanded, 'Who *doesn't* like apple pie? Eh?' We all did.

I used to enjoy, on those long summer evenings, looking

through the dining-room window at a mother sheep playing with her half-grown lamb. Before dinner one night I could only see the mother. Came the main course – shoulder of lamb. When, at the end of the week, the menu offered mutton stew … I ate nothing but cheese and biscuits till we left.

I loved working in this, to me, totally new way. Telling the story off the cuff. Since those days, of course, it's done all the time, and I wish I had the chance to do it again. I wish too that David would get the chance to do more. He was, like John Duncan and Frank Dunlop, an inspiration.

In 1983 the BBC, in their wisdom, had decided to drop the hugely popular variety series, *The Good Old Days*. The show, recorded at the City Varieties Music Hall, Leeds, purported to be a reconstruction of an evening at a music hall. It was a very cleaned-up, homogenized version of the original entertainment, but featured all the famous songs and, in my case, all the original jokes! The audience attended in Victorian and Edwardian costume and the whole hour was kept together by the chairman, Leonard Sachs, a very good actor whose talent for using outrageously long words became the show's trademark. It ran for thirty years on BBC TV and there was a two-year waiting list for audience places. The atmosphere was great and the audiences a piece of cake. Because the producer, Barney Colehan, hid his cameras among the audience it was easier for comedians who were inexperienced on TV to feel at home. So many comics made their TV debuts on the show: Les Dawson, Norman Collier, Hylda Baker and me.

Anyway, one day I got a call from a chap called Roger Bolton, who now does *Feedback* on BBC Radio 4, but in

1984 was a big pot at BBC TV Manchester. I went to see Mr
Bolton, and the brief was to come up with a show similar to
The Good Old Days. I had an idea for one called *Halls of
Fame*, on which I, as the host, would take the show to a
famous theatre, tell its story and introduce the turns – who
either came from where the theatre was or had a connection
with the place. Roger gave us the go ahead with a director
called Barry Bevins and a producer called Rod Taylor. I
wrote the linking material and together we picked the
performers.

We did six shows – in Manchester, Wolverhampton,
Bristol, Aberdeen, Sunderland and London – and they were
a success. Rod was ace at persuading names to appear, Barry
shot the turns beautifully, Don Shearman did great
arrangements and Kenny Clayton conducted the orchestra
with sympathy and wit.

The line-ups we had for each show were fantastic,
ranging from Anita Harris, Vince Hill, Alan Randall, Marti
Webb and Johnnie Ray at the Palace Manchester, to Danny
la Rue, Ted Hockridge, Marion Montgomery, Acker Bilk,
Billy Burden, Anna Neagle and Stubby Kaye at the Bristol
Hippodrome. The night at the Victoria Palace in London
was a memorable one: Max Bygraves, Chas & Dave and the
very last appearance on television of The Black and White
Minstrels – they got a standing ovation.

Rod, Barry, Roger and I were all pleased with the shows
and the first couple got good ratings. Then the powers that
be started moving transmission schedules around: a
different day and time each week – fatal when you want to
build an audience. I was told Michael Grade didn't want a
show featuring variety, which is odd when you think of his

background. But he was the BBC big chief at the time, so the show was quietly dropped. This was a damn shame as so many of the turns had never been presented properly on television before and for some it was their last public performance. I recently got the recordings out to have a look at the shows again and they stand up well. The crafty blighters who video'd the series now have collectors' items. One of my great regrets is not being allowed to capture any more top variety acts.

Christmas 1984 meant a happy return to the place where Debbie and I met: the Theatre Royal, Nottingham. I was playing the Hamlet of panto roles and, of course, my favourite – Buttons. The Ugly Sisters in that one were an inspired pairing: the diminutive comic Joe Black and the gargantuan Bernie Bresslaw. The Broker's Men was another odd pairing: Les Henry (Cedric of the Three Monarchs) and half of a double act, Ted Durante, of Ted Durante and Hilda. Hilda, his wife, was playing the Fairy Godmother. Ted and Hilda did a terrific cod acrobatic act – how that fitted into the plot we'll never know. One afternoon they had a mishap in the act and she was sent to a local doctor, who asked how she sprained her ankle.

Her reply was a classic, 'I fell off my husband's head!'

But back to Debbie and I ... After debating with myself (well, you meet a nicer type of person) I decided, despite all my worries about messing up another marriage, to take a chance and propose to Debbie. I thought proposing on her birthday would be good, but picking the right venue was important. Though she is pretty sloppy when it comes to romance I had to make 'the big ask' somewhere different – somewhere she'd never forget. I'd had the ring in my pocket for over a week – all the while looking for the right location.

I'd just finished two shows of *Roy Hudd's Very Own Music Hall* at The Grand Theatre Wolverhampton, and we were driving home down the M1 ready for the next day's *Huddlines* recording.

'Let's have a bite at the next service station,' I suggested, and we pulled in ready for tepid tea, tired tagliatelle and worn-out waffles. Just before we got out of the car I glanced at my watch and it was just gone midnight: her birthday had arrived.

'Hang on a second,' I said. 'I've just remembered I've got to ask you something. What was it? Oh yes! Will you marry me?'

She looked at me for a long moment and said, 'Don't be so silly. What are you having? Sausage, egg and chips, I suppose. I must try and stick with a salad. I weigh nearly seven stone. Oh, yes – I will.'

The ring came out of my hot little hand, and was on her cold-with-fear one before you could say, 'We've been together now for forty years'. I did all the usuals – 'Don't drop it or you'll be in for seven years' bad luck!', 'I had a hell of a job getting it out of the bull's nose'. But not a laugh: she was amazed I'd asked and so was I.

We gave each other a better kiss than Wayne Rooney has ever given Ronaldo and went into the café. Debbie waved the ring around and declared to everyone, 'I've just got engaged!'

'Wait a minute,' I protested. 'I only just met her in the car park!'

We eventually got ourselves an engagement breakfast – Debbie had the full works and I had a cup of tea, a cigarette and a good cough. The girls behind the counter were thrilled for us both. They gave Debbie extra baked beans and me a box of matches.

We floated back to the car and back to Clapham. You can stick the River Seine by moonlight or the Taj Mahal at daybreak – the most romantic place for us is Watford Gap at midnight. Even though the cafe has changed beyond recognition – they've got tables and chairs now – we always squeeze each other's hands as we pass and give a quietish cheer.

The following year, after I made my annual trip to the City Varieties, Leeds for a week's music hall, I hurriedly dashed back for a date at St Paul's Church, Clapham. On 25 September 1988, Debbie and I got married. My brother Peter was best man, and the choir were Charles Young and his lads and lasses from *Roy Hudd's Vintage Music Hall*. Among many favourites, they sang a hymn 'A Perfect Day', which had been sent to us by its composer, Les Reed.

We'd kept the whole thing hush-hush and it was just our families and Morris and his wife, Sheila. The cake was a replica of The Theatre Royal, Nottingham, where we first met.

We went to Jersey for the honeymoon. The cabin crew found out we were just married and fed us champagne the entire flight. I'd hired a car to take us to our hotel and it was a miracle we made it there.

We went to bed – and fell straight asleep! Thank you cabin crew!

I'd bought a new suit for the occasion and new shoes. They were very trendy-looking but too tight and put huge blisters on my heels. Our first morning of wedded bliss was spent looking for a pair of backless black slippers. I rushed back to London – in my backless black slippers – for the *Huddlines* recording and then back again to Jersey.

The hotel was *very* posh and, as so often in the most beautiful hotels, the staff thought they were doing us a favour by keeping everyone away from us. The clientele were very unfriendly. Meals were taken in total silence – it was like eating in a library. Not for us. We explored the island until we found a restaurant that was full of locals who enjoyed their food. The children eating there liked good grub too, and sat and ate happily, without tantrums or crying or embarrassing anyone. Wherever we go, on holiday, or to work, we always look for where the locals go.

Just a few words about the girl – and I can only ever think of her as a girl – who changed my life so much: Deborah Ruth Hudd.

Of course, everyone said it wouldn't work. She's twenty-two years younger than me. She has never mentioned the age gap to me. Never. And the only time I ever thought about it was when the day of our marriage was getting closer. Was I ruining her chances of marrying a young, handsome contemporary? You bet I was!

So far, the partnership has lasted twenty-one years and I hope it'll run and run.

Let me give you a little pen portrait of the lady wife. She is one of the most intelligent people I know, ultra-enthusiastic, all action and bursting with ideas, yet can organize things very coolly. She loves being in charge and, rather like yours truly, is inclined to want to do everything herself. I learned, and passed it on to her, that the art of delegation is the secret. She proved the worth of this when she became the youngest ever Queen Ratling in the history of The Grand Order of Lady Ratlings (the female branch of the Water Rats).

She listens to me most of the time, but can still, infuriatingly, nod and smile, make agreeing-type noises and *still* go away and do something quite different. Usually something much better than I'd suggested in the first place.

She is the greatest at putting on surprise parties and has caught me out on every birthday. A great triumph was my fiftieth. We went to the West End for supper with two special chums, the actors Geoffrey Toone and Frank Middlemass. On our way to the restaurant we passed The Prince of Wales (the theatre, not the geezer), the place that held so many happy memories for me. It was where *Underneath the Arches* had played. The theatre manager, Mike Churchill, was outside the place, up a ladder replacing light bulbs.

'Hello,' said Mike. 'What are you doing here?'

I, not thinking for one moment that he wouldn't be doing stuff like that on a Sunday evening, told him it was my birthday and that we were off for dinner.

'Oh, great,' said Mike. 'Come into my office and have a drink.'

I looked at Geoffrey, who had supposedly booked the meal. He looked at his watch and after a bit of grumbling (well acted) he said OK, we had time for a quickie.

As we approached Mike's office a great shout rang out and a bar full of family and friends appeared from behind every available pillar. Debbie always knows just the right people to invite, folk who I genuinely love, and they were all there. The icing on the cake was that Evelyn Laye came – she even sang a song for me.

My seventieth birthday was another surprise. Debbie had booked every seat for dinner at the Brick Lane Music Hall. I was amazed at how many of the same guests that were at my fiftieth were also at my seventieth – and how many did the same jokes!

On one of my recent birthdays, after a very jolly evening I did get a laugh out of her by whispering, 'Be careful, tonight you could feel old age creeping over you!' (a line borrowed from an era long gone).

Debbie has played every female part (and the ghost) in panto especially to be with me. She graduated to choreography and is now an excellent director – well, she does love being in charge. The mere fact she is asked back to the same places year after year shows she's 'the business'. She instinctively knows what can be achieved with lighting and what stage crews are capable of. Dancers like her because she was one of them, and comedians love working with her because she laughs at their stuff, even though she's heard it all before. Which is one of the reasons I love her.

Debbie's terrific with the children's chorus in panto. She has saved my bacon so often, shepherding them away just as I'm about to blow my top. She's on the kids' wavelength, knows the way they think, when to give them a cuddle and when to give them a telling-off. And they take it all from her because she can't disguise her love for them.

We tried very hard to have our own children, but the nearest we got was losing one just a few weeks into the pregnancy in 1995. She would have been a smashing mum. She gets on well with my son, his missus and, need you ask, especially well with their daughter Emma. I often catch those two whispering together – the telltale sign of two girls getting on. A great one for keeping in touch with her own family, Debbie's always the one who rings, never forgets a birthday and spends lots of time talking to her nieces.

Totally loyal to me, Debbie cheers me up when I'm down and will defend me to the last. Gawd, she sounds like a dog! She is anything but. She has a face that, when it breaks into a smile, gives my heart a real thump, and a Lancashire accent that always turns me on – as long as she doesn't sing!

Lest this should sound too much like a Mills and Boon, let me say that we've had a few punch-ups. Cases have been packed and front doors slammed, but, thank God, she's always come back to me, and me to her. (Well, she's a great cook ... and now she's growing her own veg.)

She has been through and read every chapter of this book with me – apart from this bit. Now she's seen it I hope she won't be too embarrassed, but I do want to say thank you, Debbie, for allowing this ugly old clown into your life. All my love, 'Orrible 'Uddy.

CHAPTER TEN

'Tell me, Mr Hudd. Didn't you used to do comedy?'

In the late eighties and well into the nineties I did series after series of that good old warhorse of a panel game, *What's My Line?* There are still folk about who remember the original series back in the black-and-white days. Eamonn Andrews was the host and Lady Isobel Barnett, Barbara Kelly and Gilbert Harding were the regular panellists, with a variable fourth in the team, usually someone to get the laughs.

I thought this was the very best game of them all. It didn't rely on greed and big money prizes, all a winner got was a certificate to say they'd beaten the panel. Such a simple idea. The guests would be folk whose job we had to guess. They would begin by miming something to do with the job, and then we'd ask them questions that could only be answered 'Yes' or 'No' – and we were only allowed ten 'Nos'.

I used every trick in the book to discover what the jobs were before the programme started, especially the ones that I could get a few laughs out of. I remember one of my better enquiries was to a bra manufacturer: 'Does it involve lifting at all?'

I wasn't told anything at all about the majority of guests, and I rarely got any right. I did, however, have one major triumph. A bloke came on, did his mime and, as a complete shot in the dark, I said, 'You're a chicken sexer!' – and he was! Somewhere at the back of my mind, I remembered a man doing the very same action the contestant had mimed on the Thomases' farm in Northamptonshire, to where I had been evacuated all those years before. Everyone swore I'd been told beforehand but, as sure as God made little yellow furry things, I hadn't. At last I had respect!

The very best 'catch' I can remember, though, was when they caught me for *This is Your Life*. One of the spots in *What's My Line?* was when the panel were blindfolded and then had to guess the identity of a mystery celebrity. On one particular show we put on the blindfolds and the mystery guest answered all our questions in a hammy Welsh accent.

'Well, I'm damn sure you're not Neil Kinnock,' said I.

To which the voice replied, 'Perhaps you'd recognize me if I said "Roy Hudd – this is your life!"' I did. It was Michael Aspel and I was whisked off to Thames TV to collect the red book. I think the programme's budget took a bit of a tumble once Eamonn Andrews died as the furthest any of my friends and family came was from Walthamstow and Croydon. It was a good 'do' though and just after it was recorded I was elected King Rat of The Grand Order of Water Rats for their centenary year.

Denise Coffey, my chum from The Young Vic, 'discovered' what was purported to be a play by William Shakespeare. I don't think it was. The co-author of *The Birth of Merlin* was one William Rowley, who was the clown with one of Shakespeare's companies. My theory was that our Will may have given our Billy the idea for the piece or perhaps suggested a few things, but he didn't write it. It's too good a part for the comic and there are too many opportunities to ad-lib. Or perhaps that was just in Denise's production.

We did it at the Clwyd Theatr in Mold, and it was one of the strangest pieces I've ever been involved with. But I would happily undertake anything to be directed by Denise. It was also the hardest piece I've ever had to learn, and it was only through the encouragement of Denise, Debbie and my partner in the show, Anna Karen, that I ever got on. Denise did let me play the ukulele though. Well, perhaps Shakespeare did write it – for George Formby Senior.

One night, after the show, I had an unexpected guest: Ken Dodd. I suppose I shouldn't have been that surprised – Ken is fascinated by comedy of any sort. But I soon discovered his visit was far more important than that. I went to meet him in the bar and was greeted by that familiar voice.

'Ah! There you are, young man. What will you have to drink?' A phrase rarely heard from the lips of the King of the Diddymen.

'I'll have a bitter please.'

'Certainly. A *half* of bitter for this young man, please!' A fairly important visit, then.

He had come to ask if I would be a character witness at his forthcoming trial: the Inland Revenue versus Doddy. Of course I would.

Ken wisely insisted the trial should be held in Liverpool. He was quite well known there! His defending counsel was the amazing George Carman QC, who was famous for taking on, and winning, lost causes. As the writer and producer Mike Craig said, 'He's the man who got Stevie Wonder a driving licence!'

So, in July 1989, Debbie and I arrived in Liverpool and booked into the Adelphi Hotel – of blessed memory. All expenses, of course, were to be paid for by Ken. No sooner had we got inside the room, than the phone rang. It was George Carman. I quickly ran through all I intended to say, adding, of course, the tale of us in Dartmoor Prison and Ken agreeing to do the gig with the comment, 'There but for the grace of God ...'

'We don't want that bit thank you!' Carman exploded. Fair enough, I thought.

Throughout that evening Carman was on the phone: with one call he'd tell me to tell the Dartmoor story, with the next he'd say not to under any circumstances. The final call said, 'Don't do it.'

The next morning, Ken's character witnesses – Eric Sykes, Reg Swinson MBE (General Secretary of the EABF), the television producer, writer and historian of comedians, John Fisher, and myself – arrived at the court. We were all counted in by a great pal of mine, and someone who has been totally loyal to Ken since his earliest days, publicist Laurie Bellew. Eric got the first laugh.

'Mr Sykes,' asked the judge. 'How old are you?'

'Let's put it this way, your honour,' said Eric. 'I'm a trifle past my sell-by date.'

The judge soon put a stop to these 'music hall japes' and we all did our two penn'orth. Just as I was called, I got a message from Carman to definitely tell the Dartmoor story. I played it dead straight and it got a good reaction. We broke for lunch.

'The judge hates us,' Carman told us. That cheered us all up.

We went back in to court for the winding-up speeches. The prosecuting counsel advised the jury to disregard everything that Messrs Sykes, Swinson, Fisher and Hudd had said about the defendant. To which the judge, bless him, responded: 'I disagree with the prosecuting counsel. These gentlemen have painted a picture of a man of the theatre, an eccentric, who only cares about his work. Take heed of what they said.'

I think that did the trick. The jury said 'Not guilty' and Ken was acquitted, thank God. There was every chance that, if found guilty, he'd have gone inside, and if that had happened I don't think Ken could have coped. Without the love of his audiences what would there be for him?

As he stepped out into the Liverpool sunlight, the crowd welcomed Ken like a Steven Gerrard European Cup goal. He was, and still is, greatly loved, and went on to turn his most frightening experience into a good extra twenty minutes of laughs in his act. So his second house audiences definitely had to have taxis home.

Only Liverpool could get away with this one – when it really did seem as if he might go inside, at Walton Jail a bed sheet appeared, hanging from a cell window. On it, it said, 'Coming soon – Ken Dodd!'

I'd wondered for years where one of my favourite songs, 'Try To Remember' came from, and Ian Talbot, who was then artistic director at The Open Air Theatre, Regent's Park, came up with the answer. He booked me to be in *The Fantasticks*, a quaint American musical that had run 'off Broadway' for a record forty-two years. 'Try To Remember' is the first song in the show.

I knew my career was changing: alongside Anthony O'Donnell I played one of the two *fathers* of the romantic leads in this one.

The Fantasticks was my first brush with The Open Air Theatre. When it was offered to me I asked Bernie Bresslaw, who had played there loads of times, whether I should do it.

'People either love the Park or hate it,' said Bernie. 'And you, I guarantee, will love it.'

I did and still do: it's got the biggest bar in London. Again, it's the team aspect I so enjoy. Us against the weather, for a start. It's the spirit of the Blitz all over again.

When it comes to 'proper' acting, how lucky I've been to be kicked in the right direction by people like Alexander Dore, Frank Dunlop and John Duncan. Ian Talbot is another to add to that list. Being a terrific comedy actor himself, Ian's just what a comic needs to guide him or her.

The Fantasticks was a huge success in London but then it was mooted we would tour the show. I was dead agin it – and made my views heard. The show had a huge cult following all over the world and people came from everywhere to Regent's Park to see it. But were there enough fans of the odd little show to pack out the provincial theatres for a whole week? No. It did nothing like the business it did in Regent's Park and we lost money – but no one ever listens to me. The final date on the tour was the Forum Theatre, Billingham. As I was getting changed after the show two old girls were chatting outside the dressing room window. Their verdict? 'Well, fancy Roy Hudd putting his name to that!'

The next year, Ian granted me the privilege of playing Bottom in *A Midsummer Night's Dream*. He himself had played the part more often than Robert Atkins and was, indeed, the top Bottom. This time he was directing – and he was terrific. Ian had a collection of comical wheezes that he'd developed for Bottom over the years and we were to benefit. He explained to me every detail of what the bloke and the play was all about. Ian made Bottom real for me, and he must have been as bowled over as I was with the inventiveness of Bottom's 'gang': Quince (David Gooderson), Flute (Matt Bardock), Snug (Gavin Muir), Starveling (Ian Mullins) and Snout (Keith Osborn). I name them here because they were such a joy to work with and every one of them made me laugh. They all wrung every ounce of comedy out of the piece – especially in the play-within-a-play, *Pyramus and Thisbe*.

The constant threat of rain in the Park makes every performance an adventure. If it does rain (and actually it doesn't very often), the actors run for cover and the audience repair to the bar. When it stops we all come back again. One memorable evening it rained and stopped five times. By the time we got to *Pyramus and Thisbe* at the end of the show, the audience were in an extremely jolly state of mind – it never ever went as well.

One afternoon we'd all just done a smashing matinee to huge laughs and I was having a cup of tea on the lawn next to the bar. A lady came over and said what fun she'd had. I glowed, till she added, 'Tell me, Mr Hudd. Didn't you used to do comedy?'

My last time in the Park was as Pseudolus in *A Funny Thing Happened On the Way to the Forum*. It was a chance to reprise a role I'd first played over thirty years previously in the company of 'Monsewer' Eddie Gray and Charlie Naughton in Coventry. Ian directed it and he let me have a ball. He even, very nearly, approved of some of the ad-libs. I was ashamed not to be able to get myself round the song 'Pretty Little Picture'. In the end Ian cut the number from the show, and I felt rotten until a friend of Frankie Howerd (the first English Pseudolus), told me that *he* couldn't learn it either. I felt a bit better.

My advice? If you want to introduce anyone to Shakespeare, get them down to the magical Open Air Theatre to see *A Midsummmer Night's Dream*.

In 1991 I was in panto at my very favourite modern theatre, the Theatre Royal, Plymouth. One evening the phone in the dressing room rang and a voice said, 'Hello. This is Dennis Potter.'

'Of course it is,' said I. 'And this is Martin Bormann!' and put the phone down. I didn't recognize the voice, but I was sure it was one of the *Huddlines* writers. Not a very good gag – there was no tag – and why would the bad boy of TV ring me?

The phone rang again.

'This *is* Dennis Potter!' said the same voice.

'Hey up,' I thought, 'stranger things have happened. Could it be him?' I let him carry on talking and, blimey, it *was* him.

As I always used to do, whenever a phone call got interesting, I reached for a fag and my lighter – then I remembered I'd stopped smoking. I sat there sucking a pencil and heard Dennis explain he thought I might be right for a part in his next TV series. Could I go to see him at Twickenham the following Sunday? Could I! This was the man who changed the whole face of TV drama with pieces like *Pennies From Heaven* and *The Singing Detective*. I'd have walked to Twickenham if necessary.

Came Sunday, and Debbie and I drove off for the big meeting. Well, Debbie drove and I 'back-seat drove'. Of course, she always ignores my knowledgeable advice ... so she should – I can't drive. I have never, except if a part required it, sat behind the wheel of a car.

We arrived and I was shown in to meet Mr Potter and his director, Renny Rye. The two of them told me what the part was all about, but I wasn't listening. I was just fascinated to be there with someone whose writing I admired so much. Eventually they stopped talking and I assured them I would like to do the part.

I was on tenterhooks worrying if I'd done everything by the book when it came to how you should behave on these occasions. Did I push myself too much – or not enough? Was I trying too hard to get laughs? Was I being too po-faced?

Dennis asked how I'd travelled to the meeting and I said my missus had driven me.

'Where is she?' he asked.

'Outside in the car.'

'Bring her in and we'll have a drink.'

In came Debbie who, in her subtle way, ventured an enquiry.

'Well, has he got the job?'

I blanched and thought, 'You saucy mare! You don't say things like that to these sort of people! That's it! I've had it!'

But Dennis laughed. 'She doesn't mess about, does she!' he said.

I apologized, my humorous explanation for the lady's

bold demand being, 'Well she *is* from Lancashire.'

We all had a few glasses of red wine, very jolly, and 'the saucy mare' and I went back to Plymouth. A few days later – YES! I had got the job.

The series was *Lipstick On Your Collar*. I played Harold Atterbow, a lecherous cinema organist who lusted after and did get a bit of joy from a beautiful usherette. It was a brilliant piece, with a cast to die for. All the good 'uns wanted to work for Dennis.

Director Renny Rye, who Dennis respected, banned him from the set while we were shooting. Like Spike Milligan, Dennis always wanted to add bits to the scenes – not a good idea when a director is working against the clock.

I remember I had a scene in a hospital bed and waited behind the set while it was being arranged. There, lurking, with a glass of red wine in hand, was Dennis with some additional lines.

'Don't tell Renny,' he said. 'Just say the words. They'll all think what a marvellous ad-libber you are and keep them in.'

I did – and they did.

The usherette who Harold fancied was a gorgeous blonde, a model, Louise Germaine. She was something. One of the older members of the crew said, 'She's another Diana Dors.' She was, I thought, even better. Thankfully I've never had any sex scenes to worry about. I've lost my trousers quite a lot, but only for comic effect. All of the organist's naughtiness with Louise happened off-camera, but there was one scene with us both parked up in a car that did get a bit fruity.

In return for a few bob, poor old Harold was allowed to touch the lady's breast.

'Cor!' said the lads in the crew. 'Get in there, son!' etc., etc.

This Jack the Lad was petrified: red-faced, bashful, nervous and, believe it or not, shy, and wishing he was somewhere miles away. The scene was all lined up.

'Action!'

We did the business and that, I prayed, was that. But no.

'Sorry,' said the cameraman, 'we'll have to go again – camera jam.' We went again.

'I'm getting a nasty flare off the car window,' said the lighting bloke. We went again.

'There are finger marks all over the car door,' said the prop man.

By now, I was a white-faced, shaking, totally embarrassed wreck.

Lou was quite happy, she was laughing … she knew the rotten sods had got the shot first time but just kept making me do it again to enjoy my sweating discomfort.

Not only a cracking looking girl with a great sense of fun, Lou was a very good actress and got great notices for the show. She was taken on by the American William Morris Agency and was all set to fly. Then she got married, had a couple of kids and chucked it all in. I have a Christmas card from her every year and I think she's the very happiest of ex-sex symbols.

Early in the shooting Dennis said, 'Do you want to see some of the rushes?'

'See the rushes!' A phrase I'd only ever heard in Hollywood films. I now *knew* I was a proper actor. We watched them together.

'That lad,' I said at one point. 'He's marvellous. Whatever

scene he's in you can't take your eyes off him.' He was Ewan McGregor.

'He is marvellous,' said Dennis. 'I know how to pick 'em.'

Lipstick On Your Collar was a real milestone for me. If Mr Potter employed me I must be all right and lots of nice parts came as a result.

In 1993 Dennis called me to have lunch with him at The Ivy restaurant. Now I *knew* I'd made it: The Ivy was – is – the show business eating place. Even now you have to have at least a Knighthood, an Oscar, several BAFTAs or have been in *Big Brother* to even be considered for a place at one of their tables.

Dennis, I believe, had a permanent seat there, and I entered in great trepidation. I tend to feel uncomfortable going into those sort of places – the staff always seem so much more important and sophisticated (and pompous) than the customers.

He told me about a new series he was planning. The main character would be me, playing a comedian. Dennis described him as a just past it, radio comic who had been well known for his gimmick of talking in spoonerisms. He said the comic just had the opening scene, and described it thus.

The camera starts on a peeling poster outside a seaside theatre and tracks along the 'out of season' windswept promenade. Rain is pouring down. The camera stops outside a tatty boarding house and slowly moves in towards a window. Its painted frame is peeling and the glass is cracked. The grey lace curtain is pulled aside and the comic looks out at the weather. He shakes his head and comments: 'Rucking fain!'

'That's all I've got so far,' said Dennis. 'What d'you think?'

As if it mattered what I thought. But I carefully considered what he'd told me and, two seconds later, said, 'I'll do it.'

That's how we left it. He would send me the first draft when he could. My feet didn't touch the ground – from The Ivy to Clapham Common.

Not long after that, the phone rang at home and Debbie answered it. It was Dennis. He said how sorry he was that the idea he'd told me about over lunch wasn't going to happen, but added that the TV people were going ahead with his new piece, *Karaoke*.

'There's a smashing part in it for Roy,' he told Debbie. 'And I've retained the idea of the spoonerisms for his character.'

Debbie told him I was only upstairs in the office and that she'd fetch me.

'No,' he said. 'I don't want to talk to him. He'll get upset. You tell him.'

'Tell him what?' asked Debbie.

'I've got terminal cancer and I've six weeks to live.'

'Oh, Dennis,' she said, 'What can I say?'

'Nothing,' he said. 'All is well. Now I've got to go and write. He's got a good part. Tell him not to let me down.'

Anyone who saw that moving interview with Melvyn Bragg will know all was well.

Dennis was gone by the time *Karaoke* got off the starting block. I played Albert Finney's literary agent. Albert was a writer dying of cancer and my first scene with him was a real jolter. I had to pick him up from the hospital where he had just been diagnosed with the dreaded disease. At the rehearsal

I walked into the waiting room to see Albert's back view. He was wearing an identical corduroy suit to the one Dennis always wore. The writer Albert played was, of course, Dennis.

They always say the bigger the star the nicer they are. I think so too, but perhaps I've just been lucky. Albert was a diamond: a superlative pro and a funny, generous and thoughtful workmate. As far as I know he only ever directed one film himself, *Charlie Bubbles*. He should do more. His knowledge of the technicalities of filming was amazing and he certainly helped me understand all the bits I needed to know.

As you know, I've never learned to drive and whenever the part requires it I've had to suffer the indignity of sitting in a car, which, in turn, has been loaded onto a trolley and towed along. For a scene in *Karaoke* I had to be seen actually driving a Jag. Albert was in the car with me.

'You just steer the thing,' he said. 'I'll handle the rest.' I did and he did. With his right foot across mine, he accelerated, braked and changed gear while doing all his dialogue – he could have been doing a tap routine with his left foot!

One day, in the middle of filming, I had a message that Debbie's jewellery had been stolen. While she had been in the front garden, someone had sneaked into the house. Just after I got home that night, a huge bunch of flowers arrived. They were for Debbie and the card read: '*nil desperandum* – love, Albert'. The old smoothie had never met her but just overheard me on the phone. They don't make 'em like that any more.

In yet another shake of the colander, in the early 1990s I embarked on my literary career, when a chance meeting in the bar of the Key Theatre in Peterborough led to me into journalism. Well, I say journalism – not quite. The chance meeting was with a chap who'd been in to see *Roy Hudd's Very Own Music Hall*. I always, *almost* jokingly, invite the audience to buy me a drink after the show – and this night somebody did!

He was Neil Patrick. In 1991 Neil was the editor of *Yours* magazine and he asked if I'd be interested in writing a monthly column for the publication. At first I thought he'd been in the bar for far too long. But he meant it.

I knew of the quality of the magazine and its concentration on older people. This, and his promise to let me write whatever I wanted, made me say, 'Yes, please.' Neil and I shared a similar sense of humour so he wasn't taking too much of a chance. He guided me well and, in 1993–4, I was made EMAP's Columnist of the Year. Move over William Hickey.

Our present editor, Valery McConnell, has increased the readership, persuaded the publishers to go fortnightly instead of monthly and *never* complains about my wit. So I think she's marvellous! Don't let me down, Valery!

My first column appeared in *Yours* in July 1991 and I'm still at it. I can honestly say writing the column has given me enormous pleasure. Not only the writing of the pieces, but also the feedback from readers. When the big fat envelope from 'Bauer London Lifestyle, Peterborough' plops through the letterbox, I never know just what letters I'll be getting. Some say what a wonderful fella I am because they agree with what I've written and some say what a flaming idiot I am because they don't.

I get requests for all sorts of ancient sheet music,

monologues and poems. I get enquiries from folk putting together family trees asking if I can give them info on a theatrical forebear. I get lots of good gags and stories and tales of personal involvement with my heroes – the variety stars. Some are even fit to print!

I was on the Radio 4 chat show, *Loose Ends*, which used to be hosted by my old friend Ned Sherrin, and Ned and I were talking about his recently published book of theatrical anecdotes. I told him how I'd bought several copies for the previous year's Christmas presents.

'Why don't you do one of music hall and variety anecdotes?' said Ned.

As usual I said, 'Good idea,' and, as usual, I immediately forgot all about it. The next morning a bloke rang saying he was Ned's literary agent and, he understood, I was writing a book of showbiz anecdotes. That was the way Ned did things – helping chums and putting the right people together. He was an amazing fella. He told me once that he went to the theatre almost every evening – be it a West End opening night or the eighth month of an Agatha Christie tour in Salford. If you needed a certain type when casting a role, he was the one to talk to.

Once, when we were looking for a new lady for *The Illustrated Weekly Hudd*, I asked him whom he thought would be good. He suggested Marcia Ashton and told me she was appearing in a show in Guildford. Morris and I duly went to see the show. It was a panto and Marcia was playing the Wicked Witch, with a green, wart-covered face and a huge hooked nose. We had to wait for her to come out of the stage door to see how pretty she really was. She got the job.

However, the outcome of the literary agent's phone call

was a collection of stories, *Roy Hudd's Music Hall, Variety and Show Biz Anecdotes*, and I'm proud to say it made the top twenty in the non-fiction books published that year. I wasn't quite so lucky with the follow-up in 1997, *Roy Hudd's Cavalcade of Variety Acts: A Who Was Who of Light Entertainment 1945–60*. This one was a real labour of love. A collection of facts and photographs of all sorts of variety acts remembered by myself and an old time producer, Phil Hindin. We loved it and so did all those who bought it. Sadly, not enough did, but it is still being used by researchers of the period today.

Then, just before the Labour Party Conference at Blackpool in 1996, I had a phone call from Alistair Campbell, then Tony Blair's oppo. Knowing how totally against the government *The News Huddlines* was (we were, of course, against any party that was in power), Mr Campbell wondered if our writers could come up with some good lines for the forthcoming conference. Our lads and lasses were only too pleased. They all desperately wanted the Tories out.

I carefully watched Tony Blair addressing the voters and came to the conclusion that he was to stand-up comedy what Oliver Reed was to Alcoholics Anonymous. Tony's deputy, though, was a fish of a different colour. John Prescott not only looked like a Northern club comic, he sounded like one and delivered gags as expertly too. He, like Michael Heseltine for the Tories, was always the last turn on at the conference. He was also there to get some laughs, give the opposition a going over and send the party away buoyed up and cheerful.

I assembled all the lines our writers had come up with and sent them off, and suggested that Prescott would be the man to deliver the slings and arrows. He did and stopped the conference with one of Dick Vosburgh's lines. Referring to Heseltine he commented, 'Michael Heseltine – the *Kama Sutra* of British politics. He's been in every position but he can't get into number ten!' This got a roar and he followed it up by saying. 'I hope my Mum's not here this afternoon – she'd never forgive me!'

Somehow I think more shocking events were awaiting Mrs Prescott Senior ...

1994 was, for me, the ultimate panto season: *Babes in the Wood* at Sadler's Wells. The show I'd written and nursed all over the country had arrived at the theatre in which our most famous pantomimist, Joseph Grimaldi, had made his reputation. I've no idea how long it had been since the theatre of dance had presented a panto, but we were there and raring to go. I was so proud of our show and the man who was the very best Bad Robber of them all, Geoffrey Hughes, was with me again. In so many shows I had had to drive the comedy, which I liked, but playing the Good Robber, 'Orrible 'Uddy, it wouldn't have been right to be the one in charge. Geoff was everything to me that Oliver Hardy was to Stan Laurel. He bombasted his way through the show, leaving me to lay back and be much more gentle, and dafter, than I'd ever been. Jack Tripp was 'discovered' yet again by the national press, and Keith Barron camped it up as The Sheriff of Nottingham.

Babes was ever so well received, and was chosen to be the representative pantomime by The Theatre Museum. It was filmed and is stored in the museum archive – forever!

We were so looking forward to bumper business but

Sadler's Wells had no concessions for children – I ask you. So many times I met mums who would say they wanted to see our show, but Hackney Empire, just down the road, gave good deals for families and especially children. The theatre priced itself out. The front-of-house staff at the Wells were so offhand and patronizing you knew they thought the whole idea of a pantomime was anathema to them.

At the end of the season, the powers that be asked if I would be interested in writing a new panto just for Sadler's Wells. I suggested *Dick Whittington*. Obvious, because London was about to elect its first mayor.

The director was to be Gillian Lynne and we had several very productive meetings. We sparked each other off.

I was then called to the theatre office, where it was explained to me that the management wanted a 'real' pantomime – 'along the lines of *Oliver!*' I couldn't believe it. On Morris's advice, I bowed out.

The finished product, heralded by all sorts of pseudo-intellectual cobblers in the press, was awful. It was neither fish nor fowl. Not a musical, 'real' or otherwise, and certainly not a pantomime. The kids in the audience were bored to tears and, until the interval (when we left), there wasn't a single laugh.

In December 1995, Jack Tripp had said that, after Sadler's Wells, he would retire. Paul Elliott, for whom Jack and I had worked for the last twelve pantos, asked if I could persuade him not to. I tried and Jack said he would do one more, but he wanted to play *the* dame role, Mother Goose in his hometown, Plymouth, and he wanted me to write and direct. When the idea was mooted at Plymouth, they said, 'Yes, please!' And it was all on.

I wanted so much to see Jack handle the comicking, the nastiness and the pathos, and I gave the script my all. He loved it and Paul gave me £250,000 for scenery and costumes. That was quite a budget in 1995.

He gave me a good cast, too. Debbie played Virtue (a character role!), Jason Donovan wasn't in it but his father, Terry Donovan, played The Squire, Judi Spiers did a great job as Vanity, I had the best goose in the business (who gave it to me I can't remember) and our Priscilla was Noël Butler. Jack and I played mother and son, with Caroline Dennis as my brother. It was Jack's finest hour. We did all our old routines and worked up some others that he had remembered.

It should have been Jack's great swan song, but he did another the following year. He shouldn't have. It was without me. Yes, it was great for me to work with him, he taught me such a lot but, all the time we were working together, I sensibly made sure all his appearances were presented properly and that no one trod on his toes. People said I was a mug to take so much trouble, but I've always been a sucker for sheer talent. With no one shouting and hollering for him, he couldn't give the show his best shot. I so wish he'd finished on top in Plymouth.

From the early 1990s to 2002, when the theatre closed for refurbishing, I wrote the Christmas show for the Watford Palace. I covered every possible panto subject and persuaded Chris Emmett to play in skirts. From a tentative first go I've seen him develop into one of our very best old-fashioned dames. No female impersonating, just a sporty, jolly old mum (he now cavorts every Christmas at the Brick Lane Music Hall). Watford always gave their panto great sets and excellent performers and I gave them lots of good, clean(ish), fun, situations the comics could develop and storylines that started on the first page and finished on the last. I also gave them Debbie as choreographer. She did a great job there and now directs pantos in her own right.

When I first heard the score for *Hard Times: The Musical*, I was convinced it was a winner. (Mind you – what do I know? I was the one who 'advised' Cameron Mackintosh not to do a musical based on T. S. Eliot's *Old Possum's Book of Practical Cats*.) I was really pleased when I was offered the part of the circus proprietor, and even more pleased when I found I had a terrific song, 'There'll Be Another Town Tomorrow'.

The musical had been written by the *Daily Mail* film critic Christopher Tookey, with a pal while at university. Christopher had nurtured the idea of a professional production for years and, with his own money (Oh dear, Oh dear), he mounted it.

The show was a play within a play, and Charles Dickens/Gradgrind was played by that shy little flower, Brian Blessed. Brian's a fiery fellow. Short-tempered? Yes, but mostly with himself. During rehearsals he was, amazingly, wracked with self-doubt. He stopped in the middle of a scene, let out an animal-like cry of pain, hurled a prop walking stick across the room and went. Encouraged by Christopher I chased after him and persuaded him to come back.

For some reason I've always been the one designated to persuade members of a company who have had enough to return. During rehearsals for *Much Ado About Nothing* at

The Young Vic, our director, that great hero of mine, Frank Dunlop, silently walked out of rehearsals at one point. I followed him and enquired, 'What's up?'

'I've watched actors trying to remember their lines before,' said Frank. 'I'll come back when they know 'em.'

But back to the Blessed Brian. He can, when in the mood, talk for England, and has opinions on everything from fast food to extrasensory perception. Opinions always expressed in that sergeant major roar that has become his trademark.

We tried out *Hard Times* at the Theatre Royal, Windsor, and Brian and I shared a dressing room. A friend asked me how I was getting along with him.

'He arrived on Monday morning,' I said. 'I said "Hello". That was a week ago, and I haven't said a word since – can't get in!' I didn't mind really (says me through gritted teeth) because Brian was a good talker and his tales of his mountaineering exploits were fascinating. He was the oldest man to attempt to climb Everest.

We did quite well in Windsor. So much so that Christopher and his backers got us into the beautiful Haymarket Theatre in the West End. On my way to the theatre for the opening night I trod in a dirty Fido and went base over apex. I felt nothing, but after the show I discovered I'd done the evening with a broken wrist.

The opening night went well. All shows in the West End do – well the place is full of backers, family and friends. According to Dickens, Mr Sleary, the circus proprietor, had a heavy speech impediment. I did my best with it and in the interval Debbie, earwigging in the bar to find out what the audience thought, heard a man say to his wife, 'Roy Hudd's developed a shocking lisp.'

'It's called acting, dear,' replied his wife. The first time I've ever been accused of that!

Sadly, though, the critics didn't like it. They gave us a real seeing-to. I still wonder if it wasn't the fact that a critic had written and produced the show that caused the savaging from his brother scribes.

The plot line was a bit confusing, but the songs and production numbers were excellent. The choreographer was 'Mr Nasty' from *Strictly Come Dancing*, Craig Revel Horwood, and he was then exactly like he is on the telly today – say no more.

The dancers and principals were all top class and, from poor business following the reviews, the audiences did start to pick up. Alas, not quickly enough to make it worthwhile to risk investing more. We came off and a play by Jeffrey Archer took over our theatre. It had a shorter run than we did – and worse reviews. He was later sent to jail!

Brian Blessed was interesting to work with and always, like his delivery of lines, full of offbeat surprises. I think he just loved being in the theatre.

He was always 'over-excited', as my missus would say. One of his favourite 'jokes' was to hide behind bits of scenery and jump out at people. When he did it to me and saw my reaction: a jump, a scream and a long-suffering, 'Oh, bugger off, Brian!' he did it all the more.

Eventually, he'd used every available bit of scenery to hide behind so he had to become more inventive. Curtain down, and I went to my dressing room, where I was greeted from behind the door with the usual leap out and roar.

'Oh, bugger off, Brian!' He did, chuckling as only he could.

The next night, I opened the door slowly and peeped round the edge. He wasn't there. But he was in the wardrobe. 'Oh . . . . . Brian!'

Next night, not behind the door or in the wardrobe, I sat down at the table to take the make-up off. Gawd help us! He was under the table and groping me like a good 'un.

The next night, on stage, he passed out during his big song.

'Get on there!' said the stage manager, so I did and was able to achieve a lifetime ambition: to ask if there was a doctor in the house.

Thankfully there was, and within minutes Brian was OK, and carried on from where the orchestra had stopped. I had to follow this 'evening with Brian' and announce that he was fine.

'You see, he's all right when he's halfway up Everest. It's when he gets down here it all goes wrong!'

That's it, I thought, he won't be doing any frightening tonight. Nevertheless, I still carefully looked all round the room: not behind the door, in the wardrobe, or under the table. Relief. A roar filled the room. Where was he? The roar came from the window. I opened the curtains and there he was. *Outside* the window – standing on the sill! Perhaps it was a good thing the show did come off or he'd have been leaping and roaring from the top of the Post Office Tower.

A couple of years back I went to see Brian as Captain Hook in *Peter Pan*. I waited outside the stage door to say hello. He was very nice, but I don't think he knew who I was.

CHAPTER ELEVEN

'Congratulations. It'll be good experience for you ...'

These days, I think I'm far too grand to go and read for a part. People know what I do and they either want me or not. But in 2002 I was asked to go to Granada Television in Manchester and do just that. I was there as soon as I could get a cheap day return. It was for a part in *Coronation Street*. I was a huge fan of the show – turned on to it by my Lancashire missus. When I told her what was in the wind she put me into my hat and coat and bought me my cheap day return.

I read for the producer, the director and the writer. They wanted me to play the local undertaker, Archie Shuttleworth, invented by Darren Little. The character was well written and had a great catchphrase. Eyeing up anyone he was introduced to he would guess how tall they were and declare 'Five foot eight! [or whatever] I'm not wrong am I!'

They gave me the part and I was in heaven.

The day I arrived on set, one of the younger members of the cast asked me, 'How did you get the job?'

'Well, I read for the part,' I said, 'and they offered it to me.'

'Congratulations,' she said, having no idea I'd been in the business for nigh on a hundred years. 'It'll be good experience for you.'

From day one in Manchester I felt at home. For anyone who goes into the *Street* the problems are the same. Yes you do call all the actors by their *Street* names – you can't help yourself – they are all so familiar. People always ask you what the members of the team are like. A popular character when I was there was Fred Elliott the butcher, played by John Savident. Anyone less like Fred – I say, anyone less like Fred – you couldn't find. John is a good singer, with a Donald Sinden-type speaking voice. And when you think how authentic his Northern butcher was, a bloomin' good actor too.

I was so delighted to have the chance to work with them all, from Bill Roache (Ken Barlow) to Jack Shepherd (David Platt), who's become as good a rotter as he was a cute schoolboy.

Most of my big storylines were with Blanche Hunt, played by Maggie Jones and Audrey Roberts, played by Sue Nicholls. When you look into an actor's eyes and see the truth you can't go wrong and with those two it was easy.

Now I mustn't go picking out favourites. Suffice to say they are all the most believable characters on the box. Brilliant casting, of course.

But there were a few little surprises. The ones who made me laugh off the screen were Eileen Derbyshire (Emily Bishop) and Barbara Knox (Rita Sullivan) – for me, the French and Saunders of the *Street*. The funniest letters I get are from David Neilson (Roy Cropper) and Malcolm Hebden (Norris Cole) was, and is, a good audience for rude gags, and always had a dirtier ad-lib to top me. Anne Kirkbride (Deirdre Barlow) was always up for it and is very inventive, too.

Almost the first scene I had to do was on the Barlows' doorstep with Ken, Deirdre and Blanche. From the house opposite came a pregnant girl who was helped into an ambulance and driven away to the hospital. Just out of shot were two firemen, preparing their hoses to soak the cobbles for the following scene. As the ambulance turned the corner the firemen turned on their hoses. Anne clutched me and said, 'My God! Her waters have broken!' She endeared herself to me when, at a rehearsal for one of my funerals, an enormous fart issued from the coffin. It was a remote-controlled machine placed there by our Deirdre. (Whisper it, but I've bought a similar machine for June Whitfield for this Christmas. Like me, she loves a good raspberry.)

The two years I spent in Manchester with the team were so enjoyable. We did a couple of charity shows which were organized by one of the *Street*'s assistant directors, the permanently stage-struck Peter Shaw, and the effort these national favourites put in – after six days a week recording – was amazing.

Bill Tarmey (Jack Duckworth) sang the Flanagan and Allen duets with me. Andrew Whyment (Kirk Sutherland) played guitar and sang. Bruce Jones (Les Battersby) did some country and western stuff with his own band. Sue Nicholls tap-danced and did a duet with her real-life old man, Mark Eden (he played the rotter Alan Bradley who tried to push Rita under a Blackpool tram – and he still gets old ladies waving their umbrellas at him in supermarkets). Bill Roach told a story that got roars – mainly because Bernie Clifton's ostrich was trying to goose him. Malcolm Hebden came on in a ballet tutu – nobody asked him why.

Archie's catchphrase, 'Five foot eight – I'm not wrong am

I!' became as popular as my Quick Brew commercial, and kids would shout out in the street, 'Here, Archie! Got any empty boxes?' I really do like being recognized. Ego I suppose.

I think my favourite offstage comment ever came from an assistant director, John Foulkard. An actor, no longer with the show and a bit of a pain in the butt, was unhappy about the quality of the sound at the location where we were working.

'These acoustics are dreadful,' he complained. 'It's just like acting in an empty theatre.'

'Really?' said John. 'We bow to your superior knowledge of empty theatres ...'

I left the show because they didn't really want me to do anything else while I was playing Archie. But the fart is always looking for new ways out of the colander, so I wanted to tackle other things. I didn't want to be tied down on a regular basis. I've been back a couple of times since and hope to return. To share the company of the Weatherfield mafia is always nothing less than a perfect joy.

After several bits of nastiness in south London, Debbie and I decided that we should get out of town and, having had several great holidays on the Broads, Norfolk was the first place we looked. We searched and searched but nothing was quite right. We had been used to a tall, thin Victorian house with high ceilings in Clapham, and we didn't find one.

We spent so much time looking at places on the computer that the four months it's taken me to put this book together seem like a long weekend.

I saw one that took my fancy but Debbie said, 'I've seen

that one lots of times. I haven't chased it up because it's not Georgian, it's got low beams not high ceilings, and it's in Suffolk – not Norfolk. But apart from that, it's perfect!'

'It's got a pond,' was my pathetic hard sell, so we went to have a look.

The owner was Roger Moore. No, not that one: I wouldn't have been able to afford a garden shed of his. We'd hardly got into the house when I whispered to Debbie, 'I could live here.'

The outcome was, we do. It's actually three little cottages knocked into one, and five hundred years old. Unfortunately it is a listed building. That might sound rather grand, but all it means is that any change to the place has to conform to the listed building demands – and that costs.

Thankfully, we sold our house in Clapham when prices were more than healthy, so we were able to afford all the improvements we wanted. Debbie, whose brothers, Colin and Roy, are both in the building trade, consulted with them regarding the drastic things she planned to do. I say drastic, but that's not really true because, to me, a drastic alteration means moving a chair. But she planned, and had executed, a brilliant home for my lifelong collection of music hall songs, books and ephemera. She organized a smashing office for me, and I've even allowed her in a couple of times (not too often – she will Hoover and throw away rubbish).

The local council was quite happy with what we'd done inside. But the outside was different. I wanted the house painted blue – a beautiful colour we'd seen on no end of Suffolk houses. The lady from the local council who says yea or nay said we couldn't have the house that colour as, in her opinion, it would be 'too dominant on the landscape'.

However, she assured me, we could apply again.

'Who to?' I asked.

'Me,' she replied.

'But you've already said we *can't* have it painted blue.'

'That's right,' she said.

I put my hand to my brow and ran away. Debbie negotiated with the lady and we finished up with a Suffolk Pink house.

When we first moved in, Debbie confided to friends, 'I can't see him staying. You know how much he loves London, he'll never get used to all this peace and tranquillity.' It took me a quarter of an hour to get used to it. For me, living here is a return to those happy wartime years of evacuation in Northamptonshire.

My county, because that's how I look at it now, is a bit scruffy because it is a working county. Our neighbours are farmers who earn their livings by doing what farmers have always done. When I say it's a bit scruffy, I mean it hasn't been tarted up like some of the trendy counties have. Not too many 'Ye Olde Bakehouse' or 'Toadstool Farm' signs on newly built 'spacious family dwellings (with swimming pool)'.

The pace of life is slower and so, for me, much more enjoyable. When variety was still happening, one of the great pleasures was having time to chat. Suffolk folk *insist* there's time to chat. Debbie has always found time to chat, and so people like her. The old cliché, 'You're a stranger until you've been here fifty years,' isn't true in Suffolk.

The other thing about living the country life is that we can have a dog who enjoys a bit of freedom. I've always been a dog man – ever since a pal in the RAF introduced me to the book *Thurber's Dogs*. Once you've bought a copy of *A Fart in a Colander* for all your friends, do try to find James Thurber's masterpiece. In short, it's his recollections of the dogs he and his family have had.

We've had a few belters – all lovable but for different reasons. The first dog we had was an accident. Way back in the sixties, Ann and I were in Belfast doing panto. Our landlady had a much-loved dog, and I can't remember whether it died or was run over. In our ignorance we thought what she needed to get over her sorrow was another dog, so we got one for her from the dog's home. He was a scruffy old mongrel with a winning smile and an ever-wagging tail. Perfect, we thought. At the end of the season we presented it to the landlady. She didn't want it. No way. So he came back to Croydon with us.

He'd only been with us a few days and had spent most of the time sniffing around our little garden. One morning we heard a crashing sound and rushed outdoors. In the middle of the back fence was a dog-shaped hole (designed by Hanna-Barbera) and the Irish pooch was never seen again – by us.

When Ann, Max, mother-in-law Alice and I moved to Oxfordshire we had a bigger garden and this was our chance to have a big dog. She was, whisper it, my very favourite of all. She was a bouncy boxer and, like most of her ilk, she thought she was a small dog. Just two minutes after you sat on the sofa to watch television you would be joined by a snorting, dribbling, licking thing surreptitiously creeping onto your lap. When she thought you hadn't noticed her she'd put her head on your shoulder and snoringly nod off. Some loathed this. I loved it. We christened her Lily after

Morris's mum Lilian Aza. He wasn't amused.

Lily was mated, and what a special delivery she gave us. On New Year's Eve she went into labour and Max saw the first puppy arrive. It arrived, as puppies do, perfectly packaged in what to him looked like clingfilm. We all sat round her while another came, then another, then another. Now we started to laugh, nervously, but with wonder as more and more arrived. She stopped at eleven and we relaxed. Too soon. An afterthought came along: a round dozen. It was days before she'd leave them – even for a couple of minutes to have a wee. When, eventually, I dragged her into the garden (the first and only time she ever growled at me) it was like a dam bursting. She was on her way back to them while still at it.

We all wanted to keep the lot but the food bill alone would have meant all four of us doing full-time jobs. The pups were sold to heavily vetted dog lovers, including two to Bernie Winters. One, the runt of the litter (the late arrival, I suspect) was her mother in miniature. We called her Maud and kept her. She was fairly bad-tempered and that made her a great guard dog – she wouldn't even let me in.

There was a King Charles spaniel named Albert who was put on this earth to be chased by Maud, but he didn't do an awful lot for me. Albert had a mad look: you know, when you can see white all round the edges of their black eyes. Especially scary when you catch them looking at you surreptitiously.

Max had a gun dog called Duchess, the most stunning looking flat-coated retriever, she was as thick as she was beautiful. But Max worked very hard on her and I was terrifically impressed when one day he sat her in the middle of a huge field and hid, with me, behind a hedge. Duchess didn't move. In fact I think she's still there.

Max first met his wife, Janet, in a pub near the Phoenix Theatre in the West End, where he was working backstage on *Blood Brothers*. Janet is a pretty New Zealander and she was working behind the bar. When the landlord and his wife emigrated to Australia, they left behind a Lhasa Apso cross, a barrel on legs called Barney. They couldn't afford to take him with them so, that collector of waifs and strays, Debbie, took him in. He was hers from the moment they met – and dead jealous of me. He'd push himself between us when we sat together and would defend her to the death.

Barney, like most dogs, didn't like being laughed at. I laughed at him just once and he bit me on the nose. He was a pub landlord's dog – he even looked like Al Murray. He was fat because his only exercise was once round the block after closing time and a Sunday run in Hyde Park, but he soon lost the weight on Clapham Common and he was, without doubt, the most intelligent dog we've ever had. He understood loads of different commands and Frank Ginnett, a pal of mine from the circus who'd had a dog act, told me he thought Barney would be very easy to train because he loved doing things to please. Dogs do seem to enjoy doing tricks: I've never seen a dog act where all the tails haven't been going like the clappers.

Our latest dog is Bella. We bought her as a puppy from a farmer in Suffolk. She was sharing a big box with six sisters, all twice her size. When we said she was the one we liked he said, 'You don't want 'er, do you?'

'Yes,' we both said.

'Oh well,' he said. 'You can have 'er cheap.'

Though not quite my favourite (I can't forget Lily), I am very fond of this one. Debbie calls her a typical blonde (this is Debbie talking not me!), beautiful but daft. It's true. Just as her predecessor was Albert Einstein, this one is Stan Laurel. She will sit there with her head on one side melting your heart, but you know she doesn't even remember her name. She will only eat dog biscuits after you've nearly choked yourself showing her how to do it. Just as you're nodding off after Sunday lunch she'll force you judderingly awake by letting go a stream of raucous barks, howls, yaps, growls and whines. All directed at some, unseen-by-human-eyes, thing in the corner of the room. Just hearing the cacophony puts the fear of God up anyone who knocks at our door, as long as we keep her out of sight. If she should actually appear the game is up. People laugh. She isn't a giant throat-tearing Rottweiler, but a tiny white bunch of wriggling, loving, backward, friendly Lhasa Apso.

The longer we spend in the rural idyll, the less we want to go to London. When we do go I have to forcibly restrain Debbie from ripping down the posters that say: 'Come to Suffolk!' She'd prefer 'Stay away from Suffolk – it's mine!' Mine too. Ooo arrh! Yes, we both happily 'sits among the cabbages and peas'.

After twenty-six years of having a go at the entire House of Windsor on radio, I was amazed to get an OBE in 2004. It was, I'm so chuffed to say, for 'services to entertainment'. (Or was it for the conference jokes sent to Tony Blair? The 'gags for gongs' scandal!)

On the day, the Queen, who did the business, recognized my Water Rat emblem as she pinned the gong to my lapel, and said how much her husband (a companion of our Order) enjoyed the company of the Rats. He's certainly always been good fun when he's been with us.

My day at the Palace was shared with an old friend and Brother Water Rat, John Styles. I first met John when he entertained my son Max and his chums at Max's fifth birthday party. John was receiving an MBE for 'services to the arts (especially Punch and Judy shows)'. Quite right too.

Later that year, things weren't quite so happy. I went to Belfast to do a little part in a radio play. The lead was Patricia Routledge and she had asked for me. We got on well during the two days we were there and that, I thought, was that. But no.

Almost the last play the great American writer, George S. Kaufman wrote, in cahoots with Howard Teichmann, was *The Solid Gold Cadillac*. I was asked to play a tough American wheeler-dealer Edward McKeever, while Pat was the female lead, Laura Partridge. When I knew I'd be with Patricia I immediately said I'd do it. I shouldn't have. It was nothing to do with Pat, but I started to have worries I'd never had before.

I don't know why but, totally unlike me, I couldn't stop thinking about the show being a failure, me being a failure in it and, for the first time ever, I couldn't get my mum's suicide out of my head. In short, I had a bit of a nervous breakdown. I had to come out of the show while we were playing – guess where – Guildford! The company and the cast, especially Pat, all gave me terrific encouragement and within ten days I was back. Doctor Theatre they call it.

I'd been told how difficult Miss Routledge could be, but she wasn't. She is one of those performers who wants it right.

If it isn't, then she might be difficult. We both did our best to work well together and I think we did. I found her difficult to talk to offstage. We just weren't on the same wavelength. Pat was a little too unpredictable for me. I never mind if someone is prickly all the time or if someone is jolly all the time. It's when you don't know what to expect that I find it difficult.

I have to say, however, that onstage Pat was impeccable. She would lay back and let me do my thing. She never killed a laugh or moved or made noises on a tagline. She was the ultimate 'pro' and, by example, she made me behave the same way. Those three months at the Garrick Theatre were an education for me.

I did enjoy playing an American. I did it like Jimmy Durante. One evening I came out of the stage door and an American lady (it could have been Jimmy Durante in drag) said, 'I tawt yore accent wuz t'rific!'

'You sound just like me,' I said.

'Dat's why I tawt it wuz t'rific!' said she.

When the show finished, Debbie helped me get my head together again and I cooked up a new one-man show. We – Debbie, Max, the brilliant accompanist Ian Smith and I – went on the road with *Roy Hudd's Extremely Entertaining Evening* (I can't help hiding my light under a bushel). It was really me doing songs, anecdotes and monologues – bits from shows I'd been in. We packed 'em out.

The touring did me a power of good. I could – had to – concentrate on the job in hand, because every Monday is an opening night and audiences are different all over the country. I've never stopped doing one-nighters first with *Roy Hudd's Very Own Music Hall* and now with the new show, Music Hall still pulls 'em in and I've enjoyed loads of one-nighters as part of Ian Liston's *Hiss and Boo Music Hall*. Ian puts together really good bills and, as Mr Chairman, compères them superbly.

I also enjoy touring with plays, too. Particularly anything by the master farceur, Ray Cooney. He is one of the very few who can write belly laughs.

I indulged myself and recorded forty-odd of my favourite monologues on CD. No record company wanted to do it so I did it myself, and I'm happy to say I made my money back in a fortnight and to date it's sold like a good 'un.

This was also the year I was offered a trip to the jungle to eat insects, argue with people, look dirty and start to smell – yes, *I'm a Celebrity . . . Get Me Out of Here!*

'Your profile doesn't need raising yet – don't do it,' said Morris.

I didn't.

While we're on the subject of health (well, sort of), I thought I'd put all my medical adventures together in one fell swoop. In most autobiographies, particularly those of actors, there always seem to be in-depth references to the illnesses and medical woes the subject has encountered throughout their life. Very boring. So I thought I'd get them over with for you. If, like me, you don't enjoy folk talking about their operations, skip the next few pages.

I only include this stuff because the older you get, the more it comes home to you just how important it is to stay healthy in show business. I've been lucky. Without really trying I've managed to keep reasonably fit and very rarely have I missed a performance.

I have always had trouble with my weight. Both sorts of trouble – too little and too much. Yes, I know when you see me now you say, 'So Tessie O'Shea *did* have a son!' but it took a lot of time and effort for me to get to the size I am now! I was a sad thin case when I came into the game. Eight and a half stone when wet! I really was a six-foot bag of bones. As Eric Davidson once wrote about me: 'Take his clothes off and you can hang your hat on nine different places!'

Not only did I look like a white Gandhi, I also used to get awful stage fright. I would often throw up just before I went onstage. My old doctor advised that there were only two things that could help: smoking or whiskey! Of the two, he told me smoking was the least harmful. Can you believe it? I'd never smoked – except for the odd Wild Woodbine nicked from Auntie Ivy when I was a lad. So I had to sit down and really work hard to make myself smoke … but I did succeed and started to enjoy it – or was it that I couldn't do without it? It did do the trick regarding the stage fright though.

The next milestone – or was it a gallstone – was stomach trouble. About three or four times a year I started to get a feeling in the belly – a feeling like a hedgehog doing forward rolls. This was followed by passing out and violent sickness and the other end – not necessarily in that order. No one could find out what it was, I just had to suffer in anything but silence. Then a doctor friend (not the old one) told me that the astronauts carried a pill with them to help these problems if they occurred in space. I got some and they really worked. What had been a recurring nightmare seems to have disappeared.

There's more! There's more!

After years of belting it out without any training, my voice started to peter out in the middle of sentences. This was no good at all as it was often the tag of the joke that disappeared. An ear, nose and throat specialist was recommended to me. I can't forget his name, Kenneth Rotter, and he told me I had corns on the vocal chords. I was in good company. The unique voice of Al Bowlly was threatened with the same problem – as was Shirley Bassey's. They got through it and so did I.

Mr Rotter removed the corns at the hospital of St John and St Elizabeth near Lord's Cricket Ground. Then, the hospital was mostly staffed by nuns and, after coming round from the operation, I said to the sister I hoped I hadn't sworn during the session.

'Mr Hudd,' she said. 'No need to apologize. You did swear – for fifteen minutes non-stop and you never repeated yourself once. It was a master class in blasphemy – I learned a lot.'

She was my kind of nun.

So many friends enjoyed coming to see me in the hospital because I wasn't allowed to speak. I communicated by holding up a series of cards with phrases on like: 'Hello!', 'I'm fine', 'Tell me', 'That's enough', 'Now **** off'! Not being allowed to speak for ten days was purgatory, but I've tried to make up for it since.

I wonder if you're like me? Whenever I hear a radio programme about any sort of skin disease I start to itch; brain trouble and my head starts to throb; pregnancy and I get a pain in the wallet. I'd heard a documentary about pressure behind the eyes. Apparently it was quite a common problem so I went to see the man. David Watson had been recommended to me by Lionel Blair and I wondered if Lionel had got it in for me when I first met him. Mr Watson was nothing like the surgeons on the telly. He was a softly-spoken toff with a waistcoated suit and Victorian side whiskers. I thought, 'Hello. He'll be getting out the leeches in a minute.' He gave me the full going over and he reassured me there was nothing wrong with the pressure but that I had got perforated retinas.

'I can fix them,' he said. 'When can you come in?'

I started to calculate when I would finish in *Run For Your Wife*. 'In about ten weeks' time,' I said.

'No. What time can you come in *tomorrow*?'

If it had been left any longer, apparently, I would have been walking with a white stick. It was done and all was well. This time the nurse who I apologized to about the 'Lord Mayoring', was very upset at my language and was quite huffy with me. She wasn't a nun.

A couple of years later the same thing happened and the same chap did the same business. It worked and I haven't had to give any nurses a mouthful since.

Regarding the weight, originally I just couldn't seem to put any on and I said as much on a TV chat show. All sorts of weird and wonderful suggestions arrived in the post. The only one that appealed to me was a glass of Guinness with a port in it. I forced myself to try it and soon found I was forcing myself on a regular basis. I put on a couple of stone and felt better for it.

I had a great way of taking off any pounds that crept on. Pantomime. Whatever weight I was when we started rehearsals, by the end of the season I'd always dropped a least a stone. When I eventually stopped doing the slapstick stuff it started to creep up again.

Eventually all the brainwashing, and a growing breathlessness, made me give up smoking. To 'combat my stage fright' I'd got up to sixty cigarettes a day! I was a sad case. I loved smoking. I *enjoyed* it.

Every morning, before my feet had even touched the floor, a fag was lit. Breakfast was a cup of tea, a cigarette and then another. I couldn't answer the phone or put pen to paper without the dreaded crutch. It got so bad that if I ran out in the middle of the night I'd have to find an all-night garage to keep me sane. Something had to be done.

I read Allen Carr's famous *Easy Way to Stop Smoking* and it is a good 'un. But for all Allen's sensible arguments I needed something more to help. I went for the nicotine patches and they worked for me. It wasn't anywhere near as bad as I anticipated. I was fag free, but to be honest, if there was a safe way of smoking, I'd take it up again tomorrow. I miss not having a 'prop' to gesture with, and the air of mystery a carefully puffed smoke ring creates. But, a mixed blessing for audiences, I can now hold on to notes longer when I sing. And I can run, a few feet, without collapsing in a shaking heap.

The only real downside was, within a few nicotine-free weeks, the appetite really perked up and the weight started to pile on. I made pathetic attempts to control it – and failed. I even told my doctor I'd go back to the fags. She hastily told me nicotine didn't take weight off. It just stopped it going on.

I got up to nineteen stone and so, in desperation, I joined a slimming club. To date, I've lost two stone – with a couple more to go.

The strangest health scare was during a return to *Coronation Street*. I'd been brought back to bury John Savident (Fred Elliott the butcher). One scene was me, as the undertaker, sorting out Fred in his coffin. John had a great idea to start the scene.

'As you bend over the coffin,' he said, 'why don't you reach in and do up my flies?'

I did – and as I stepped back, I collapsed. John was out of the coffin like lightning. He called for a glass of water and sat me in a chair – and then got back in the coffin! Oh, if only the camera had been running. I managed to wobble through the scene but felt terrible.

Granada were terrific. They put me up in a smashing quiet hotel, while Sue Nicholls got Debbie up from home. The hospital did the full MOT and tests. Next thing I knew the press heard about it and proclaimed that I'd had a heart attack. What damage the press can do, honestly. Those words, 'heart attack', sound so final.

I had stacks of letters wishing me a speedy recovery and, even today, folk write and say they hope I've got over the attack. Managements were very wary of employing me – in case I died on their time. It wasn't true. Nothing to do with the heart – in fact it was entirely the other end. I'd had a urinary infection and within four days I was back in Weatherfield burying whoever I could get my tape measure on.

But there you are – my medical record – and then you wonder why BUPA turned me down. They must have read the papers.

Just last year came another exit from the colander I'd never found before – Opera, or rather Operetta. Again, without me asking, the English National Opera enquired whether I'd be interested in *The Merry Widow*. Even I resisted the temptation to say, 'Depends what she looks like.' Or, 'Does she have a few bob?'

I remembered the hundred-year-old Franz Lehár musical as the good old standby for 'am drams' around the world. I'd never actually seen the piece but did know all the terrific tunes. The part on offer was Njegus, the servant to the comedy lead. It was a very small part, but both Operetta *and* the London Coliseum were completely new to me, so it had to be done.

Someone – it could have been Jude Kelly who was originally to direct, but had to pull out for family reasons, or John Copley who did direct – found out that in the first London production of the *Widow,* in 1905, my part was played by a well-known comedian, W. H. Berry. He, apparently, was happy to do it but only if he had a song, so Lehár wrote one especially for him, which, I was told, never saw the light of day once Berry left the show.

After lots of encouragement from John, the choreographer, the dancers, the ENO chorus, the orchestra and all the principals, it stopped the show. How could anyone go wrong with that lot on your side? I shared a dressing room with Richard Suart (the ENO's greatest Ko-Ko and my boss in the *Widow*) and the tenor, Alfie Boe. Let others say what they will, but I was in the best room in the house. Laughs galore and not a smidgeon of 'you common little concert-party comic'. Well, not to my face anyway!

I knew from the first day of rehearsals that John Copley was my man. He was enthusiastic, full of ideas and would always, when things got a bit fraught, tell us some outrageous true story from his years in the business. And, when I felt it was all a bit beyond me, put his arm round my shoulder and encourage me to have another go. The first time he did it I said, 'If you offer me a sweetie, I'm off!' From then on we spoke the same language.

The show rehearsed for five weeks. It had to because the chorus were in two current shows and rehearsing for forthcoming productions. Even though I only had a spit and a cough, I turned up every day.

The night before we opened, I said to Alfie, 'When do we get the rehearsal money?'

'What rehearsal money?' he said.

I explained that in my side of the business we always get a few bob to cover travel, etc. during rehearsals.

'The principals don't get paid for rehearsals,' he told me.

And I'd turned up every day! I tried like crazy to persuade the powers that be that I was chorus and needed rehearsal money. The chorus did their best to help me and, as I write this, I'm looking at a framed certificate, signed by the Chorus Master, that declares:

'This is to certify that Mr Roy Hudd is hereby elected an honorary member of the English National Opera Chorus.'

It didn't help but I shall return! (But won't rehearse!)

Later that year Jude Kelly, the director who had had to bow out of *The Merry Widow* production, remembered me and asked me to play the Wizard in *The Wizard of Oz* at, of all places, the Royal Festival Hall. The production had lukewarm notices, but I thought Jude's conception was good.

It was difficult – and daring – to try to turn the Royal Festival Hall into a theatre, but the designer did and, apart from some very odd projected slides, it worked. I made a mistake in agreeing to play the title role because it is a rotten part. The Wizard comes on at the beginning of the play for about five minutes and isn't seen again until just before the end. He doesn't have any funny lines, or any fun at all really. Everyone else does – but not the Wizard. Jude worked hard with me to make him something worthwhile but it just didn't happen. I think it was the thought of working in the Royal Festival Hall that made me say yes in the first place. Next time I'll read the script!

At the end of 2008, Morris Aza told me that he was going to retire. Oh he gives up so easily. He'd only been my agent for fifty years. Doesn't he realize good wine takes a long time to mature?

We still chat on the phone and, whisper it, I think he misses the biz. How could he not? He's spent longer than me at it and, together, we've seen all sorts of changes: the death of Variety, cassette tapes, video, the end of concert party, the horrendous growth of reality TV (no good to agents at all) and the unpleasant growth of effing and blinding from comedians. If I didn't think my career was only just beginning, I'd retire too.

When I asked Morris for any particular memories he had regarding our fifty years together he came up with lots – most too rude to put in this book. However, there was one meeting I'd almost forgotten.

In 1974, BBC television offered me the host's job on a magazine programme, *The 607080 Show*. As you can guess, it wasn't for teenagers, it was for the older generation.

Because of my relationship with my gran I wanted to find out more, and an evening meeting was arranged with two charming and extremely posh ladies, the producer, Brigit Barry, and her boss, Sheila.

All four of us met at an old haunt of mine – the Arts Theatre Club off Leicester Square. It was 7 o'clock, and dusk was falling.

We all had a drink at the bar and then proceeded up a flight of narrow squeaky stairs to a room we'd booked for our meeting; a room tucked away in the club; a room with no windows.

For the first half-hour all was going well. The ladies had lots of ideas for the show's content, and I was in full flow, telling tales about old comedians and singing music hall songs. Morris was trying hard to get in and ask about the money.

Suddenly, all the lights went out and we were left in pitch blackness – we couldn't see a thing, let alone each other. Sheila and Brigit played a blinder pretending not to notice the lack of light – in fact they carried on chatting as if nothing had happened. But it wasn't easy talking to people you couldn't see and, at last, affable chat petered out.

The ladies became a trifle distraught. Morris swears they thought we'd arranged the whole thing. White slave traffic?

Feeling his way carefully, *very* carefully, around the room he located the door and opened it. The whole building was in darkness. We apologized to the ladies, who responded from somewhere in the void.

'Excuse me,' said Sheila in querulous tone. 'But how do we get out?'

Then the real adventure began. Morris stood by the door and guided us there. The four of us collided and, in his words, 'became quite intimately entwined'! Now there was the narrow staircase to tackle.

Three steps down and neither of us knew which lady we were escorting till we suddenly realized we both had hold of the same one, Brigit. No sign of Sheila, or vocal response. She was gone. Where?

I worked my way back up the stairs and down again, crying out her name: but nothing. Poor Brigit was where I'd left her – hanging on to the handrail and Morris. Sheila had disappeared.

By now weak with laughter, we shuffled down the staircase and one of us felt a doorknob. The knob was turned and we were in the bar – with light. Candles were on the counter and leaning against it was Sheila.

She said just five words, 'What can I get you?'

'A large one of anything,' I replied, 'and the same for my friends.'

The outcome was I got the job of presenter, alongside Irene Thomas, a very clever, pretty lady who'd been BBC Radio's *Brain of Britain*.

One of *my* favourite Morris stories, and one that sums us up completely, is the one about him taking me to see *Oedipus* at the Old Vic. Gawd knows why he wanted to go, but go we did.

We couldn't get seats together, so he sat in the stalls and I was in the circle. The whole thing was a trifle beyond me, but the tag at the end of the piece wasn't.

The play finished – I think – and everyone exited the stage, leaving a giant penis centre stage.

As it was disclosed, just two laughs rang through the theatre – one from the stalls and one from the circle. After much shushing I made my way out. It had to be the end – nothing could top that enormous erection. Nothing did and, of course, it was the end. In the foyer I met the only other person who laughed and was making his way out: Morris Aza. We were both having a Guinness in The Windmill before the rest of the audience had decided the play was over.

And that's just one of the reasons he was my agent for fifty years.

A few years back, comedy was referred to as the 'new rock and roll'. Lots of present-day performers think they invented a new kind of comedy – but they didn't. Comedy hasn't changed but *comedians* have: in some cases for the better.

My earliest recollections of working with comedians was in pantomime, and they were mostly very big or very small men. They all seemed fairly old, but I suppose when you're young anyone grown-up seems old. They nearly all seemed to wear camelhair overcoats and homburg hats and most smoked cigars. They looked like affluent businessmen. I remember thinking, how can these boring-looking blokes be the great harbingers of joy? How can these, usually sour-faced, frequenters of the best bars in town be able to charm and amuse a panto audience?

Whichever town or city you were in they knew someone – someone who could get bolts of cloth cheap; someone who 'knows where the body's buried'; someone who would let them open a credit account; and someone who was on intimate terms with trainers and jockeys. They knew the ladies who had the best 'digs' in town and *might*, with the right encouragement, 'do you a favour'. They were streetwise, and their comedy, for their audiences, was based on the people and the places they knew; they were 'one of them', but perhaps a bit cleverer. They were, above all, warm and human.

There were so many more different types of comedians then. Visual slapstick ones, sharp fast-talking ones, slow reflective ones, posh ones, common ones, acrobatic and juggling ones, simple ones and professorial ones. I miss this variety.

Offstage, today's comedians, the ones I've met, are, of course, young. So they should be. They're usually quite serious, well read, and write their own material. They're very 'politically correct', and much more interested in doing television than chancing their arms playing with a live audience.

Onstage, so many of today's comedians are similar in style and delivery: they seem to come off an assembly line. Going around the comedy clubs, I see comic after comic doing the same sort of material.

Whereas the previous batch of comics represented the majority, the present batch represents a much smaller proportion: their own kind, and their constant exposure on television is disappointing to someone like me who believes original comedy should be encouraged. What would be original today would be someone who made you smile when he or she walked on. Someone who didn't swear on every tag. Someone who looked as if they liked their audience.

Don't get me wrong, there are some who are totally original today. Peter Kay is one. He's a sort of throwback in that he talks about things *all* his audience know. Ricky Gervais doesn't look as if he likes us, but I forgive him that for his original thinking. Joe Pasquale is an original – if you don't remember Cedric and the Three Monarchs. Harry Hill is a favourite of mine for looking funny as well as, astutely and wittily, pointing out just how dumbed down and ludicrous most of television has become. Billy Connolly, if you can take the swearing, is a terrific entertainer but, to me, none are as good as the number one, eighty-years-young Ken Dodd.

What next? Concert parties, variety, summer revues have almost disappeared. Most have been replaced by one-man/woman shows, and I'm well into them. I have two: *Roy Hudd's Very Own Music Hall* (where I tell the story of music hall and get to do the songs, jokes and anecdotes of all my favourites); and *Roy Hudd's Exceedingly Entertaining Evening*, is me telling my own history with songs, jokes, excerpts from shows, anecdotes and scandalous personal stories. Although I do miss being part of a team at least I can cut, ad-lib and, hopefully, improve the shows without having to consult a committee. Now I've finished this book both shows will be back on the road soon – you have been warned!

Ever on the lookout for more exits from the colander, apart from the bits and pieces on the telly, I've been involved in some interesting projects recently – all involving music. Musicians are my favourites and I've worked with some good 'uns. I've never got over watching a big band sitting together behind their music stands chatting. It's usually mundane things like, 'How are your tomatoes coming on?' and, 'How's the wife?' Then the conductor taps his baton and, with hardly a beat, they'll pick up their instruments and play the most difficult piece they've never even glanced at before.

I've been lucky enough to have some outstanding musicians and good buddies working with me. My favourite drummer through many years of cabaret, pantomime, variety and musicals was, and is, Bobby Cook. Bobby is perhaps the last of that unique breed – the show drummer, someone who can 'follow the act'. Without writing out lots of rim shots, drum rolls, paradiddles, whistles, cymbal crashes and cow bell effects, the show drummer knows, without having to be told, *exactly* what noises enhance the turn. Try to imagine a juggling or acrobatic act without the necessary effects. Someone with this sort of talent is essential for slapstick routines in panto. Having had to spend many unnecessary hours explaining what sounds are required to embryo percussionists, the real show drummer is a gift from the Gods.

The first time Bobby worked for me was a one-night cabaret at a venue he'll never forget, The Old Coach House at Stanstead Abbots. Anxious to impress, apart from his drum kit he brought along every accessory known to mankind. The Coach House set up was a tiny stage in the corner of a tiny restaurant. Once the piano was on, there was just room for me to half turn to all corners of the room. I'm sure the pianist was sitting outside the building and playing through the window.

Bobby could only get a drumstick-and-a-half and a side drum into the place. He couldn't get on the stage, so he joined a party of three and took an unoccupied seat at their table. With my band parts taking up the place where his dinner should have been, we got underway. Halfway through the act the customer sitting next to Bobby offered him a chip on a fork. Eyes fixed on the music as he played along, Bobby smiled and said, 'Thanks, love, but not while I'm working!'

Bobby is now the resident drummer at the Brick Lane Music Hall. Aren't they lucky.

And wasn't I lucky to have Don Shearman as musical director for longer than anyone else. Don is the very best arranger and conductor I know and, like so many good musos, the possessor of an off-beat sense of humour. When the post arrives I look forward to spotting his handwriting on an envelope – it will always contain a great cartoon or comment on the current news.

When I take out either of my one-man shows my accompanist is Ian Smith. I first met him in Leicester and, on the tour of *Oliver!*, he conducted the show.

I have read about actors being so 'into' the role they're playing that they forget they're giving a performance at all. This has happened to me just twice – once playing Fagin – and I can feel what it was like even now. Scary. Onstage that night I *was* the old villain: his talent in keeping the kids under control, his inventiveness, his paranoia, his greed, his loathing of violence, his Jewishness, his self pity, his arrogance – all the things that make him such a fascinating character to play. Yet this night I *wasn't* playing. It was real. I came off sweating and shaking. Ian came round at curtain down, sweating and shaking too.

'That was amazing,' he said. 'I forgot I was conducting a show. I was watching Fagin.'

It wasn't hard to relax and lose yourself in the songs when Ian was on the stick. Talk about following the act. He watched every move and every nuance. He is exactly the same when he plays for me on solo piano. He makes me do the stuff well. His arrangements gently push me into telling the stories in the songs be they funny, sad, bawdy or romantic. I still get a tingling when he plays the overture.

But back to what's next. I narrated *Wind in the Willows* with the King's Singers at the Snape Maltings. I played Stanley Holloway's part in a concert version of *My Fair Lady* at The Sage Gateshead with the Northern Symphonia – and to sing with and hear those marvellous tunes, played by that brilliant young orchestra was just terrific. I did a workshop with the National Theatre of a new musical, *Feather Boy*. It is a very successful children's novel and this version was written by the novel's author, Nicky Singer, with music by Debbie Wiseman and lyrics by an old chum, Don Black. The cast included thirty-odd boys and girls (some very odd!). The story began with the kids visiting an old folks' home to do a project. Yes I *was* one of the residents. The plot develops in a fascinating way and it'll be interesting to see what happens with the musical.

POSTSCRIPT

Putting this book together has been a bit like solving a Rubik's Cube – moving all the memories around until they form some sort of whole.

Well that's it, so far. What more could anyone want out of a life? How lucky can a bloke be? To be brought up, advised and most importantly, made to laugh, by a grandmother who should have been on the halls. To be taught to perform by people who were in the game to entertain audiences *not* to be famous or for the money, people who would look at triumphs and disasters, in the same eccentric, whimsical way. To have been allowed to spend half a century performing a labour of love alongside the very best, dedicated professionals, from Paul Schofield to Hylda Baker, from Max Miller to Ian McKellen. To be able to count, on the fingers of Dave Allen's right hand, the number of fellow workers I haven't liked. To hear of show-business feuds, jealousies and selfish self-interest, and to have been able to avoid most of them. To have been involved with ladies who were all, without exception, grafters. Ladies who were good at the job and would always roll up their sleeves and get on with whatever was required *and* make me laugh. They're the ones that really turn me on. 'Gran! Will you marry me?' To have had the irreplaceable joy of being able to make an audience laugh and to still be allowed the privilege of trying to do it again.

And, by writing this book, to have the chance to share my love of laughter, and what I do for a living, with you.

INDEX